Asia's Middle Powers?

ASIA'S MIDDLE POWERS?

The Identity and

Regional Policy of

South Korea and Vietnam

Edited by
Joon-Woo Park, Gi-Wook Shin,
and Donald W. Keyser

SHORENSTEIN
APARC
STANFORD

THE WALTER H. SHORENSTEIN
ASIA-PACIFIC RESEARCH CENTER

THE WALTER H. SHORENSTEIN ASIA-PACIFIC RESEARCH CENTER
(Shorenstein APARC) is a unique Stanford University institution focused on
the interdisciplinary study of contemporary Asia. Shorenstein APARC's mission
is to produce and publish outstanding interdisciplinary, Asia-Pacific–focused
research; to educate students, scholars, and corporate and governmental
affiliates; to promote constructive interaction to influence U.S. policy toward
the Asia-Pacific; and to guide Asian nations on key issues of societal transition,
development, U.S.-Asia relations, and regional cooperation.

The Walter H. Shorenstein Asia-Pacific Research Center
Freeman Spogli Institute for International Studies
Stanford University
Encina Hall
Stanford, CA 94305-6055
tel. 650-723-9741
fax 650-723-6530
http://APARC.stanford.edu

Asia's Middle Powers? The Identity and Regional Policy
of South Korea and Vietnam
may be ordered from:
The Brookings Institution
c/o DFS, P.O. Box 50370, Baltimore, MD, USA
tel. 1-800-537-5487 or 410-516-6956
fax 410-516-6998
http://www.brookings.edu/press

Walter H. Shorenstein Asia-Pacific Research Center Books, 2013.
Copyright © 2013 by the Board of Trustees of the
Leland Stanford Junior University.

Library of Congress Cataloging-in-Publication Data
Asia's middle powers? : the identity and regional policy of South Korea and
Vietnam / edited by Joon-Woo Park, Donald Keyser, and Gi-Wook Shin.
    pages cm
ISBN 978-1-931368-32-2
1. Korea (South)—Foreign relations—Vietnam. 2. Vietnam—Foreign relations—
Korea (South) 3. Korea (South)—Foreign relations. 4. Vietnam—Foreign relations.
5. United States—Foreign relations—East Asia. 6. East Asia—Foreign relations—United
States. 7. Nationalism—Korea (South) 8. Nationalism—Vietnam. I. Park, Joon-Woo.
DS910.2.V5A75 2013
327.5—dc23

                                                                    2013025048

First printing, 2013
ISBN 978-1-931368-32-2

Typeset by Classic Typography in 10½/13½ Minion Pro

Contents

Tables and Figures

Tables

Figures

Contributors

LEIF-ERIC EASLEY is assistant professor in the Division of International Studies at Ewha University and a research fellow at the Asan Institute for Policy Studies. At Ewha, Easley teaches international security and political economics. His research interests include contested national identities and changing levels of trust in the bilateral security relationships of Northeast Asia. He received his PhD from Harvard University's Department of Government and was the Northeast Asian History Fellow at the Shorenstein Asia-Pacific Research Center at Stanford University.

DONALD W. KEYSER retired from the U.S. Department of State in September 2004 after a thirty-two-year career. He had extensive domestic and foreign experience in senior policy positions, conflict resolution, intelligence operations and analysis, and law enforcement programs. His career focused geographically on U.S. policy toward Northeast Asia. Fluent in Chinese and conversant in Japanese, Russian, and French, he served three tours in Beijing and two tours in Tokyo. A Russian language and Soviet/Russian area studies specialist through MA work, he served 1998–99 as Special Negotiator and Ambassador for Regional Conflicts in the former USSR. He was the 2008–09 Pantech Fellow at Stanford University's Shorenstein Asia-Pacific Research Center. He is currently a nonresident senior fellow at the China Policy Institute, University of Nottingham, U.K.

SU-HOON LEE received his PhD in comparative international development and sociology from The Johns Hopkins University in 1986. He is professor of sociology and political science at Kyungnam University and the director of its

Institute for Far East Asian Studies (IFES) in Seoul. His monographs include *State-Building in the Contemporary Third World* (Westview Press, 1989), *World-System Analysis* (in Korean, 1993), and *World-System. Northeast Asia. Korean Peninsula* (in Korean, 2004). He has published numerous articles and book chapters on the world order, Northeast Asia, and the Korean Peninsula. Lee has served on various ROK government advisory committees; since August 2005 he has assumed the chair (ministerial-level position) of the Presidential Committee on Northeast Asian Initiative.

PHAM QUANG MINH is associate professor of history and politics at the University of Social Sciences and Humanities (USSH), Vietnam National University-Hanoi. After receiving his PhD in Southeast Asian studies from Humboldt University in Berlin in 2002, he first became deputy head, and then head of the International Studies Department at USSH, and in 2012 Minh was promoted to vice-rector for research affairs at the university. His main teaching and research interests include world politics, Asia-Pacific international relations, and Vietnam's foreign policy. His articles have appeared in *International Relations of the Asia-Pacific*, the *Journal of Vietnamese Studies, Asia-Pacific Review*, and *Asia Europe Journal*; he has also recently contributed a chapter, "Images and Perceptions of the EU in Vietnam: Media, Elite and Public Opinion Perspectives," to *The EU through the Eyes of Asia / Volume 2, New Cases, New Findings* (World Scientific, 2009).

JOON-WOO PARK was appointed by President Park Geun-hye as South Korea's Senior Secretary to the President for Political Affairs in August 2013. A Korean career diplomat for thirty-three years, Park served as the ambassador to the European Union, Belgium, and Singapore. Other overseas assignments included the United States, Japan, and China. Park was the 2011–12 Koret Fellow at the Shorenstein Asia-Pacific Research Center at Stanford University, where he taught a graduate class on Korean foreign policy, and later was a visiting professor at Yonsei University's Institute for State Governance.

GI-WOOK SHIN is the director of the Walter H. Shorenstein Asia-Pacific Research Center; the Tong Yang, Korea Foundation, and Korea Stanford Alumni Chair of Korean Studies; the founding director of the Korean Studies Program; a senior fellow of the Freeman Spogli Institute for International Studies; and a professor of sociology, all at Stanford University. As a historical-comparative and political sociologist, his research has concentrated on social movements, nationalism, development, and international relations.

Shin is the author/editor of a dozen books and numerous articles. His recent books include *History Textbooks and the Wars in Asia: Divided Memories* (2011); *South Korean Social Movements: From Democracy to Civil Society* (2011); and *One Alliance, Two Lenses: U.S.-Korea Relations in a New Era* (2010). His articles have appeared in academic journals including the *American Journal of Sociology, Comparative Studies in Society and History, Political Science Quarterly, International Sociology, Nations and Nationalism, Pacific Affairs,* and *Asian Survey.*

SCOTT SNYDER is senior fellow for Korea studies and director of the program on U.S.-Korea policy at the Council on Foreign Relations (CFR), where he had served as an adjunct fellow from 2008 to 2011. Snyder's program examines South Korea's efforts to contribute on the international stage; its potential influence and contributions as a middle power in East Asia; and the peninsular, regional, and global implications of North Korean instability. Snyder is also the coeditor of *North Korea in Transition: Politics, Economy, and Society* (Rowman and Littlefield, 2012), and the editor of *Global Korea: South Korea's Contributions to International Security* (Council on Foreign Relations, 2012) and *The U.S.-South Korea Alliance: Meeting New Security Challenges* (Lynne Rienner Publishers, 2012). He served as the project director for CFR's Independent Task Force on policy toward the Korean Peninsula. He currently writes for the blog, "Asia Unbound."

TUONG VU is associate professor of political science at the University of Oregon and has held visiting appointments at the National University of Singapore and Princeton University. His book, *Paths to Development in Asia: South Korea, Vietnam, China, and Indonesia* (Cambridge, 2010), received a 2011 Bernard Schwartz Award Honorable Mention. He is coeditor of *Dynamics of the Cold War in Asia: Ideology, Identity, and Culture* (Palgrave, 2009) and *Southeast Asia in Political Science: Theory, Region, and Qualitative Analysis* (Stanford, 2008). His articles have appeared in many scholarly journals, including *World Politics, Journal of Southeast Asian Studies, Journal of Vietnamese Studies, Studies in Comparative International Development, Communist and Post-Communist Studies, South East Asia Research,* and *Theory and Society.* Currently he is completing a book about the Vietnamese revolution as a case of radical movements in international politics.

ALEXANDER L. VUVING is associate professor at the Asia-Pacific Center for Security Studies in Honolulu. A native of Vietnam, he received a PhD in political science from the Johannes Gutenberg University, Mainz (Germany), and has been a research fellow at Harvard University's Belfer Center for Science and International Affairs and assistant professor in the Department of Political Science at Tulane University. His work focuses on Vietnamese politics and foreign policy, China's economic growth and foreign relations, Asian security, international relations theory, and soft power. His research articles have appeared in *Asian Survey*, *Asian Politics and Policy*, and *Asien* as well as the edited volumes *Negotiating Asymmetry: China's Place in Asia* and *Living with China: Regional States and China through Crises and Turning Points*, among others. He has also contributed three chapters on Vietnam to the annual review *Southeast Asian Affairs*, published by the Institute of Southeast Asian Studies.

BRANTLY WOMACK is professor of foreign affairs at the University of Virginia, where he holds the Miller Center's C. K. Yen Chair. He is the author of *China Among Unequals: Asymmetric International Relationships in Asia* (World Scientific Press, 2010), and *China and Vietnam: The Politics of Asymmetry* (Cambridge, 2006), as well as over a hundred articles and book chapters. He edited *China's Rise in Historical Perspective* (Rowman and Littlefield, 2010) and *Contemporary Chinese Politics in Historical Perspective* (Cambridge, 1991). Current research projects include a general theory of asymmetric international relationships, structural transformations of international order, and political modernization in China and Vietnam.

Preface: About the Koret Series on Korea

This volume is the fourth in a series of policy-related studies on contemporary Korea. The Koret Foundation of San Francisco made the project possible by a generous grant to the Korean Studies Program at Stanford University. The Koret Foundation's gift allowed Stanford's Walter H. Shorenstein Asia Pacific Research Center, of which the Korean Studies Program is a part, to establish a Koret Fellowship to bring leading professionals in Asia and the United States to Stanford to study United States–Korean relations. Koret Fellows conduct their own research on Korea and the bilateral relationship, with the broad aim of fostering greater understanding and closer ties between the two countries.

Acknowledgements

In recent years, South Korea has been the focus of innumerable academic conferences, think tank symposia, and book-length studies. These have examined such familiar policy issues as national reunification, dissuading North Korea from pursuing its nuclear ambitions, reshaping and modernizing the Seoul-Washington treaty alliance, and adjusting to China's increasing regional weight. As we at the Shorenstein Asia-Pacific Research Center at Stanford University contemplated an organizing theme for the Center's fourth annual Koret Conference, we judged this turf to have been well ploughed. We elected instead to look at South Korean foreign policy options and behavior through a different prism, one that might yield fresh insights and perspectives.

The resulting March 2, 2012, conference—whose essays are collected in this volume—was called "Korea and Vietnam: The National Experiences and Foreign Policies of Middle Powers." The focus was chosen for a number of reasons that seemed not only logical but also compelling. Enhanced understanding of South Korea's policy environment and options can plausibly be attained through comparison with other nations similarly oriented and endowed. Vietnam and South Korea share broadly similar histories, cultures, population size, and regional "weight," yet they are also sufficiently different that such a comparison might yield interesting insights useful both for academic theory and for contemporary policy analysis. Both nations are visibly exerting greater influence within their respective subregions and upon the larger region they inhabit. Yet one finds a dearth of systematic comparative work on the two, at least in the English language. Finally, South Korea and Vietnam in 2012 marked the twentieth anniversary of diplomatic relations.

Their leaders, celebrating the unanticipated success of their new ties, agreed to joint commemorative activities and a stepped-up pace of political, economic, and cultural exchanges. We hope that the essays in this volume will contribute to these ongoing Vietnamese-South Korean reflections on shared experiences and practical means of fulfilling the promise both sides perceive in deepening their bilateral cooperation.

As always, we are indebted to the many people who made the convening of the conference and publication of this book possible. We are particularly grateful to the Koret Foundation and its chairwoman, Susan Koret, for generous support of both the conference and this publication. The fourth Koret Fellow at the Center's Korean Studies Program, Joon-Woo Park, a recently retired senior career diplomat and Korea's former ambassador to the European Union and Singapore, played a leading role in all aspects of the conference and book publication. Twelve of the conference participants were from outside Stanford community–from countries including the United States, Korea, and Vietnam. We would also like to thank all those who contributed to the conference as discussants: Michael H. Armacost, David Elliott, Donald Emmerson, Donald Keyser, James Ockey, Victor G. Raphael, Daniel C. Sneider, David Straub, T.J. Pempel, and Philip Yun.

Finally, we appreciate the dedication and hard work of all Shorenstein APARC staff members who contributed to this project, especially Heather Ahn and George Krompacky, responsible, respectively, for arrangements for an efficient and pleasant conference and for the professional editing of this publication.

The Editors

Asia's Middle Powers?

1 Introduction
Asia's Middle Powers: South Korea and Vietnam

Donald W. Keyser and Gi-Wook Shin

Koreans have historically seen their nation as a "shrimp among whales," with good reason. Neighboring China, Japan, and Russia—whose areas, populations, and resources dwarf those of Korea—have in the past indisputably resembled and indeed acted as hungry predators. Since the 1990s and especially the turn of the millennium, however, political leaders and scholars in the Republic of Korea (hereafter ROK, or South Korea) have begun to speak of the nation as a "middle power" capable of exercising significant influence within the Northeast Asian region and beyond. Such middle-power aspirations reflect South Korea's enhanced position in the world. In 2011 its gross domestic product (GDP) ranked thirteenth in the world, eighth in exports, and eighth in reserves of foreign exchange and gold. With roughly 49 million people, it ranked twenty-fifth in population—ahead of nations such as Spain, the Ukraine, and Poland.[1] South Korea maintains approximately 650,000 active duty military personnel (the eighth-largest number in the world), and 3.2 million in active reserve status.

Vietnam, like Korea, is dwarfed by China and feels, profoundly, the weight of Chinese history and culture, along with contemporary China's immense military and economic power. Yet Vietnam's middle-power aspirations are grounded in what that nation's leaders deem to be a realistic appreciation of the nation's current gravity in its region and future potential. Vietnam is the world's fourteenth-most-populous country, with an estimated 91.5 million citizens in mid-2012—some 10 million more than Germany, the most populous nation in Europe (not counting Russia). Though still a developing country seeking to overcome the ravages of civil and foreign wars and failed socialist policies, Vietnam emerged—prior to the 2008–09 global financial crisis—as one of Asia's newest "tiger economies." Today its gross domestic product (GDP) is forty-second in the world, it is the fortieth-largest exporter and thirty-second-largest importer, and its reserves of foreign exchange and gold put it in the top one-third of the world's nations.[2] Vietnam has around 485,000 armed forces personnel on active duty (the estimated thirteenth-largest number in the world, and the largest in Southeast Asia).[3]

Being a middle power is not, of course, merely a question of development level, population size, military prowess, and other such measures. It depends more on a nation's regional capabilities and influence, and predisposition to look to regionalism (as opposed to bilateral ties or ad hoc groupings) as a primary mechanism for addressing national interests. South Korea has amply demonstrated a rising self-confidence in its international status and diplomatic capabilities in the variety of roles it has taken in recent years: as host of the G-20 Leaders Summit (2010); member of the Organisation for Economic Co-operation and Development (OECD) Development Assistance Committee (2010); host of the Nuclear Security Summit (2012); and vigorous advocate of and participant in the ASEAN+3 system (the Association of Southeast Asian Nations, plus China, Japan, and South Korea), the East Asian Summit, and annual tripartite meetings with China and Japan at the levels of finance minister, foreign minister, and prime minister. All of this bespeaks not shrimp-like timidity but a bold vision—and actions corresponding to classical notions of middle-power niche diplomacy focused on regional issues and the broader international common good.

Likewise, during the past decade Vietnam's leaders have begun to articulate a middle-power vision and to project this in practical diplomacy within the Southeast Asian region. Vietnam in 2006 became the World Trade Organization's 150th member, in 2008 it was elected to serve as a nonpermanent member of the United Nations Security Council, and in 2010 it became a partner in developing the Trans-Pacific Partnership (TPP) trade agreement. Since acceding to ASEAN in 1995, Vietnam has visualized its evolving regional identity and pursued its middle-power ambitions through that organization. Although Vietnam is far behind South Korea in all customary measures of economic power, its emphasis on regional diplomacy and its corresponding influence within its subregion are perhaps stronger. Both countries are also inclined—in the classic mode of middle powers—to assign a particularly high importance to the encouragement and utilization of regional and international conflict resolution mechanisms.

Thus, there is good basis for taking Vietnamese and South Korean leaders at their word and comparing the two nations through the prism of middle-power aspirations and behavior. Both countries share broadly similar histories, cultures, population size, and regional "weight," yet they are also sufficiently different that such a comparison can yield interesting insights useful both for academic theory and for contemporary policy analysis. Both nations are visibly exerting greater influence within their respective subregions and upon the larger region that they inhabit. Yet one finds a dearth of systematic comparative work on the two. In this book we use "middle power" as a conceptual framework to comparatively understand South Korea and Vietnam in terms of their respective national identities, regional behavior, and international relations. As Leif-Eric Easley aptly points out in chapter 8, current studies of middle powers tend to focus on European countries or nations with a European heritage such as Canada and Australia,[4] while research on contemporary East Asian international politics tends to focus on great powers (i.e., China, Japan, and the United States) or the development of regional institutions (e.g., ASEAN). We hope that the essays in this volume will contribute to comparative understanding of the two important East Asian nations and also to a growing but previously excessively Eurocentric literature on middle powers.

Middle Powers

The term "middle power" lacks an agreed-upon definition in the international relations (IR) literature; indeed, the comparatively few scholars specializing in the field forcefully contest the attributes, roles, typical behaviors, and specific examples of middle powers. The word "power" itself signifies a relative concept that defies empirical measurement. Ranking states' power by objective criteria has proven as unavailing an exercise as parlor games that challenge participants to rank English poets or professional athletes according to "greatness."

It follows that pinning down the concept of "middle power" or the quality of "middle-powerness" has proven all the more elusive. Allan Gyngell, the founding executive director of the Australian Lowy Institute for International Policy and subsequently the director-general of the Australian intelligence community's Office of National Assessments, exposed the dilemma by explaining Australia's middle-power character in terms of what it is not: "We are not a great power, we are not a small power."[5]

Apart from somewhat whimsical suggestions that one might trace the middle-power concept back to the era of independent city-states in northern

Italy, the seminal work in contemporary IR theory is credited to Professor A. F. K. Organski. Introducing his power transition theory in 1958, Organski posited a global pyramidal structure in which the "dominant power" or "hegemonic state" controlled the preponderance of resources such as population, territory, military power, natural resources, economic and technological capacity, and political stability. Beneath Organski's dominant power were "great powers" that might potentially challenge it; "middle powers" that emulated the international "dominant power" within their region, but lacked the wherewithal to threaten the dominant power or the overall system; and the rest of the world's nations, "small powers," that were devoid of significant capacity, power, and influence.[6]

The archetypal middle powers of the Cold War period were Canada, Australia, Norway, Sweden, the Netherlands, and Belgium. Each of these punched well above its weight within the newly established United Nations, via overseas development assistance programs and, for the Scandinavian and Benelux countries, in the European integration efforts that culminated in the European Communities and then the European Union. These self-identified middle powers placed a premium on the application of their unique national assets and superior diplomatic capabilities in narrowly circumscribed areas. In the logic of middle-power diplomacy, such actions positively supported the system, enhanced the credibility and international stature of the nation, and served to offset national vulnerabilities arising from relative material weakness vis-à-vis dominant powers in the region and the larger global system.

For example, Canadian political leaders, pundits, and scholars asserted a national identity explicitly in terms of middle-power behavior: Canada was allied with the United States and a member of the North Atlantic Treaty Organization (NATO); was linked by history, culture, and economy to the United States and Western Europe; but evinced high-minded multilateralism, ad hoc coalition-building, innovative regional problem-solving, and the promotion of international stability. Ottawa usually avoided rocking the boat with Washington, instead complementing U.S. policies where opportunities presented themselves. Yet, on occasion, Canada tacitly underlined its national independence and altruistic commitment to the rules-based international system—sometimes in the face of U.S. policy. For example, Canada strongly endorsed the UN consensus opposing South African apartheid (from which the United States, under presidents Reagan and Bush, Sr., was noticeably absent); led the international effort to ban landmines; and—both bilaterally and within the Organization of American States—pressed for a policy approach toward Castro's Cuba substantially more flexible than Washington's.

By the end of the past century most treatments in IR literature sought to combine elements of the differing IR approaches. Eduard Jordaan saw middle powers as those "states that are neither great nor small in terms of international power, capacity, and influence, and demonstrate a propensity to promote cohesion and stability in the world system."[7] M. A. Rudderham offered this definition of middle powers: "actors that are inferior to great powers in both realist and structural senses, but that emphasize multilateral solutions, that are capable of exerting leadership on the world stage, and that are particularly concerned with second [i.e., economic] and third [i.e., environmental, human rights, other transnational] agenda issues."[8] William Tow and Richard Rigby proposed a similar synthesis: middle powers are those "which have sufficient material resources and diplomatic standing within the international community to exercise leadership of key issues relating to international rule-building and rule-adherence, but are not 'great powers.'"[9]

Scholars and policy analysts have recently challenged the utility of the middle-power concept on multiple grounds: its uncertain relevance in the post–Cold War, globalized international environment; the dearth of analytical instruments to identify and compare regional or middle powers;[10] the inherent vagueness of the term, which has led a lengthening list of "astonishingly heterogeneous" states to self-identify or otherwise be defined as middle powers[11] (one academic points out that self-proclaimed middle powers behave in a wide range of styles and roles, while those defined as such by analysts are more likely to have similar behaviors);[12] the "troubling parochial bias"[13] and "ideological overtones"[14] introduced by the preoccupations of scholars researching the subject; and the impression of a substance-free "artifice" put forward by nations to advance and justify their national interests.[15]

Such reservations notwithstanding, a middle-power framework has analytical utility when considering the current identities and policy behaviors of Vietnam and South Korea. As Pham Quang Minh points out in chapter 5, the vibrant bilateral relations of Vietnam and South Korea reflect their shared commitment—given analogous security challenges—to play "an active and constructive role" in "the building of an emerging Asia-Pacific security architecture." Easley believes that both nations are "navigating the same geopolitical spectrum," with the United States and China at two poles, and in response are developing middle-power identities.

One could argue, meanwhile, that *neither* Vietnam nor South Korea acts like a middle power. Neither dominates its mini-region, and neither (thus far) has shown a disposition or ability to contribute to common goods on a regional scale—let alone a global one. And—to put any comparison of the two into question—the regional context of each nation is strikingly different: both are concerned about rising China, but Hanoi need not devote the same attention and creativity to ties with the United States, Japan, and Russia that Seoul must. Conversely, ASEAN, central to Vietnam's emerging identity and diplomacy, remains an afterthought for South Korea.

Still, as South Korea and Vietnam are increasing their regional influence—in Northeast and Southeast Asia, respectively—we see the analytical value of the middle-power framework, and of comparison. As Brantley Womack points out in chapter 7, the major utility has to be heuristic: to rise "above the idiosyncratic study of each to confront questions of similarities and differences in context and path." The two nations, he observes, had been pivots in Cold War confrontations, to their sorrow, but had emerged to become two of the more consequential actors in contemporary East Asia. Without doubt, their role in East Asia will only increase in the coming years.

For the purposes of our study, former Australian foreign minister Gareth Evans' working definition of middle-power diplomacy is apropos: "[it is] the kind of diplomacy which can, and should, be practiced by states which are not big or strong enough, either in their own region or the wider world, to impose their policy preferences on anyone else, but who do recognize that there are international policy tasks which need to be accomplished if the world around them is to be safer, saner, more just and more prosperous . . . with all the potential this has, in turn, to affect their own interests; and who have sufficient capacity and credibility to be able to advance those tasks . . . The characteristic *method* of middle power diplomacy is coalition building with 'like-minded' countries. It usually also involves 'niche diplomacy.'"[16]

With this broad definition of middle power in mind, we examine a number of interrelated issues: evolving national identities, the way that policy choices and behaviors are shaped by the weight of history and culture, the lessons of national unification (both accomplished and thwarted), the influence of political ideologies, the challenge of globalization, enduring territorial and maritime conflicts that implicate national pride and economic interests, and the role and promise of subregional and regional groupings. Achieving a deeper understanding of how these factors may play out in conceptual and practical policy terms for Vietnam and South Korea, two aspirant middle powers, can help to illuminate the meaning of middle-power diplomacy in the East Asian geopolitical arena.

National Identity

National identity is a complex and slippery concept. External threats motivate internal cohesion on behalf of autonomous survival. History—and the "significant other"—further shape identity. Of particular importance is how history is taught, remembered, and used to express past national grievances, articulate future goals, and pursue international reputational ambitions.

As Tuong Vu puts it in chapter 9, Vietnam and Korea have inhabited roughly "the same neighborhood" from ancient times, and "have traveled broadly similar paths" as independent (but tribute-paying) states within the Confucian Chinese world order, as late-nineteenth-century victims of colonialism, as divided states arising from Cold War conflicts, as protagonists in military conflicts involving China, and as twenty-first-century states whose identities feature a strong element of assertive nationalism. Historically, as Alexander L. Vuving observes in chapter 4, both Vietnam and Korea faced "an insurmountable power asymmetry in favor of China," while both nations' elites embraced—up to a point—the Chinese civilization and worldview. Some experts even claim that, while geographically Southeast Asian, Vietnam is culturally and historically Northeast Asian, with experiences most similar to Korea's.

And yet, as Vuving observes, the two states adopted unique styles of accommodating imperial Chinese authority: Korea's rulers followed the precept of *sadae* ("serving the great with respect"), while Vietnam's elites practiced the approach of *trong de ngoai vuong* ("inside emperor, outside king"). Their respective histories began to diverge sharply as China, and the region, came under sustained military—and civilizational—assault by Meiji Japan and Western imperial powers. Vietnam, placed under colonial rule by a distant Western power, France, was divided into three separate administrative districts under distinct legal regimes. Korea, which decades later fell under imperial Japanese dominion, had a unified colonial administration. The colonial experiences were deeply felt, had an undeniable impact on the subsequent shaping of national identities, but were fundamentally different in terms of preparing the two nations, once independent, for state-building tasks. Japanese colonial administration, for all its undoubted harshness, afforded (South) Korea better preparation for modern governance and economic development than the French administration did for Vietnam.

There is also a sharp divergence in how the two countries experienced the Cold War. Both Korea and Vietnam were divided into communist and anti-communist states. But while North Vietnam unified the nation under communist rule following decades of bloody civil strife and war against outsiders, North Korea failed in its effort to unify Korea by military force between 1950 and 1953. The ironic consequence is that Vietnam emerged from the Cold War period formally united but impoverished, while Korea remained divided—into a communist, desperately poor north and a rapidly modernizing, prosperous, and increasingly democratic south. These evolving historical contexts led both South Korea and Vietnam to search for appropriate national identities.

Easley seeks to construct a matrix for understanding the "shared and conflicting" identities that tie South Korea and Vietnam to China, and to each other—and potentially for predicting what changes might occur, and at what pace, along each nation's "geopolitical spectrum" vis-à-vis the U.S.-China contest for influence in East Asia. Easley, Vu, Minh, Womack, and Vuving all point to the continuing relevance of the South Korean and Vietnamese legacies of membership in an ancient China-dominated regional order whose enduring Confucian traditions still infuse society and bureaucracy. But as Easley observes, there are different elements of embedded identity that matter more today: ethnicity, especially as opposed to the "other" that is China; the historical memory of struggle against outside pressure, influence, hegemony, and colonization; liberation wars against foreign colonial rulers; national divisions drawn in the Cold War context; and pride in national achievements, including an economic modernization that has lifted millions out of poverty. Added to this are South Korea's sharp political cleavages over how to address incomplete unification, versus Vietnam's domestic preoccupation with political pressures arising from democratization, economic reform, and globalization. Easley's matrix of the salient aspects of identity and their evolution yields an impression that South Korea and Vietnam are converging somewhat, even while growing apart from China. This, he posits, helps to explain and predict the "geopolitical convergence" of Seoul and Hanoi and their concomitant tendency to balance or buffer China.

Vuving agrees broadly with the thrust of that analysis. He demonstrates persuasively that for Vietnam, China is beyond question the primary reference point and "significant other"—a model in some sense both for anti-Western socialist ideologues and for Western-oriented economic reformers. For the ideologues, China is a desirable strategic ally; for the reformers it is the major potential threat to Vietnam's independence, security, and territorial integrity. Vuving, Minh, and Womack all show that Vietnam's embedded identity was challenged—and fundamentally altered—by successive shocks following the victory over the United States in 1975 and national unification in '76; a decade of armed conflict with China; the collapse of the Soviet Union, the Soviet alliance, and the spirit of socialist triumphalism; and profound disillusionment at home as socialist commandism failed to forge national unity and prosperity. Womack proposes an analytical framework that emphasizes the interplay of developments in the spheres of economics, politics, the surrounding international environment, and national ideology. Such a framework, he shows, helps reveal how a shifting national identity in the short term can significantly affect foreign policy decision-making in the long term.

Two other factors—religion and the degree of ethnic homogeneity—might influence Vietnamese and South Korean national identities, ideologies, and foreign affairs. South Korea is 98 percent ethnic Korean, although gradually becoming a multicultural nation in outlook and to some extent in demographics owing to growing numbers of resident guest workers and foreign spouses (a significant percentage of both being Vietnamese). Yet while South Koreans see this phenomenon in largely positive terms as reflecting the nation's broader, more "global" outlook, Vietnamese have expressed anger, resentment, and wounded national pride over anecdotal accounts of the alleged ill-treatment of Vietnamese workers and brides in South Korea. Vu discusses the gravity of the situation for the Vietnamese, especially considering the Confucian tenets of honor and chastity and their implied violation in the de facto purchasing of brides by richer foreigners. Vietnam is 86 percent ethnic Vietnamese, and increasingly showing a disposition to acknowledge and protect the rights of minorities under law. Whether any of these trend lines suggest an ongoing or future change in identity that might shape a different foreign policy agenda requires further empirical study.

The role of religion in forming national identity is another topic that needs proper research attention. Vietnamese and Korean responses to the introduction of Christianity, meanwhile, seemed to play only a small role in shaping their respective identities. The religion had been introduced to Vietnam earlier than in Korea, but it was popularly perceived to be the faith of the French colonial ruler and thus something to be rejected in terms of Vietnamese national identity. In Korea, however, Christianity largely enjoyed the status of the religion of national opposition to the Japanese colonial ruler, although it never became a basis for emerging Korean national identity. Vu suggests that Christianity was further marginalized as an element of Vietnamese identity owing to the officially atheistic state ideology imposed after 1975 by the victorious north.

Geostrategic Imperatives

Today most East Asian nations have to face a geopolitical situation in which they must deal with two giants. As Vuving expresses it, "navigating a course between China and the United States has become the common business that all other governments in the region have to pursue." Each of the authors in this volume concludes that new East Asian geostrategic imperatives behoove Hanoi and Seoul (1) to accept the reality of intensifying U.S.-China bipolar contention, (2) to adjust to China's rising economic and military weight, (3) to encourage America's continued balancing—hopefully stabilizing—involvement in the Western Pacific, (4) to avert having to make any choice between Beijing and Washington, and thus (5) to support regional multilateral cooperation and integration.

In chapter 6 Su-Hoon Lee presents the underlying logic of President Roh Moo-hyun's Northeast Asia Cooperation Initiative in much the same terms, although he also underlines the salience of inter-Korean relations, the evolving strategic priorities and regional security posture of the United States, and sharp domestic divides within South Korea over optimal policy approaches. In chapter 3 Scott Snyder emphasizes that South Korea, reliant upon China for economic growth but upon the United States for security, has a large stake in the maintenance of cooperative Sino-U.S. relations. Moreover, Snyder notes— affirming an insight made by Korean-American scholar J. J. Suh—that the "sunk costs" of investment in the U.S. relationship discourage a fundamental strategic realignment, as does South Korean doubt that building an independent military capability would be feasible financially or a sufficient deterrent against major powers in the region. Easley, as earlier noted, conjectures that embedded identity is one reason why both Seoul and Hanoi are distancing themselves from Beijing's perceived regional ambitions. Minh suggests that South Korea and Vietnam share an interest in fostering a new Asia-Pacific security architecture; he draws encouragement from what he sees as the meaningful bilateral cooperation of two Asian middle powers toward that end.

Womack, meanwhile, assesses Vietnam's position and options vis-à-vis China: Vietnam's identity is suffused with the idea of heroic resistance to Chinese aggression; contemporary disputes over island sovereignty and fishing rights in the South China Sea have only deepened Vietnamese resentment; yet no other Southeast Asian nation is so dependent upon trade with China (nor runs as high a chronic trade imbalance). Womack sees policy shifts in both Hanoi and Seoul signifying new (or renewed) interest in forging closer ties with Washington, not because of any inherent trust in the goals and exercise of American power but rather to balance against the rising threat from China and to buy time to support stabilizing mechanisms in the region. Vuving and Vu postulate that Hanoi—far from being hamstrung by an opaque, passive, and short-term diplomatic strategy—has cultivated a subtle, realistic chess master's long-term approach to national security that entails continual assessment of, and concomitant adjustment to, the respective capabilities and intentions of Washington and Beijing.

Each essay in this volume brings to light important details in the general picture of Vietnamese and South Korean foreign policy today. In both nations, historical and identity factors predispose political parties and ruling elite factions to favor one or another foreign policy grand strategy. In South Korea the principal divide is between conservatives and progressives;[17] in Vietnam it turns on the contest for supremacy between anti-Westerners and modernizers, or those emphasizing socialist ideology versus those laying greater stress on economic development.

In chapter 6 Lee writes from a South Korean "progressive" perspective, arguing that Seoul's continued economic prosperity and goal of peaceful reunification will be impossible to achieve absent Chinese goodwill and policy support. He contends that Lee Myung-bak—by abandoning peace initiatives toward the north, assigning paramount importance to the U.S. alliance, and even encouraging Sino-U.S. contention—left South Korea in an unenviable strategic position vis-à-vis China, North Korea, the United States, and the larger Northeast Asian region. South Korean conservatives, of course, would robustly counter those arguments. Snyder sees the strategic underpinning for Seoul's policy of *Nordpolitik* (including normalization with China and "sunshine" toward North Korea) as its plausible belief that Chinese cooperation is needed for successful reunification. He observes, however, that the past decade has exposed stark differences between how China and South Korea envision the future of the Korean Peninsula. South Koreans' frustration and disillusionment with China are on the rise: Beijing has lent diplomatic cover to North Korean nuclear ambitions; declined to pressure or even criticize North Korea for its provocations against the south; and, on a lesser but highly emotional matter, failed to rein in nationalistic Chinese scholars who have laid historical claim to the Koguryo Kingdom as falling within "China's" ancient boundaries. All such actions, Snyder shows, serve to play "on South Korean anxieties that

China's rising influence may be accompanied by Chinese attempts to replicate a historical hierarchical relationship . . . in which Korea was at a distinct disadvantage."

Minh makes the interesting observation that one reason why East Asia is failing to achieve greater regional integration can be found in the China-Japan relationship. France and Germany, the somewhat analogous leading powers on the European continent, overcame their historical legacy of competition and warfare to lead the postwar drive toward European integration. In East Asia, the two major powers have yet to settle their historical issues. As powerful (and opposing) members of the two Cold War blocs, they never reconciled their differing memories and interpretations of imperial Japan's invasion of China;[18] meanwhile, Japan remains the major U.S. alliance partner in Asia and the publicly praised "linchpin" of the American security posture in the region. Conflicting claims to the Diaoyu/Senkaku islands; to fisheries; and to potential deep-sea petroleum, gas, and mineral resources have exacerbated Sino-Japanese differences. Because the U.S. maintenance of a robust hub-and-spokes alliance system is now tacitly aimed at balancing or containing Chinese ambitions, Minh continues, Washington lacks credibility as a potential outside facilitator of regional integration. Without China, Japan, or the United States playing roles akin to those of postwar France and Germany, the region must find other means of fostering stability and eventual integration.[19]

And here, Minh concludes, is where Vietnam and South Korea, as significant middle powers, have the potential to enhance cooperation. For Minh, the ASEAN+3 format offers the greatest promise for these two nations—sharpened as they are by historical experiences as weaker powers—to utilize their diplomatic skills in forging an East Asian regional architecture able to promote and preserve stability. Vuving seems more agnostic with respect to the potential for meaningful Hanoi-Seoul cooperation to affect relations with China and the United States, but agrees that any such cooperation will occur within the framework of regional multilateralism.

Vuving looks at Vietnam's post–Cold War adjustment to geostrategic imperatives through the complex but convincing optic of that nation's political contention rooted in the sequential domestic traumas occurring after 1975. He identifies two major tendencies, or blocs, within Vietnam's ruling elite that harbor profoundly conflicting elements of identity, ambition, and strategic choice that have maintained a precarious, shifting balance since 1975. These are: (1) *anti-Westerners*, who accord primacy to party over nation, who identify politically and viscerally with an older vision of socialist internationalism, and who thus resist integration into the Western-led world order; and (2) *modernizers*, who hold that the nation must stand above the Communist Party and must, to achieve rapid development, integrate Vietnam's economy with the existing world order.

The interplay between these tendencies shapes Vietnamese choices in both domestic and foreign policy, but ought not to be understood as a formulaic contention between "pro-China" and "pro-U.S." camps. To the contrary, Vuving emphasizes that the Vietnamese "game" has at least four players: either of the Vietnamese blocs, China, or the United States can shift the balance in Hanoi and reorient thinking about policy choices. Moreover, they are the usual psychological and external factors, including the perceived international balance of power, differing historical memories, and human ambition playing out on a canvas of domestic politics. Every player has a complex worldview that overlaps with others at both the strategic and tactical levels. Both Vietnamese blocs, for example, recognize the potential threat posed both by American "imperial ambitions" and by China's hegemonic assertiveness and military-backed expansionism within the region. Virtually all Vietnamese hold an image of China—the omnipresent "other"—as a major world power, a fountainhead of East Asian cultural values, and an indispensable economic partner. Further, China stands as a model for both Vietnamese blocs: (1) for the anti-Western keepers of the socialist flame, China shares an ideology, a set of higher ambitions, a one-party system, and similar governing and control mechanisms; (2) for the modernizers, China has successfully cast off the shackles of socialist planning, modernized rapidly by embracing market mechanisms and integrating into the global economy, and raised the living standards of a massive population not long ago mired in the direst poverty. From all this, Vuving distills the essence of the grand strategy pursued by each Vietnamese camp: Anti-Westerners aim to ally with China on the basis of a shared ideology and a common enemy (i.e., Western imperialism and hegemonism), and to resolve territorial and other disputes by appealing to China's commitment to the higher good; modernizers seek to balance China by, for example, inviting greater U.S. involvement in the region, and to enmesh China in a web of mutually beneficial economic and power relationships.

Embracing the Region

Each essay illuminates how South Korean and Vietnamese leaders aim to avoid becoming embroiled in Sino-U.S. regional rivalry while avoiding the necessity of making an unpalatable policy choice favoring either the existing or the nascent superpower. Vietnam's strategy since the late 1980s has featured an active embrace of the ASEAN, other regional and subregional organizations, discussion forums, and a variety of ad hoc multilateral conflict-avoidance mechanisms. In South Korea, prominent university scholars, national think tanks, and political progressives have offered detailed schemes for how to position the nation at the center of robust new security architectures in Northeast Asia. However, successive post–Cold War South Korean governments have endorsed many such proposals in the abstract, but only infrequently manifested a vigorous commitment to regionalism as a centerpiece of national diplomacy. One might then wonder whether there is more to regionalism, for either Hanoi or Seoul, than a device to buffer against a rapidly rising China. Should one interpret Hanoi's strong and Seoul's qualified embrace of regionalism as mainly a China-centered strategy with both balancing and bandwagoning elements? Or might one chalk it up to classical middle-power behavior—that is, coalition-building and niche diplomacy, with an eye to the common regional good?

Womack finds evidence that Vietnam's regional diplomacy since the mid-1990s has not been narrowly aimed at China. The 1997–98 Asian financial crisis exposed the fragility of many Asian economies, Vietnam's among them; China emerged, surprisingly, as a regional stabilizer and economic savior at a juncture when the United States seemed incapable of rendering timely and effective assistance. For Vietnam embracing the region was a collective effort, with China fully participating, to take out a kind of group insurance policy against any repetition of the financial crisis. As the ASEAN expanded its membership to include Cambodia and Myanmar, and broadened its agenda to embrace regional political, security, and transnational issues, Vietnam participated more actively and began to take on a new regional identity. Despite significant differences among the ASEAN member states in terms of geographic area, population, stage of economic development, and governmental system, members held more interests and attitudes in common than not. For Vietnam and other nations, membership in the ASEAN—and its associated structures, including ASEAN+3, the ASEAN Regional Forum (ARF), and the annual ASEAN post-ministerial conferences—served to multiply the influence that each nation could bring to bear acting independently. Vietnam's entry into the Asia-Pacific Economic Cooperation (APEC) had similar reasons: ending the country's international isolation, increasing its identification with the region, and spurring economic development. On a separate track Vietnam successfully negotiated a trade agreement with the United States that smoothed the way for its entrance into the World Trade Organization, a step that integrated

Vietnam into the global economy and intensified its trading relationships within its immediate region. Finally, Vietnam has taken a leading role in sub-regional organizations focused on Mekong River resources and environmental concerns. All of this is arguably consistent with Gareth Evans' understanding, cited above, of contemporary middle-power diplomacy.

The South Korean case is less clear-cut. In contrast to the recent peace seen among the mainland and island nations of Southeast Asia, the northeast is a region still rife with power rivalries, competing nationalisms, territorial disputes, and living memories of armed conflicts. The major powers—the United States, Russia, and China—whose interests intersect and clash are nuclear-armed, while North Korea pursues a military nuclear capability and both Japan and South Korea are widely presumed to have the requisite scientific expertise and stocks of enriched uranium to "go nuclear" in short order. The Korean Peninsula remains divided almost sixty years after the signing of the armistice; Taiwan remains a flashpoint, as China continues to define unification with Taiwan as a core national interest and to underline its resolve, despite recent warming trends, by deploying some 1,500 missiles targeting the island; Japan has neither formally concluded a peace treaty with Russia nor effectively addressed Chinese and Korean grievances dating back to imperial Japanese aggression and colonization; and the United States maintains robust security alliances with Japan and South Korea that North Korea deems hostile and China considers in part designed to thwart its legitimate, long-deferred national ambitions. While there is an economic logic to regional integration, tendencies toward increased regional cooperation in political and security affairs have not manifested themselves.

Against that profoundly unpromising backdrop, South Korean president Roh Moo-hyun (2003–08) articulated a hope to construct an integrative, "community-like" order in Northeast Asia similar to the European Community and then the European Union. In chapter 6 Su-Hoon Lee, a principal architect of the NEACI, offers a detailed examination of the scheme's strategic intent, domestic political considerations, incorporation into the Six-Party Talks working group agenda, and ultimate failure to gain traction among the stakeholders as Roh's time in office ran out. The rhetoric attending formal rollout of the NEACI was undeniably ambitious, even visionary: " . . . an initiative that seeks to accelerate economic, security, and socio-cultural cooperation among regional and concerned nations to build a peaceful and prosperous Northeast Asia." In spring 2005 President Roh, speaking in elaboration of his NEACI concept, asserted that South Korea might become the "balancer of Northeast Asia."

Lee terms this a "controversial" notion, as indeed it was. Other participants in the Six-Party Talks greeted it with perplexed bemusement, wondering how a formal treaty ally of the United States anticipated playing, credibly, the role of disinterested "balancer." The South Korean conservative daily *JoongAng Ilbo* editorialized: "The notion of being a regional balancer is unrealistic, given our current military capabilities, (and) that is why we have been putting so much emphasis on the alliance with the U.S."[20] Some American officials, seeing a thinly veiled distancing from Washington at the idea's core, even conjectured darkly that President Roh might have unwittingly tipped his hand to reveal a future intent to withdraw his nation from the U.S. security framework.

Lee would argue, however, that these reactions misunderstood the true aims of the NEACI. Lee explains that the concept had three mutually complementary strategic elements: (1) containing various ripple effects associated with China's "rise"; (2) restructuring and modernizing the U.S.-ROK military alliance to address Korean popular resentment of asymmetries favoring Washington; and (3) promoting emergence of regional security arrangements that would alleviate North Korean fears and thereby encourage inter-Korean reconciliation leading to reunification. President Roh's National Security Council energetically offered backgrounders to the Korean and foreign press. It asserted that the ROK is "a major actor, not a subordinate variable" in Asia; has no history of hegemonism and can thus be trusted; is ideally suited to playing the roles of mediator, harmonizer, facilitator, and initiator; and can maintain "existing alliances" through combining hard power with soft power.[21]

Above all, Lee states, President Roh's plan sought to deter emergence of a new Cold War–type bipolar system in which U.S.-China hostilities would very likely draw South Korea into the conflict. To this end, President Roh sought to lay the foundation for South Korean defense capabilities and to upgrade ROK-China relations to a "comprehensive and cooperative partnership." During the latter stages of President Roh's tenure in office, he took encouragement from partners' slightly greater receptivity toward the NEACI. A meeting of the Six-Party Talks endorsed Seoul's proposal to explore the feasibility of promoting the NEACI, and formed a working group to establish a Northeast Asia Peace and Security Mechanism (NEAPSM) to serve as a future multilateral vehicle to promote regional security beyond the resolution of the North Korean nuclear crisis.[22] President Bush, who throughout his first administration had regarded such ideas as anathema, agreed late in his second term to inclusion of the topic on the agenda for his final bilateral summit meeting with President Roh. But the initiative died as the Six-Party Talks ground to a halt, new presidents assumed office in Washington and Seoul, and North Korea betrayed no intention of abandoning its nuclear ambitions.

The fate of South Korea's NEACI proposal obliges one to consider whether any meaningful Northeast Asian "regionalism"—let alone a formal regional economic and/or security architecture—can emerge at this point in time. If not, South Korea may find it difficult to play a classical middle-power role.

In fairness, President Roh's plan did not emerge, full-blown, from the fertile imaginations of key thinkers, whether within his administration and advising from outside. It built upon ideas that had begun to gestate within South Korea as the nation democratized, the Cold War ended, and elites focused anew on strategies for effecting reunification. The acceleration of European integration, the apparent utility of the ASEAN structure, and the U.S.-Mexico-Canada North American Free Trade Agreement (NAFTA) all inspired South Korean academic and governmental interest in emulating those successes in the Northeast Asian region.

President Kim Young-sam's government, which continued his predecessor Roh Tae-woo's Nordpolitik along with further opening to China, proposed in 1994 that Northeast Asian nations join together in a so-called Northeast Asian Security Dialogue to consider ways to build and institutionalize economic and security cooperation. That proposal never gained traction with South Korea's neighbors. South Korea next enthusiastically embraced the multinational Korean Peninsula Energy Development Organization (KEDO), created to implement provisions of the 1994 U.S.-North Korea Agreed Framework, committing KEDO founders (South Korea, Japan, the United States) and other original members (Australia, Canada, New Zealand, the European Atomic Energy Community) to construct a light-water nuclear power plant in North Korea. To some, the KEDO promised to metamorphose into a permanent security structure that could address broader regional concerns. That hope soon foundered, however, amid Republican opposition in the U.S. Congress and North Korea's noncompliance with its framework obligations. KEDO became moribund early in the first term of George W. Bush, and never recovered.

In the early 1990s the two Koreas, China, Russia, and Mongolia launched the Tumen River Area Development Program (TRADP), with support from the United Nations Development Programme (UNDP), as a joint program to develop the downstream area of the Tumen River, where North Korea, China, and Russia come together. South Korea, with periodic lip service support from Russia and China, has also backed a railway project that would link the two Koreas to the Asian continental heartland. While all of these schemes remain on the books, progress has been negligible. Governmental and private sector funding has been paltry; North Korea has shown reserve, evidently fearing a Pandora's box of domestic pressures and instability; China and Russia have competed for railway routes, prospective profits, and the regional upper hand; and North Korea's nuclear program has dominated regional attention and put a brake on any cooperative impulses from other nations.

The 1997 onset of the Asian financial crisis, which struck South Korea's economy with devastating force, prompted a reaction similar to what took place in Southeast Asia: renewed enthusiasm for regionalism, especially regional cooperative mechanisms that could ensure economic survival and safeguard against recurring crises. Emulating decisions taken by ASEAN members, the three major Northeast Asian countries stepped up the pace of bilateral and trilateral dialogue. They broadened the trilateral agenda beyond short-term economic/financial responses to the crisis to include such topics as energy, environmental protection, upgraded transportation networks, and consideration of free trade agreements. In December 1997 leaders of China, Japan, and South Korea attended the first ASEAN+3 summit convened in Kuala Lumpur. That mechanism has since been institutionalized, as have the summits of China-Japan-ROK leaders and foreign ministers. Yet none of these now routine annual affairs, which typically generate warm public rhetoric and voluminous "action plans," have yielded any discernible movement toward a broader regional architecture. Similarly, the periodic calls by Washington, Tokyo, and Seoul for the creation of a Northeast Asia Regional Forum—explicitly modeled on the increasingly expansive ARF—have generated little enthusiasm in other capitals.

This two-decade record of disappointment and futility invites a difficult challenge: South Korea has many of the attributes and aspirations of a legitimate middle power, but can it command the material and diplomatic capabilities to advance its strategic vision for regional institutions? So long as the North Korean nuclear dilemma defies resolution and exacerbates regional rivalries and strategic mistrust, closer economic integration and multilateral security cooperation in Northeast Asia do not seem possible.

Vietnam and North Korea: A Useful Comparison?

While this book focuses on South Korea and Vietnam, a comparison of Vietnam and North Korea—or even of pre-unification North Vietnam and North Korea—is worth considering. North Korea is inarguably the outlier in its subregion, in Asia, and in the international community. Often characterized as the last surviving "Stalinist" state, North Korea is perhaps more accurately understood to be a one-of-a-kind outlier. It combines features of premodern hereditary monarchies, a closed autarkic economy resembling Maoist China's, and a system of totalitarian governance and social controls borrowed from Russia's early Soviet period. The Kim dynasty is sustained by a massive, politically empowered military; omnipresent organs of surveillance, control, and draconian punishment; a regime elite materially rewarded but ever mindful of its absolute vulnerability; and a mythology-laced state ideology that promotes a North Korean identity suffused with extreme nationalism, a sense of superior moral virtue, and grievances toward "hostile" outsiders. Its domestic legitimacy rests upon historical memories—however false or inflated—of the heroic struggle against the Japanese colonizer and the victorious war to repulse the U.S. aggressor; the respect evidently accorded its military prowess by all potential adversaries; and its claimed right to represent "all Koreans" in completing the sacred task of national reunification.

North Korea's grand strategy amounts to a diplomatic sleight-of-hand: posturing itself as strong, disciplined, and resolute in order to mask its fundamental weakness vis-à-vis the more powerful nations in its immediate environs. Pyongyang publicly extols "fraternal socialist solidarity" but rejects enmeshment in the trappings of formal alliance relationships such as regular policy reviews and military coordination, for these could reduce its freedom of action and even threaten its independence. It favors instead a diplomatic style that Metternich would have acclaimed: playing off allies against one another, doing likewise vis-à-vis adversaries, and engaging in protracted negotiations to buy time and exploit the fissures and weaknesses of the other party.

North Korea under founder Kim Il-sung, his son Kim Jong-il, and his grandson Kim Jong-un has consistently sought—and significantly depended upon—outside economic, technological, and political support, mainly from its erstwhile Soviet and current Chinese "allies." Perennially facing substantial domestic shortfalls in farm production, extensive malnutrition, and episodes of widespread famine, North Korea has solicited and received external food assistance from South Korea, the United Nations, international nongovernmental organizations (NGOs), the United States, and China. But these actions, entirely consistent with the North Korean regime's calculated shifting of favor and emphasis among outside powers, bespeak sheer necessity rather than any disposition to integrate into alliance, regional, or international structures.

It is therefore impossible to conceive of North Korea under its current regime as playing any type of positive regional role, let alone a classical middle-power one. It is the primary target of actions intended to promote regional security, not a prospective contributor to the region's common goods. North

Korea has repeatedly drawn the UN Security Council's admonishments and sanctions for its nuclear and missile programs, and has been targeted for bilateral economic sanctions and multilateral actions (e.g., the so-called Proliferation Security Initiative) by the United States, Japan, and dozens of other nations. It only grudgingly accepted discussion of its nuclear program within the Six-Party Talks, preferring bilateral talks with the United States and ultimately using the multilateral talks to exploit divisions among the other participants in order to extract concrete assistance. It has evinced no interest in the sort of regional arrangements anticipated by President Roh's NEACI. It has even balked at less ambitious initiatives proposed by Moscow, Beijing, and Seoul for joint economic development of the Tumen River region.

While Vietnam maintains diplomatic relations with both North Korea and South Korea, its important economic and political ties are with the latter. As Vuving, Womack, and Minh show in their essays, July 2003 marked a watershed in Vietnam's national security strategy. For the first time, Hanoi dispensed with the ideological underpinnings of its foreign policy, describing its aims and relationships in terms of "partners" (*doi tac*) and "opponents" (*doi tuong*) rather than socialists and capitalists (or imperialists). Any notional predisposition on the part of Hanoi and Pyongyang to compare and learn from each other's experiences as "fraternal socialist nations" facing similar challenges in economic development, national unification, and foreign policy had surely dissipated by the late 1980s and vanished wholly by the new millennium.

Tuong Vu offers the final and definitive word on the relevance of a Vietnam–North Korea comparison: "in all areas, from politics to economy to culture, the North Vietnamese communist state ranked equal to North Korea, and far exceeded South Korea, in terms of its domination over society. . . . [In North Vietnam and North Korea] the totalitarian mode of control stifled development in the long term, causing both countries to fail miserably. . . . The reunification of Vietnam was carried out by force and incurred staggering costs. . . . The lessons from Vietnam are perhaps more useful for North Korea since it is far more prone to taking this violent course of action than South Korea."

ROK-Vietnam Bilateral Ties: Achievements, Opportunities, and Challenges

The year 2012 marked the twentieth anniversary of the normalization of relations between South Korea and Vietnam. Once enemies, they have become important partners whose relationship has developed, in the words of Minh, "rapidly, beyond any expectation." He approvingly quotes former deputy pre-mier Vu Khoan's positive appraisal of Vietnam-ROK ties as an "endless line of water that starts from a shallow stream, grows into a big river, then flows into the ocean . . . [This development] over the past two decades could be considered 'the Pacific miracle.'" Ambassador Park is less effusive but still very positive on the fruits of bilateral engagement. He observed at the outset of his luncheon remarks, "We have achieved much more than we expected in 1992." That progress was clearly mirrored in the official language of joint communi-qués. From tentative beginnings, the relationship was termed a "comprehen-sive partnership" in the early 2000s and was upgraded, during South Korean president Lee Myung-bak's 2009 visit, to a "strategic partnership."

Park and Minh draw attention to the statistical evidence of this "miracle": South Korea is the leading foreign investor in Vietnam, with over 3,000 proj-ects valued at $23.5 billion and generating some 400,000 jobs in the local economy. South Korea is the second-largest official development assistance (ODA) provider to Vietnam, which is South Korea's number-one destina-tion for ODA; there are currently 34 projects under way with a total worth of $1.2 billion. At Vietnam's request, South Korea has focused assistance on the areas that spurred its own early success in light and heavy industries: sci-ence and technology education and training coupled with targeted invest-ment in the high-tech and information technology sectors. Bilateral trade has blossomed from $500 million twenty years ago to $12.9 billion in 2011. South Korea is now Vietnam's fourth-largest trading partner, while Vietnam represents South Korea's ninth-largest export market. Approximately 600,000 South Korean tourists visited Vietnam in 2011. Some 65,000 Vietnamese guest workers labor in the South Korean economy, and another 35,000 are long-term residents there. Approximately equal numbers of South Koreans are in Vietnam for business and official purposes, and to study. Moreover, there are currently 45,000 Vietnamese-Korean families, the vast majority represented by Vietnamese brides now residing in South Korea. While this has generated some misunderstandings and frictions, it has also increased mutual aware-ness of each other's society and promoted a visible multicultural trend in South Korea.

The impetus for Vietnam and South Korea to normalize diplomatic ties in 1992 was pragmatic. Vietnam was facing a serious socioeconomic crisis, and saw in South Korea a source of investment capital and government assistance, a prospective market for Vietnamese exports, and, particularly for Vietnamese modernizers, a model and spur to the domestic program of economic and social reform. South Korea for its part sought to develop a new and promising market in Vietnam for its booming export-driven economy. Given these powerful incentives, Hanoi and Seoul were able to put aside unhappy memories of Cold War opposition, rivalry, and even armed conflict (when ROK troops fought alongside their U.S. allies during the Vietnam War).

Park and Minh both suggest that the new relationship flourished not only owing to mutually beneficial economic arrangements but also because of cultural affinities and geostrategic commonalities. Conference discussant David Elliott recalled that some years earlier he had found a younger South Korean diplomat in Hanoi to be far and away the most acute observer and analyst of Vietnamese politics he had as yet encountered.[23] This, Elliott remarked, seemed to illustrate the simple human dimension of the new relationship: Vietnamese and South Koreans liked each other, understood each other better than most, no longer represented any sort of threat or challenge to the other, and substantially shared a perspective on the Asian region. Minh makes the same point in different words: since the Cold War and continuing to the present, the two countries have been "finding themselves in a broadly comparable geopolitical strategic position; sharing many historical, cultural, and political similarities; and emerging as two recognized middle powers." Park notes that Vietnam and South Korea now hold an annual dialogue that covers a wide spectrum of bilateral, regional, and global agenda items. China, Park declared during his luncheon address, has become "one of the main topics" of the discussions.

The open question is whether the thickening ties between Seoul and Hanoi will yield substantial cooperation in tackling, as middle powers, the most pressing challenges in the region. At present, as earlier mentioned, Vietnam has embraced its regional ASEAN identity, while South Korea sees that structure, including even the ASEAN+3 (China, Japan, South Korea) meeting, as having marginal potential utility for resolving security issues in Northeast Asia or advancing Korean reunification. Minh and others suggest simply that the potential is there to be explored and developed by the two nations. Easley offers a menu of China-focused topics for concrete Seoul-Hanoi cooperation: (1) in economic affairs, enforcing trade and investment agreements, strengthening the content and transparency of rule-of-law mechanisms, fostering stable and equitable access to energy resources, and promoting regional environmental standards; and (2) in security affairs, increasing the transparency of regional defense programs, formulating mechanisms for addressing territorial issues peacefully, and implementing a strengthened code of conduct for South China Sea navigation, fishing, and resource exploitation.

Should such a menu excite any interest in Hanoi and Seoul, the challenge is altogether daunting. China has repeatedly and forcefully made plain its disinclination to pursue multilateral resolutions to such issues, insisting that it will only discuss and negotiate them bilaterally. Chinese officials have also underlined their deep anger at what they see to be mischievous American "interference" in the region; they suggest in no uncertain terms that nations favoring multilateral approaches are but stalking horses for U.S. hegemonic intentions. Cast in this rhetoric, China's position seems to offer nations of the region precisely the stark choice between Beijing and Washington that they would prefer to avoid.

We hope that this volume will contribute to the growing literature, heretofore perhaps unduly Eurocentric, on the theory and practice of middle-power diplomacy. Acknowledging the continuing academic controversy over how to define a middle power—and whether Vietnam or South Korea fits logically within the generally agreed-upon parameters—the authors seek to examine relevant dimensions of Vietnam's and South Korea's status and ambitions. However one judges the merits of the specific case for either country, it is clear that South Korea and Vietnam share historical experiences and cultural traditions, diverge sharply in their modern development and policy choices, yet today face broadly similar geopolitical challenges. This comparative study might be useful in holding up a mirror to the publicly articulated policy goals of the two nations. Moreover, as the authors make plain, the two countries can potentially learn important lessons, both positive and negative, from each other's experience: Vietnam can draw upon South Korea's highly successful developmental model, while South Korea can usefully study Vietnam's experience in national unification and historical reconciliation.

Selected Bibliography

Ban, Kil-Joo. 2011. "The ROK as a Middle Power: Its Role in Counterinsurgency." *Asian Politics and Policy* 3 (2): 225–47.

Beeson, Mark. 2011. "Can Australia Save the World? The Limits and Possibilities of Middle Power Diplomacy." *Australian Journal of International Affairs* 65 (5): 563–77.

Boag, Gemma. 2007. "The 'Middle Power' Approach: Useful Theory, Unpopular Rhetoric." Undergraduate research paper presented at the Inquiry@Queen's Undergraduate Research Conference, March 2007. http://qspace.library.queensu.ca/handle/1974/1067.

Choi, Young Jong. 2008. "South Korea's Middle Power Diplomacy and Regional Security Cooperation." Asian Voices Seminar Series, Sasakawa Peace Foundation USA, Washington, DC, October 2. http://www.spfusa.org/program/avs/2008/oct2choi.pdf.

Cooper, Andrew F., and Jongryn Mo. 2011. "Middle Power Leadership and the Evolution of the G20." Working Paper No. 11-02, Hills Governance Center at Yonsei, Seoul. http://csis.org/files/publication/110818_hgcy_working_paper_No_1102.pdf.

Cooper, Andrew F., Richard A. Higgott, and Kim Richard Nossal. 1993. *Relocating Middle Powers: Australia and Canada in a Changing World Order*. Vancouver: University of British Columbia Press.

Cooper, D. A. "Challenging Contemporary Notions of Middle Power Influence: Implications of the Proliferation Security Initiative for 'Middle Power Theory.'" *Foreign Policy Analysis* 7 (3): 317–36.

Efstathopoulos, Charalampos. "Reinterpreting India's Rise through the Middle Power Prism." *Asian Journal of Political Science* 19 (1): 74–95.

Evans, Gareth. 2011. "Middle Power Diplomacy." Inaugural Edgardo Boeninger Memorial Lecture, Chile Pacific Foundation, Santiago, June 29. http://www.gevans.org/speeches/speech441.html.

Feffer, John. 2008. "Japan as a Middle Power." *IPS Asia-Pacific*, November 24. http://www.ipsnewsasia.net/bridgesfromasia/node/132

Gilley, Bruce. "Middle Powers during Great Power Transitions: China's Rise and the Future of Canada-US Relations." *International Journal* (Spring 2011): 245–65. http://www.web.pdx.edu/~gilleyb/Gilley_MiddlePowersAndChina.pdf.

Hasegawa, Tsuyoshi and Kazuhiko Togo, eds. 2008. *East Asia's Haunted Present: Historical Memories and the Resurgence of Nationalism*. Westport, CT: Praeger.

Harris, Tobias. 2009. "The Emergence of Middle Power Asia." *East Asia Forum*, May 7. http://www.eastasiaforum.org/2009/05/07/the-emergence-of-middle-power-asia/print/.

Hiep, Le Hong. 2012. "Vietnam Eyes Middle Powers." *The Diplomat*, March 5. http://the-diplomat.com/new-leaders-forum/2012/03/05/vietnam-eyes-middle-powers/?print=yes.

Higgott, Richard A., and Andrew Cooper. 1990. "Middle Power Leadership and Coalition Building: Australia, the Cairns Group, and the Uruguay Round of Trade Negotiations." *International Organization* 44 (4): 589–632.

Higgott, Richard A., and Kim Richard Nossal. 1997. "The Politics of Liminality: Relocating Australia in the Asia–Pacific." *Australian Journal of Political Science* 32 (2): 169–85.

Holbraad, Carsten. 1971. "The Role of Middle Powers." *Cooperation and Conflict* 6: 77–90.

———. 1984. *Middle Powers in International Politics*. London: Macmillan.

Hundt, David. 2011. "Middle Powers and the Building of Regional Order: Australia and South Korea Compared." *Korea Observer* 42 (1): 69–94.

Hynek, Nik, and David Bosold, eds. 2010. *Canada's Foreign and Security Policy: Soft and Hard Strategies of a Middle Power*. Oxford: Oxford University Press.

Ikenberry, G. John, Michael Mastanduno, and William C. Wohlforth. 2009. "Unipolarity, State Behavior, and Systemic Consequences." *World Politics* 61 (1): 1–27.

Jordaan, Eduard. 2003. "The Concept of a Middle Power in International Relations: Distinguishing between Emerging and Traditional Middle Powers." *Politikon* 30 (1): 165–81.

Juergens, Margaret M., and Nayef H. Samhat. 1997. "Middle Powers and American Foreign Policy: A Model for Managing World Politics with Lessons from Irano-U.S. Relations, 1968-1978." Paper presented to the 36th Annual Meeting of the Kentucky Political Science Association, Bowling Green, KY, February 28–March 1. http://www.kpsaweb.org/Hughes/samhatpaper.html.

Ko, Sung-Bin. 2006. "South Korea's Search for an Independent Foreign Policy." *Journal of Contemporary Asia* 36 (2): 258–73.

Koutri, Anastasia. 2011. "Turkish Foreign Policy and Turkey's Role as a Middle Power." Thesis, Istanbul Bilgi Üniversitesi, June 21. acikerisim.bilgi.edu.tr/browse/77417/ANASTASIAKOUTRI.pdf.

Lesage, Dries, and Yusuf Kacar. 2010. "Turkey's Profile in the G20: Emerging Economy, Middle Power and Bridge-Builder." *Studia Diplomatica* LXIII (2). http://www.ugent.be/ps/politiekewetenschappen/nl/onderzoek/onderzoeksgroepen/giis/nieuws/bijlagen/SD_2011_G8-G20_Lesage-Kacar.pdf.

Li, Yitan, Patrick James, and A. Cooper Drury. 2009 "Diversionary Dragons, or 'Talking Tough in Taipei': Cross-Strait Relations in the New Millennium." *Journal of East Asian Studies* 9 (3): 369–98, 509–10.

Mares, David R. 1988. "Middle Powers under Regional Hegemony: To Challenge or Aquiesce in Hegemonic Enforcement." *International Studies Quarterly* 32 (4): 453–71. http://www.jstor.org/stable/2600593.

Moon, Chung-In. 2007. "Peace, Prosperity and Community: Assessing the Roh Government's Northeast Asian Cooperation Initiative." *East Asian Review* 19 (2): 3–28.

Münkler, Herfried. 2006. "Die selbstbewusste Mittelmacht. Außenpolitik im souveränen Staat" [The self-assured middle power: Foreign policy in a sovereign state]. *Merkur* 60 (689/90): 847ff., cited in Brown, Allison. "Germany as a Middle Power." *German History in Documents and Images 10, One Germany in Europe, 1989–2009*. September/October 2006. http://www.germanhistorydocs.ghi-dc.org/sub_document.cfm?document_id=3732.

Nolte, Detlef. 2010. "How to Compare Regional Powers: Analytical Concepts and Research Topics." *Review of International Studies* 36: 881–901.

Organski, A. F. K. 1958. *World Politics*. New York: Alfred A. Knop.

Ping, Jonathan H. 2004. "Middle Power Statecraft: Indonesia and Malaysia." Thesis submitted for the degree of Doctor of Philosophy, Department of Politics, University of Adelaide. Subsequently published as a book: Jonathan H. Ping, Middle Power Statecraft: Indonesia, Malaysia and the Asia-Pacific (Aldershot: Ashgate, 2005), http://digital.library.adelaide.edu.au/dspace/handle/2440/22025.

Ravenhill, John. 1998. "Cycles of Middle Power Activism: Constraint and Choice in Australian and Canadian Foreign Policies." *Australian Journal of International Affairs* 52 (3): 309–27.

Robertson, Jeffrey. 2008. "Middle Powers and Korean Normalization: An Australian Perspective Revisited." Policy Forum Online 08-034A, Nautilus Institute, April 30. http://www.nautilus.org/publications/essays/napsnet/forum/security/08034Robertson.html.

Royds, Mollie. 2000. "Middlepowerism in the Post-Cold War Era: A Critique of Axworthy's Security Policy." *Journal of Military and Strategic Studies* 3 (1). http://www.jmss.org/jmss/index.php/jmss/article/view/267.

Rudderham, M. A. 2008. "Middle Power Pull: Can Middle Powers Use Public Diplomacy to Ameliorate the Image of the West?" YCISS Working Paper Number 46, York University, Canada. http://www.yorku.ca/yciss/publications/documents/WP46-Rudderham.pdf.

Scott, James, Matthias vom Hau, and David Hulme. 2010. "Beyond the BICs: Identifying the 'Emerging Middle Powers' and Understanding Their Role in Global Poverty Reduction." BWPI Working Paper 137, University of Manchester, Brooks World Poverty Institute. http://www.bwpi.manchester.ac.uk/resources/Working-Papers/bwpi-wp-13710.pdf.

Shin, Gi-Wook. 2006. *Ethnic Nationalism in Korea: Genealogy, Politics and Legacy.* Stanford, CA: Stanford University Press.

———. 2007. "Introduction: Regionalism and Nationalism in Northeast Asia." In *Cross Currents: Regionalism and Nationalism in Northeast Asia,* ed. Gi-Wook Shin and Daniel C. Sneider. Stanford, CA: Shorenstein APARC, distributed by Brookings Institution Press. http://iis-db.stanford.edu/pubs/21990/0_Intro_Shin_FINAL_CC2007.pdf.

———. 2010. "Historical Disputes and Reconciliation in Northeast Asia: US Role." *Pacific Affairs* 83 (4): 663–74.

———. 2011. *One Alliance, Two Lenses: U.S.-Korea Relations in a New Era.* Stanford, CA: Stanford University Press.

Shin, Gi-Wook, and Daniel Sneider, eds. 2011. *History Textbooks and the Wars in Asia: Divided Memories.* London: Routledge.

Shin, Gi-Wook, and Kristin C. Burke. 2008. "North Korea and Identity Politics in South Korea." *Brown Journal of World Affairs* 15 (1): 287–303.

Spero, Joshua. 2004. *Bridging the European Divide: Middle Power Politics.* Lanham, MD: Rowman & Littlefield.

Stairs, Dennis. 1998. "Of Medium Powers and Middling Roles." In *Statecraft and Security: The Cold War and Beyond,* ed. K. Booth. Cambridge: Cambridge University Press, 270–86.

Sussex, Matthew. 2011. "The Importance of Being Earnest? Avoiding the Pitfalls of 'Creative Middle Power Diplomacy.'" *Australian Journal of International Affairs* 65 (5): 545–62.

Tow, William, and Richard Rigby. 2011. "China's Pragmatic Security Policy: The Middle-Power Factor." *The China Journal* (Australian National University) 65 (January): 1–23.

Ungerer, Carl. 2007. "The 'Middle Power' Concept in Australian Foreign Policy." *Australian Journal of Politics and History* 53 (4): 538–51.

Vale, Peter. 1997. "South Africa: Understanding the Upstairs and the Downstairs." In *Niche Diplomacy: Middle Powers after the Cold War,* ed. Andrew Cooper. London: Macmillan.

Welsh, J. M. "Canada in the 21st Century: Beyond Domination and Middle Power." *The Round Table* 93 (376): 584, 586.

Wood, Bernard. 1987. "Middle Power in the International System: A Preliminary Assessment of Potential." Wider Working Paper 11, United Nations University, Helsinki (paper originally prepared for a WIDER meeting held in Helsinki in March 1986 on "The Role of the Middle Sized Economies in the Governance of the World Economic System").

Notes

1 All statistics are drawn from the *CIA World Factbook,* 2012.

2 Ibid.

3 Tom Rutherford, Social and General Statistics Section, *Military Balance in Southeast Asia, House of Commons library, Research Paper 11/79,* December 14, 2011, http://www.parliament.uk/briefing-papers/rp11-79.pd.

4 Joshua Spero, *Bridging the European Divide: Middle Power Politics* (Lanham, MD: Rowman & Littlefield, 2004); Nik Hynek and David Bosold, eds., *Canada's Foreign and Security Policy: Soft and Hard Strategies of a Middle Power* (Oxford: Oxford University Press, 2010); Richard Higgott and Andrew Cooper, "Middle Power Leadership and Coalition Building: Australia, the Cairns Group, and the Uruguay Round of Trade Negotiations," *International Organization* 44, no. 4 (1990): 589–632; Peter Vale, "South Africa: Understanding the Upstairs and the Downstairs," in *Niche Diplomacy: Middle Powers After the Cold War,* ed. Andrew Cooper (London: Macmillan, 1997).

5 Cited in Matthew Sussex, "The Importance of Being Earnest? Avoiding the Pitfalls of 'Creative Middle Power Diplomacy,'" *Australian Journal of International Affairs* 65, no. 5 (2011): 545–62.

6 A. F. K. Organski, *World Politics* (New York: Alfred A. Knopf, 1958).

7 Eduard Jordaan, "The Concept of a Middle Power in International Relations: Distinguishing between Emerging and Traditional Middle Powers," *Politikon* 30, no. 1 (November 2003): 165–81.

8 M. A. Rudderham, "Middle Power Pull: Can Middle Powers Use Public Diplomacy to Ameliorate the Image of the West?" YCISS Working Paper Number 46, York University, Canada, February 2008, p. 4, http://www.yorku.ca/yciss/publications/documents/WP46-Rudderham.pdf.

9 William Tow and Richard Rigby, "China's Pragmatic Security Policy: The Middle-Power Factor," *The China Journal* (Australian National University) 65 (January 2011): 157.

10 Detlef Nolte, "How to Compare Regional Powers: Analytical Concepts and Research Topics," *Review of International Studies* 36 (2010): 881–901.

11 Jordaan, "The Concept of a Middle Power," 166; and D. A. Cooper, "Challenging Contemporary Notions of Middle Power Influence: Implications of the Proliferation Security Initiative for 'Middle Power Theory,'" *Foreign Policy Analysis* 7, no. 3: 317–36.

12 Dennis Stairs, "Of Medium Powers and Middling Roles," in *Statecraft and Security: The Cold War and Beyond*, ed. K. Booth (Cambridge: Cambridge University Press, 1998), 270–86. Cited in Rudderham, "Middle Power Pull," 3.

13 Cooper, "Challenging Contemporary Notions," 6.

14 Carsten Holbraad, "The Role of Middle Powers," *Cooperation and Conflict* 6, no. 77 (1971): 77–90, http://cac.sagepub.com/content/6/1/77.full.pdf.

15 Sussex, "The Importance of Being Earnest?" 10; and Cooper, "Challenging Contemporary Notions," 9.

16 Gareth Evans, "Middle Power Diplomacy," Inaugural Edgardo Boeninger Memorial Lecture, Chile Pacific Foundation, Santiago, June 29, 2011, p. 3, http://www.gevans.org/speeches/speech441.html.

17 See Gi-Wook Shin, *One Alliance, Two Lenses: U.S.-Korea Relations in a New Era* (Stanford, CA: Stanford University Press, 2011).

18 See Tsuyoshi Hasegawa and Kazuhiko Togo, eds., *East Asia's Haunted Present: Historical Memories and the Resurgence of Nationalism* (Westport, CT: Praeger, 2008); Gi-Wook Shin and Daniel Sneider, eds., *History Textbooks and the Wars in Asia: Divided Memories* (London: Routledge, 2011).

19 For the arguments that the United States is not an outsider to East Asian historical disputes and reconciliation and therefore that it should play a certain role, see Gi-Wook Shin, "Historical Disputes and Reconciliation in Northeast Asia: US Role," *Pacific Affairs* 83, no. 4 (2010): 663–74.

20 *JoongAng Ilbo*, editorial, April 5, 2005.

21 Quoted by various Korean news media, April 4–7, 2005. Yonsei University scholar Moon Chung-in, an adviser to the Roh administration, explained that "the essence of the idea . . . is to mediate through open diplomacy the chronic feuds and dissonance that have plagued this region, and to establish there a new order of cooperation and integration." See also Chung-In Moon, "Peace, Prosperity and Community: Assessing the Roh Government's Northeast Asian Cooperation Initiative," *East Asian Review* 19, no. 2 (Summer 2007): 3–28.

22 Joint Statement by Six-Party Talks delegation heads, February 13, 2007.

23 Remarks made during the conference.

2 South Korea and Vietnam: Bilateral Relations

Joon-Woo Park

From January 18 to June 9, 2012, an exhibition was held in Seoul entitled "Tinh Ban—Friendship of a Millennium." The special exhibit was the first of dozens of commemorations celebrating the twentieth anniversary of the normalization of diplomatic relations between the Republic of Korea (ROK) and Vietnam in 1992. As the exhibition's title indicates, the contacts between the two peoples can be traced back for centuries: Prince Ly Long Tuong of the Ly dynasty self-exiled to the Koryo dynasty in 1226 after a coup d'état by General Tran Hung Dao; and about one hundred years earlier, in 1127, Prince Ly Duong Con of the same Ly dynasty, who first defected to the Chinese Song dynasty, came to Koryo when the Northern Song was defeated by the Jin dynasty and moved its capital to Lin'an in the south. Having settled successfully on the Korean Peninsula, Princes Ly Duong Con and Ly Long Tuong created two separate Lee clans—the Jeongseon and Hwasan—in Korea. According to a national census in 2000, their descendents numbered 3,657 and 1,775, respectively. If we include their descendants in North Korea, the number of Hwasan Lee clan members will be even greater. Senior members of the two Ly clans visited Vietnam in 1995 to make a historic homecoming after 770 years. They were warmly welcomed by the nation at their first homecoming and they now attend an annual ceremony on March 15 in Thang Long, present-day Hanoi, to pay tribute to their ancestors, including Ly Cong Uan, the first emperor of the Ly dynasty.

This chapter is the text of Ambassador Joon-woo Park's luncheon address at the Koret Workshop, "Korea and Vietnam: The National Experiences and Foreign Policies of Middle Powers," on March 2, 2012

The contacts between Korea and Vietnam continued from the sixteenth to nineteenth centuries when envoys of the two dynasties met and exchanged poems in Beijing while on tributary missions to the Ming and Qing emperors. During the colonial period, in an effort to join hands against colonial rule, patriotic intellectuals and revolutionaries from the two countries sought exchanges and collaboration with each other. Sharing similar experiences and outlooks as enslaved peoples, they published books on the history of their subjugated nations to draw lessons from their experiences under colonial rule that could serve to enlighten their peoples.

When World War II ended in 1945, the two countries again fell victim to great power politics: Korea won its independence but was divided into South and North Korea, while Vietnam suffered the same fate in 1954. In the middle of the Cold War, as a staunch ally of the United States, South Korea participated in the Vietnam War on the side of South Vietnam. More than 300,000 South Korean soldiers fought against the communists in Vietnam, which later became a hurdle in the Seoul-Hanoi negotiations to normalize relations upon the end of the Cold War. In the late 1980s, Vietnam adopted the *Doi Moi* reform policy to transform itself into a socialist-oriented market economy, and South Korea launched its *Nordpolitik* (Northern Policy) to normalize diplomatic relations with socialist countries. The end of the Cold War facilitated rapprochement between the two peoples, who were historically friendly and shared a common cultural heritage of Confucianism, Buddhism, and Taoism. Despite the memory of war and the potentially hindering history that the two countries shared, both South Korea and Vietnam agreed to put historical issues aside and to cooperate for the sake of the future. They first agreed to exchange liaison offices but soon agreed to upgrade those to full-fledged diplomatic missions at ambassadorial level on December 22, 1992, three years ahead of U.S.-Vietnam diplomatic normalization in 1995. After exchanging embassies in the two capitals, the Consulate-General of South Korea was opened in Ho Chi Minh City (previously Saigon), the former capital of South Vietnam.

Status of Korea-Vietnam Relations

Once relations were normalized, the two countries lost no time in catching up and upgrading their relations. During the twenty years following establishment of diplomatic relations, there have been frequent exchanges of visits of leaders, including fifteen visits of top leaders and more than one hundred cabinet minister-level visits. When Vietnamese president Tran Duc Luong visited Korea in August 2001, bilateral relations were enhanced to a "comprehensive partnership." Eight years later bilateral ties were upgraded to a "strategic cooperative partnership" when South Korean president Lee Myung-bak paid a state visit to Vietnam in 2009. The upgraded partnership between the two countries was reaffirmed in November 2011, when Vietnamese president Truong Tan Sang reciprocated President Lee's visit. The two leaders agreed in Seoul to strengthen strategic cooperation by expanding exchanges in foreign policy, security, and defense and to increase the already substantial cooperation in search and rescue, anti-terrorism, crime prevention, personnel training, and defense industries. The two presidents also welcomed agreement on the "Overall Joint Plan," prepared jointly by the two sides to foster the peaceful use of atomic energy in Vietnam. Under this agreement, two additional nuclear power plants are expected to be constructed in the near future. (Russia and Japan are currently in the process of constructing four reactors in Vietnam.)

As South Korean businesses vigorously invested in Vietnam, the Republic of Korea has emerged as Vietnam's number-one investor, with $23.5 billion of foreign direct investment (FDI) in more than 3,000 projects as of January 2012. This has created more than 500,000 jobs for the Vietnamese. Samsung Electronics has had its largest mobile phone manufacturing factory in Bac Ninh Province in the suburbs of Hanoi since 2009. POSCO has invested $2 billion since 2006 to construct steel mills in Ba Ria-Vung Tau Province in the south. Bilateral trade reached $13.6 billion in 2011, making South Korea the fourth-largest trading partner for Vietnam after China, the United States, and Japan. For South Korea, Vietnam is the ninth-largest trading partner and the second largest among ASEAN member countries after only Singapore. As Presidents Lee and Sang agreed in Seoul in November 2011 to achieve the $20 billion target before the scheduled 2015, and a $30 billion target beyond that year, bilateral trade is expected to double and triple before 2020.

Vietnam is also a main beneficiary of South Korea's foreign aid. The Korea International Cooperation Agency (KOICA) had already started its aid activity in 1991, one year before diplomatic normalization. Today South Korea is ranked among foreign official development assistance (ODA) providers for Vietnam, with more than $130 million in thirty-five projects over the last twenty years. South Korea has also provided $1.3 billion in Economic Development Cooperation Fund (EDCF) assistance for thirty-seven projects. Vietnam is the number one recipient of South Korea's EDCF, which is provided to fifty-six developing nations. As a former aid recipient and now donor country, South Korea has offered distinctive development aid to Vietnam in that it focuses on socioeconomic development by sharing development experience through education and vocational training. South Korea has built many vocational schools, including an IT college in Da Nang and hospitals in remote and underdeveloped areas in the central region. Vietnamese farmers are learning about the Saemaeul Movement (New Community Movement), which transformed poverty-stricken South Korean rural areas into modern farmland in the early 1970s. South Korea is also helping Vietnam invest in IT and high-tech industries through the transfer of know-how and experience in these areas. Many developing nations are eager to learn from South Korea about its success in science and technology. They know that South Korea's success in heavy and high-tech industries today is mostly attributable to the ROK government's early investment in this area at the beginning of its economic development in the 1960s.

South Korea and Vietnam have also boosted cultural exchanges. Sharing a long historical and cultural background in the Sinocentric Confucian order, Koreans and Vietnamese have found no obstacles to promoting cultural exchanges. There have been frequent exchanges of traditional and contemporary performances and exhibitions, while Vietnamese youth have shown widespread enthusiasm for Korean pop culture, or *Hallyu* (Korean Wave). The popularity of *Hallyu* in Southeast Asia is said to have started in Ho Chi Minh City, where the first Korean TV drama serials "Feeling" and "Golden Grass" aired in 1997. Today, more than 70 percent of foreign TV programs in Vietnam are from South Korea. There is also increased interest in Korean studies in Vietnam, which now boasts approximately one hundred professors at ten universities with about 2,000 students. In Korea, Vietnamese studies are established at four universities, and the numbers are growing.

With deepening bilateral relations in the socioeconomic area, people-to-people contacts have also greatly increased. In 2011 almost 600,000 Korean tourists visited Vietnam. The number is growing rapidly as tourism-related infrastructure in Vietnam improves. More than thirty municipalities from each country are bound together in sisterhood ties. More than 100,000 Vietnamese, including 65,000 workers, are living in South Korea, while about 100,000 South Koreans are living in Vietnam.

Vietnamese Communist Party General Secretary Nong Duc Manh, during his visit to South Korea in November 2007, likened relations between the two countries to those between *sadon*, a word meaning "in-laws" in Korean, apparently a reference to the growing number of intermarriages between Koreans and Vietnamese. More than 50,000 Vietnamese women have married South Korean men, making Vietnam the number one source of foreign brides for South Koreans. Our hope is that Korean-Vietnamese families will contribute to bridging the two peoples with kinship and also help the mostly homogeneous Korean society diversify culturally with a growing number of intermarriages with people of other countries.

South Korea and Vietnam have also closely cooperated in regional and global issues. Since Vietnam joined ASEAN in 1995, Vietnam has successfully held the rotating presidency of ASEAN twice and has already hosted important summits of ASEAN, ASEAN+3, APEC, ASEM and EAS. As South Korea holds membership in each of these regional bodies in a cooperative relationship with ASEAN, the two countries have worked closely together toward effecting their shared vision of peace and prosperity in the East Asian region. During President Truong Tan Sang's visit to South Korea in 2011, the two countries agreed to expand their cooperation on major global issues, such as sustainable development, climate change, nonproliferation of weapons of mass destruction, anti-terrorism, the maintenance of peace and stability, and the freedom of navigation in the waters around East Asia. As middle powers, their partnership on global issues will contribute greatly to the peace and development of the world.

When South Korea normalized relations with Vietnam in 1992, the ROK government had high expectations about Vietnam's potential future role in bringing reform and openness to North Korea. While attaching importance to economic cooperation with South Korea, Vietnam has maintained its traditional friendly relations with North Korea as former Cold War allies and socialist comrades. Vietnam is one of the few countries with which North Korea has regular exchanges and contacts. North Korea sent more than 200 fighter pilots to assist Hanoi during the Vietnam War, and Vietnam has honored the fourteen North Korean war dead as heroes in a mausoleum in Bac Giang Province. Vietnam has provided rice for North Korea since 1995 and has purchased military equipment from North Korea. Vietnam's experience as a previously divided nation places it in a unique position to play a role in ending the hostilities on the Korean Peninsula. Vietnam stresses especially the importance of peaceful reunification, while supporting a nuclear-free Korean Peninsula and peaceful resolution of disputes through dialogue. If North Korea were to move forward for reform and opening-up in the years to come, Vietnam could offer itself as one of the best models to follow. This is where Vietnam's valuable contribution is anticipated for peace and security both on the Korean Peninsula and in the region.

Future Tasks

As they celebrate the twentieth anniversary of their diplomatic normalization, South Korea and Vietnam can feel proud that they have become close partners. They have achieved much more than they expected in 1992. They have shelved the negative history of the Cold War period for the sake of a future-oriented relationship and have overcome their differences of ideology and social systems. But some obstacles to further progress remain. For example, while there have been a large number of intermarriages between Koreans and Vietnamese, some of those marriages have had unhappy endings, leading to damaged feelings between the two peoples. When the South Korean government in July 2004 brought hundreds of North Korean refugees seeking asylum from Vietnam to Seoul via two chartered 747 jumbo jets, tension rose among the three countries. When the South Korean government in 2009 promoted legislation to honor its veterans of the Vietnam War, it encountered strong opposition from the Vietnamese government and withdrew the measure. Vietnam argued that such a step would have dishonored their national unification war and served to justify South Korea's participation in the war. The veterans are mostly in their sixties and seventies, many of them suffering from the aftereffects of Agent Orange exposure. The two countries need to increase mutual efforts to get over all these hindrances. And, considering the mutually complementary nature of their relations and their geopolitical similarity, they need to expand the scope and content of their collaboration beyond bilateral relations.

East Asia is one of the most dynamic and thriving regions in the world today. We are witnessing a rapid increase in interdependence and exchanges among the countries of the region. However, complex security concerns, deep-rooted differences in perceptions of history, and the ever-worsening territorial disputes inflamed by growing nationalistic fervor represent obstacles to securing durable peace and prosperity in the region. With the rise of China and the decline of U.S. regional influence, uncertainties are growing in East Asia, where a region-wide institutional framework for cooperation to address these challenges is lacking.

As newly emerged middle powers in the region, South Korea and Vietnam can play important roles in fostering East Asian cooperation. They need to make joint efforts to enhance regional cooperation leading to integration. We should recall the roles played by the Low Countries of Benelux for over 60 years in the process of European reconciliation and integration, roles that should serve as models for Korea and Vietnam. The two countries, as facilitators from Northeast Asia and ASEAN, respectively, need to collaborate in playing a bridging role and promoting a greater East Asian community.

South Korea and Vietnam are two unique countries that share similar experiences in their relations with China and the United States. Sharing borders with China, Korea and Vietnam have maintained relatively peaceful relations with China during the long history of the Confucian tributary system. With unyielding and indomitable spirit, they have endured and survived the many challenges from their neighbors, and succeeded in keeping their national identity and integrity. Today, China has become the number one trading partner for each of these two countries. In terms of their respective relationships with the United States, South Korea has been America's key ally in East Asia since the United States defended the freedom of the Korean people during the Korean War. As a U.S. ally, South Korea shares fundamental values and security interests and has prospered economically. Vietnam overcame its animosity against its former enemy in 1995 and has emerged as a strategic partner of the United States. East Asia is counting on the role South Korea and Vietnam will play in the nebulous and complicated geopolitics of the region.

3 Korea, Between China and the United States

Scott Snyder

At the dawn of Korea's entry into the modern diplomatic era in the late nineteenth century, China, Japan, and Russia were the countries that loomed large. As Yi dynasty leaders contemplated the establishment of diplomatic relations with the United States, the faraway great power seemed an attractive counterweight to Korea's larger next-door neighbors. Strategists of the day hoped a relationship with the United States might provide options that would be unavailable to a Korea acting on its own.

South Korea's choices today may seem hardly comparable to those faced by a dynastic Korea on its last legs (although the old days may parallel North Korea's current strategic circumstances), but the Korean Peninsula's position remains unchanged. The geostrategic situation at the end of the nineteenth century provides a preamble to South Korea's modern-day strategic dilemma: how to avoid circumstances that require choosing between the interests of Washington and Beijing.

The challenge is a difficult one, as South Korea relies on China for economic growth and the United States for security. A downturn in Sino-U.S. relations would force the Republic of Korea (ROK) to make a costly strategic choice. To avoid such a predicament, the ROK has major stakes in the maintenance of good Sino-U.S. relations.

Another reason why Seoul would prefer to avoid choosing between Washington and Beijing relates to its desire for Korean reunification. Despite concerns about the ramifications of China's power and the possibility that China could prevent Korean reunification, South Koreans also recognize that cooperation with China is necessary if Korean reunification is to be achieved.

Thus, the ROK has been relatively reluctant to embrace the idea of aligning with the United States against China's rise, especially if such a choice were to foreclose the opportunity to achieve reunification. Moreover, South Korea's historical pattern of seeking protection and support from the most dominant power in the regional/global order suggests that using military means to confront that power has little salience; rather, Korea has historically underinvested in military capabilities, recognizing that such are of little use in trying to blunt the influence of larger powers.

In this chapter I will examine the potential obstacles to improved Sino-ROK political and strategic relations, including the issues of history and territory, the future of North Korea, and the role of the United States—obstacles that have emerged in the context of China's rising influence over the Korean Peninsula. I will then evaluate factors such as relative power, system type, and the sunk costs of investment in the status quo (represented by South Korea's alliance with the United States) that might influence ROK priorities and could ultimately require it to make strategic choices as it grapples with the possibility of a power transition between China and the United States.

The Evolution of South Korean Foreign Policy: The End of the Cold War and the Effects of South Korea's Democratization

Even as the establishment of the ROK was a manifestation of divisions drawn by the Cold War and reinforced by the Korean War, South Korean foreign policy was tethered to the foreign policy of the United States throughout the Cold War. The new ROK depended on the United States for its security and prosperity; the United States was the central actor around which South Korean diplomacy revolved, with supplemental interaction with U.S. friends and allies in Western Europe, Southeast Asia, and Japan. As a result, South Korea had little contact and no meaningful political relationships with the Eastern Bloc countries until the Seoul Olympic Games in 1988.

A second driver of South Korean foreign policy during the Cold War was the nation's competition for influence and legitimacy on the international stage with North Korea. This subsided as an influential factor in South Korea's foreign policy, however, as the nation successfully expanded its relationships with the Eastern Bloc in conjunction with the Olympics, and as the two Koreas entered the United Nations in early 1991.

As South Korea modernized economically, made the transition to democracy, and established and expanded normal diplomatic relations with the Eastern Bloc countries at the end of the Cold War, there was a shift in the

U.S.-ROK relationship from that of a patron and client toward a more equal partnership. South Korea's economic modernization provided an important catalyst for the development of new relationships that allowed Seoul to establish a modicum of independence from the United States in its interests and orientation. Democratization removed some of the most heated flashpoints from the management of the U.S.-ROK alliance, and also made the relationship with the United States—and the question of South Korea's historic dependence on the United States—a topic of domestic political debate for the first time. Particularly prominent was the issue of coordination in policy toward North Korea, which did much to influence South Korean perceptions of the United States.

Following the establishment of diplomatic relations with the Soviet Union in 1990 and the People's Republic of China (PRC) and Vietnam in 1992, the question of how to manage relations with the four major powers surrounding the Korean Peninsula replaced reliance on the United States as the primary organizing principle underlying South Korea's foreign policy. China's rising influence became a major variable. Roh Moo-hyun's failed effort to adopt the stance of "balancer" between China and Japan in the mid-2000s, along with emerging questions about how South Korea might most effectively manage the dilemma of its economic relationship with China while maintaining good security relations with the United States, are evidence of the influence of China's rise on South Korea's foreign policy debate. Aside from the perennial debate over North Korea policy (which is really a domestic issue for Koreans), how to effectively position South Korea in relation to China and the United States became the fundamental issue of concern among South Korean foreign policy strategists.

But this debate was soon to have a new backdrop: a South Korea with a global reach and a stronger network of relationships around the world, as symbolized by the selection in 2006 of former South Korean diplomat Ban Ki-moon as the secretary-general of the United Nations. The United States and China are dominant influences over South Korean foreign policy (even in the context of UN politics). Even so, it is important to recognize that South Korea's domestic debate over its strategic management of these two critical relationships is occurring as the nation has assumed an increasingly important and influential position in the international community.

The normalization of relations between South Korea and Vietnam is a case in point. It is evidence of South Korea's broadening relationships in the post–Cold War period, especially as Vietnam followed its own direction of reform and integration with the Association of Southeast Asian Nations (ASEAN). Vietnam and South Korea share a common history as former tributary states of imperial China. In the ensuing years they have been characterized as much by difference as by similarity. As Alexander Vuving shows in chapter 4, Vietnam's historical experience of navigating the priorities of China and the United States is informed by a shared ideology with China, a legacy of enmity and/or unfamiliarity with the United States, and a postunification strategic narrative, while South Korea's narrative has occurred against the backdrop of an alliance with the United States, a rapprochement with China driven primarily by shared economic interests, and the need for China to provide a missing piece in Korea's unsolved reunification puzzle. But China's rise could be one of several factors facilitating a newfound convergence of interests between the two countries.

South Korea has naturally gravitated toward Vietnam as an economic partner and center for locating low-cost manufacturing that can no longer be produced competitively at home. Vietnam has benefited both from its cost competitiveness and from recent South Korean concerns about overinvesting in China. The two countries—which established a "comprehensive partnership" in 2009—remember their shared history as tributaries of imperial China and now must manage the opportunities and challenges posed by today's China. It remains to be seen whether these circumstances forge stronger ROK-Vietnam links in the future.

Historical, Maritime, and Territorial Issues in Sino-ROK Relations

Despite a historical relationship between China and the Korean Peninsula that dates back centuries, it is important to recall that the relationship between the ROK (established in 1948) and the PRC (established in 1949) is only two decades old. China's support for North Korea during the Korean War meant that the PRC and ROK had a nonrelationship in the 1950s and 1960s, despite their geographic proximity. North Korea served as a buffer that removed the prospect of direct territorial conflict between South Korea and China, but also served to diminish the need and desire for contact, at least until Nixon's opening to China established a relationship between South and North Korea's two primary patrons. From the 1970s China and South Korea gradually moved closer to each other on the strength of mutual economic and political interests, finally normalizing relations in 1992, despite North Korea's strong objections. Although South Korea finally gained normalization with China, it did not win China's commitment to fully abandon North Korea, even as China succeeded in convincing South Korea to abandon Taiwan. South Korea was still unable to achieve the strategic rationale behind its *Nordpolitik*, that is, China's buy-in and/or acquiescence to a, ROK-led reunification of the Korean Peninsula. On the other hand, diplomatic normalization with South Korea allowed China to hedge its bets regarding North Korea's future, drawing South Korea away from its security dependence on the United States and strengthening China's strategic position on the Korean Peninsula vis-à-vis Japan.

Diplomatic normalization opened the way for rapid growth in bilateral trade and investment relations during the mid-1990s. The Asian financial crisis in 1997–98 slowed growth in the Sino-ROK economic relationship temporarily, but double-digit trade growth was boosted by China's entry into the World Trade Organization (WTO) in 2001. With the exception of a dispute over Chinese garlic imports in 2000, economic opportunity was a powerful driver of the relationship through the mid-2000s, with most potentially divisive political issues falling by the wayside. However, as China's economy has grown, so has its power and political influence. Thus, the emergence of historical and maritime conflicts between China and South Korea has developed against the backdrop of South Korean concerns about China's rising influence. The accumulating list of political challenges within the China-ROK relationship cannot be fully separated from South Korea's larger concerns about the implications of China's rise and South Korea's desire to maximize its independence and pursue its own strategic choices.

The Koguryo Dispute

The issue of the historical origins of the Koguryo dynasty emerged as a source of controversy between China and South Korea in 2004. In the debate, China's desire to bolster its historical claims to a unified China unmarred by ethnic separatism were pitted against South Korean anxieties that China could use its version of history to thwart eventual Korean reunification. The dispute heated up following a decision by the United Nations Educational, Scientific, and Cultural Organization (UNESCO) to designate the remains of Koguryo in China and North Korea as World Heritage Sites, even as Chinese and North Korean sources differed over which sites should be included in the list.[1] China's interest in listing its Koguryo relics developed as a part of its Northeast Project, a five-year initiative launched in 2002 that promoted research into China's northeast region as a means of strengthening Chinese claims to historical unity. Reporting on the UNESCO decision, the PRC's *People's Daily* reported on July 2, 2004, that "the capital city and tombs of the ancient Koguryo Kingdom of China" had been added to the World Heritage List.[2] The announcement drew a protest from South Korea, leading the foreign ministry to assert that "our basic stance is that Koguryo is part of Korean history," while China's official Xinhua news agency asserted that "Koguryo was a local government of China; . . . its politics and culture were heavily affected by those of the central government" and that the kingdom's remains "are a key part of Chinese history."[3]

In response to the dispute, the Chinese foreign ministry decided in April 2004 to delete historical references prior to the founding of the ROK in 1948 from the Korea section of its website, inflaming public opinion in Seoul and stimulating a major shift in South Korean public perceptions of China. The dispute deeply influenced South Korean opinions of China, both among legislators and in the general public. An April 2004 poll by *Donga Ilbo* taken just prior to the eruption of the Koguryo issue as a problem in Sino-ROK relations had shown that the majority of the National Assembly members of the ruling Uri Party believed that South Korea "should focus more on China than the US" in future foreign policy, and that 84 percent of the public agreed that it was important to give "serious consideration to China."[4] However, a *Chosun Ilbo* survey on January 1, 2005, showed that only 40 percent of the Korean public had a favorable attitude toward China, revealing the extent of the political damage to China's image that resulted from the Koguryo issue.[5] The shift in South Korean opinion is also recorded in Pew surveys from spring 2007 and 2008, which showed 52 percent and 48 percent of respondents with positive views of China, respectively, compared with the summer of 2002, when 66 percent of South Koreans had a positive view of China.[6] The dispute has been kept alive in South Korean public consciousness by a series of historical television dramas focusing on the Koguryo period, widely watched in 2006 and 2007. How to deal with China remains a topic on the minds of the Korean public.

The Koguryo dispute is clearly not just about history, but about the future of Sino-Korean relations. The dispute plays on South Korean anxieties that China's rising influence may be accompanied by Chinese attempts to replicate a historical hierarchical relationship with the Korean Peninsula in which Korea was at a distinct disadvantage. For its part, China is primarily motivated by anxieties about national cohesion and minority relations—even as the Chinese public is suspicious of the motives behind South Koreans' perceived overreaction to the issue. It would be difficult to "resolve" a historical issue like Koguryo because there is no clear way to settle ownership over contested history. The territorial boundaries of historic Koguryo existed long before the modern concept of the nation-state had defined international relations, much less before current borders were drawn. The Koguryo issue will persist as a symbol of broader anxieties about the future of the Sino-ROK relationship.

Maritime/Territorial Disputes between South Korea and China

Another expression of China's rising economic and political strength in the region is the expanded maritime capability of both of its fishermen and its navy. Since the early 2000s, there has been an increase in the number of Chinese fishing vessels encroaching on Korean territorial waters and fishing in Korea's exclusive economic zone. While there is nothing new about periodic fishing violations by Chinese trawlers in Korean waters, which have predated diplomatic normalization,[7] the numbers have gradually increased as Chinese fishermen upgrade their equipment and are able to go farther afield in pursuit of their catch. Chinese vessels have periodically been seized, and a number of Korean coast guard members have perished while enforcing Korean rights against Chinese intruders. South Korea's coast guard documented a sharp rise in the number of illegal fishing cases, from 174 in 2001 to 656 in 2004, raising concerns about accidental clashes with Korean enforcement authorities.[8] A South Korean coast guard official died in 2008 at the hands of Chinese fishermen wielding metal pipes, prompting China's ambassador to South Korea to express regrets over his death.[9]

In another incident, on December 12, 2011, a Korean coast guard officer died after being stabbed by a Chinese fisherman resisting arrest. This drew attention to the inadequacy of Korean enforcement capabilities against the growing numbers of Chinese vessels entering Korean waters and employing more aggressive tactics and new, technological means of thwarting enforcement efforts. It elicited a round of editorial comments and efforts by South Korea to strengthen its enforcement capabilities. It also sparked violent demonstrations against the Chinese embassy in Seoul, and a retaliatory incident involving a metal ball that hit the South Korean embassy in Beijing.[10] The rise in South Korean concern over border defense following the casualty of the South Korean coast guard official resulted in a redoubling of resources and better arms for the Korean coast guard. South Korea is reportedly planning to increase the number of high-speed ships patrolling the Yellow Sea from 18 to 27 and to use special forces to detain Chinese fishermen found in South Korean waters. Strengthened management of fishery-related disputes was included as part of a ROK-PRC joint statement released during Park Geun-hye's first summit meeting with Xi Jinping in Beijing in June 2013.[11]

Another latent territorial issue between China and Korea could flare up: Ieo-do, an uninhabited rock formation in the Yellow Sea, lies in an overlapping area of the exclusive economic zones of the two countries. South Korea has built an ocean and weather research station on the rock, which China protested in 2006. Although South Korea's foreign ministry has claimed that Ieo-do is not a disputed territory since it is a submerged rock, China has continued to protest Korean activity in and around the rock, including efforts to retrieve a Korean bulk carrier that had sunk near Ieo-do. China's National Marine Data and Information Service has classified Ieo-do a "Chinese territory" on its website.[12] Ieo-do is no Tok-do (which the Japanese call Takeshima),[13] but it does present the leading edge of a dispute that could be inflamed by nationalism on both sides.

Korean reunification, if ever realized, could reopen territorial disputes long considered closed. A controversy erupted in February 2007 over a South Korean women's short-track skating team that held up signs at an Asian games event in Changchun claiming Paekdusan, a mountain on the China-DPRK border (known as Changbaishan by the Chinese), as Korean land. This forced the South Korean foreign ministry to clarify that South Korea does not claim the mountain, since South Korea and China do not share a land border. Controversy also simmers over an administrative decision from the Japanese colonial period that ceded to China some land adjoining Korea and China that had previously been under Korean administration. Chinese analysts fear that Korean nationalists might use this claim to reopen expansive territorial claims to ethnic Korean autonomous areas of China, even though China and North Korea settled their respective border claims decades ago.

North Korea as an Issue in Sino-ROK Relations

China's shielding of North Korea from international criticism further fanned the flames of negative South Korean public opinion toward China in 2010. The impact of the *Cheonan* and Yeonpyeong incidents[14] has intensified debates over Seoul's policy orientation toward the United States and China. In the summer following the *Cheonan* sinking, a South Korean editorial noted that "Seoul and Washington have come to a new chapter in their strategic alliance and partnership," to which "no doubt the North's torpedo attack on the South's warship *Cheonan* in the West Sea in March has contributed." But it also argued that "the two countries should be careful not to bring about unnecessary conflicts with neighboring countries, especially China. . . . It would be better for the South to avoid being caught in the rivalry between Beijing and Washington."[15] This echoes the conventional wisdom among leading South

Korean foreign policy specialists on how best to manage the respective relationships with China and the United States. South Korean analysts appear wary of the long-term risks of U.S.-China tensions as raised by the *Cheonan* and Yeonpyeong incidents, versus the need to maintain a favorable China-ROK partnership, and privately express grave concerns about the weakening of the relationship with China.[16] A major challenge for South Korean policy is how to build sufficient trust to win more active cooperation with China on political issues, especially those relevant to the future of the Korean Peninsula in the event of North Korean instability.[17]

More fundamentally, China and South Korea appear to have different preferences regarding the desired end-state of the Korean Peninsula. From a South Korean perspective, reunification is essential for the full recovery of Korea's historical identity—and the Korean perception that a great power is opposed arouses suspicion. Although China rhetorically supports the objective of reunification, it appears comfortable with the status quo of a divided peninsula.

South Korea's goal for the peninsula is embodied in its July 2009 Joint Vision Statement with the United States, which pledges that "through our Alliance we aim to build a better future for all people on the Korean Peninsula, establishing a durable peace on the Peninsula and leading to peaceful reunification on the principles of free democracy and a market economy."[18] This objective reflects both South Korea's growing confidence as an internationally responsible player and ally of the Obama administration, and increasing pessimism that the DPRK regime is sustainable in its current form.

South Koreans perceive Chinese activities as driven by a strategic interest in propping up the DPRK regime, thwarting unification, and maintaining long-term influence on the peninsula. To the extent that China utilizes economic tools to expand its political influence in North Korea or to shore up the North's stability, such actions are perceived as an attempt to deny a unified Korea, with negative ramifications for Sino-ROK relations. For example, Chinese food and material support to North Korea in the mid-1990s arguably played a major role in forestalling North Korean instability, when famine and a deteriorating economy raised prospects of North Korea's collapse and the realization of Korean reunification.[19]

Chinese debates about the implications of Korean unification for China became more active with the onset of South Korea's Sunshine Policy toward the North. Of note is the inter-Korean joint declaration of October 2007, which stated that the two Koreas would work together to advance cooperation on building a permanent peace regime in the peninsula among "the three or four parties directly concerned"—a statement that appeared to exclude

China from the process.[20] A Chinese foreign ministry spokesman affirmed on October 9, 2007, that "China, as an important nation in Northeast Asia and also a contracting party to an armistice agreement of the Korean War, will go on playing an active role in the process."[21] Chinese analyst Ren Xiao added that in the creation of a permanent Korean peace regime, "if the United States is an indispensable power, China is an equally important player that can by no means be bypassed. . . . It is neither possible nor desirable to exclude China."[22] Shi Yinhong of Renmin University defines China's "nonnegotiables" on the peninsula: the peninsula must not (1) threaten China's security through internal disruption or chaos, (2) function as a strategic fortress for U.S. "containment" against China, or (3) damage China's territorial and national integration by any irredentist and "pan-Korean" aspirations driven by extreme nationalism.[23] This statement illustrates Chinese sensitivities and its desire to diminish both U.S. influence and Korean nationalism while maintaining stability on the Korean Peninsula.

The Role of the United States on the Korean Peninsula

China tends to look at its policies toward the Korean Peninsula through the lens of its strategic calculus vis-à-vis the United States, and continues to fear that a unified Korean Peninsula allied with the United States could leave China strategically vulnerable to external attack. Xiaoxing Yi states that Beijing prefers a "strategically neutralized Korean Peninsula . . . Beijing's long-term strategic concern is not whether there will be two Koreas or one reunified Korea, but how to reduce U.S. influence there."[24] Jing-dong Yuan of the University of Sydney argues that China would oppose "a hastily unified Korea following the collapse of the North Korean regime" as that would result in the "loss of a strategic buffer."[25]

China has made no secret of its view that American alliances are a Cold War "relic," as expressed by the Chinese foreign ministry spokesperson in advance of South Korean president Lee Myung-Bak's first visit to Beijing in 2008. The PRC spokesman asserted at the time that the U.S.-ROK alliance "would not be valid in viewing, measuring and handling the current global or regional security issues."[26] Chinese analysts were frustrated by Lee Myung-Bak's efforts to strengthen the U.S.-ROK security alliance following the seeming convergence of Chinese and South Korean interests under Roh Moo-hyun's progressive leadership (which emphasized the shared objective of stability in North Korea and also seemed to be moving in the direction of lessening South Korea's dependence on the United States). They saw Lee's move as leading to heightened inter-Korean tensions and, by bolstering the U.S.-ROK security alliance, as an obstacle to greater Chinese influence on the Korean Peninsula.

While the United States does not have strong aspirations to dominate the Korean Peninsula and has viewed its presence there as less strategically necessary than its ongoing presence in Japan, the U.S. alliance system gives the United States a responsibility both to protect South Korea from external aggression and to safeguard the security of Japan, which, like China, views a friendly Korean Peninsula as a strategic necessity to assure its security. For this reason, Japanese security analysts are keenly aware of and sensitive to any potential shifts in U.S. security policy that might result in a lessening of U.S. commitments to the security and stability of the Korean Peninsula. It is these commitments rather than any overarching U.S. strategic aim toward China that motivate continued U.S. political involvement and presence on the Korean Peninsula.

South Korea's Strategic Choice between China and the United States: Relative Power, Sunk Costs, System Type

Having reviewed major issues in Sino-ROK relations, including aspects of strategic mistrust between China and the United States that continue to inhibit Sino-U.S. cooperation despite a limited set of common interests in maintaining a stable, nonnuclear Korean Peninsula, we will now turn to an evaluation of how South Korea is likely to manage its respective relationships with the United States and China in the event that there is a power transition between the United States and China.

South Korea is unlikely to shift its allegiance away from the United States in the near term, although it recognizes the need to enhance cooperation with China and will take advantage of opportunities to improve Sino-ROK relations where possible. China and South Korea have a widening sphere of common stakes in regional stability and prosperity. This is evident from the high levels of economic interdependence between the two, as reflected in a vibrant bilateral trade and investment relationship (China is South Korea's number-one trade partner, while South Korea is among China's top five trading partners and sources of foreign direct investment). However, even though China has surpassed the United States as South Korea's largest trading partner and is a major destination for South Korean foreign investment, South Korea still recognizes that the United States has the largest economy and most effective military in the world. Moreover, South Korea's successful economic and political development is deeply tied to the U.S.-led world order that has enabled

South Korea to flourish, making it difficult to imagine that South Korea would willingly abandon that order as long as the United States remains the world's number-one power.

However, if China's growth propels it into being a peer competitor with the United States, or if China surpasses the United States in its ability to shape global institutions, influence the economic rules of the game, or wield military might, then South Korea will face some difficult decisions. Or if the power of China and the United States is roughly equivalent and South Korea is able to play a decisive role in strengthening one side or the other through its strategic choice—how will South Korea decide?

As long as both China and the United States are equivalent powers, South Korea will continue to avoid choosing between the two except in the most dire circumstances. However, South Korea is likely to continue to prioritize its relationship with the United States over China even if there is relative parity in their respective power positions. Again, South Korea's past success and future prospects are heavily tied to the existing U.S.-led global order. To the extent that South Korea can convince China not to challenge the primary factors that have enabled South Korea's success, it will try to maintain the status quo. But if power tilts toward China in ways that impose costs on South Korea or that deny it the benefits it enjoys as part of the current international system, South Korea might be pushed to adapt to a new, China-centered global order.

Such an order would not be easy for South Korea, given its comfort and familiarity with the United States and the deep influence of U.S. thinking on South Korean society. South Korea's development has deeply benefited from a U.S.-led order, and South Koreans will want assurances that Chinese global leadership would not sacrifice those features that have enabled their success.

Another factor likely to cause South Korea to hold on to the United States is the sunk costs of the strong institutional ties between the United States and South Korea. J. J. Suh of the Johns Hopkins School of Advanced International Studies points to this in his analysis of how the U.S.-ROK security alliance survived the end of the Cold War and the dramatic political changes that were part of South Korea's democratization. Many of these forces appeared to be strong direct threats to the future of the U.S.-ROK security alliance, but Suh finds that the sunk costs in the institutionalization of habits of cooperation helped sustain the alliance. If South Korea were ever to switch its allegiance to China, its cooperation with the United States would eventually be under severe pressure to unravel given China's negative views toward U.S. alliances.[27]

A final factor that would likely discourage South Korea from moving too quickly to join a China-led Asian security order is its concerns about China's political system. One Korean analyst has argued that "we should accommodate the increasing economic relationship with China, but . . . China is not a democracy and is very different from the South Korean identity as a democracy and market economy—it is very different from us."[28] South Korean opinion polls show an awareness of systematic differences with China and concerns that a China-centric system would not be advantageous to South Korean interests. The freedom for South Korea to maneuver in a China-centered world might be considerably more circumscribed than is the case in a U.S.-led world.

Conclusion

A rare, in-depth assessment of the relative importance of ROK relationships with China and the United States is found in a December 2008 report by the Korean Institute for Defense Analysis entitled *China or the United States?*—a debate that intensified in the aftermath of North Korean military provocations in 2010. The book suggests that differences between the two arise from differing perceptions of strategic competition on the Korean Peninsula and the long-term role of the U.S.-ROK alliance, especially in scenarios related to DPRK instability and Korean unification. South Koreans' preference for a continuation of the alliance risks disapproval from Chinese, who may see the alliance as targeted toward managing Chinese influence rather than deterring North Korea as the primary source of threat. Meanwhile, South Korean perceptions of the alliance as an important source of security reflect a reluctance to accept a Sinocentric regional structure.

The book also notes a potential strategy for South Korea in response to China's rising influence, namely, to strengthen horizontal ties with other smaller neighbors on China's periphery. Although the specifics of the strategy and rationale for such moves are not fully laid out, this points to the fact that Vietnam and other neighbors of China face similar strategic challenges in the context of China's rise, and that South Korea might benefit from more active cooperation in that context. The strengthening of horizontal consultations with China's other smaller neighbors seems like a desirable strategy for South Korea to pursue, especially in the context of a U.S. pivot that prioritizes relationships with the ASEAN countries in response to Chinese assertiveness, as long as Korean strengthening of consultations with ASEAN countries is not done in such a way as to arouse Chinese suspicions or backlash against China. In fact, there are many similarities in the historical positions of Korea and Vietnam, both former tributary states of the Chinese middle kingdom who have contemplated or depended on the strategic value of the United States as a counterweight to China's renewing power. The potential contributions of South Korean and Vietnamese horizontal cooperation in the face of growing Chinese influence are worth further consideration, given these similarities. Some aspects of ROK-Vietnam cooperation are well under way, but there may be particular opportunities for South Korea and Vietnam to strengthen technical and/or military cooperation, including provision of military supplies and joint maritime training opportunities, that have yet to be fully explored. A further question that deserves careful consideration is whether the United States is positioned to be a facilitator or strategic anchor for such enhanced cooperation, or whether it is best pursued bilaterally by South Korea and Vietnam.

Notes

1 UNESCO (United Nations Educational, Scientific, and Cultural Organization), "Capital Cities and Tombs of the Ancient Koguryo Kingdom," http://whc.unesco.org/en/list/1135.

2 "China's Ancient Koguryo Kingdom Site Added to World Heritage List," *People's Daily*, July 2, 2004, http://english.peopledaily.com.cn/200407/01/eng20040701_148209.html.

3 Lee Chi-dong, "China's Claim on Koguryo Kingdom Goes Too Far, Scholars, Lawmakers Say," *Yonhap*, July 5, 2004.

4 Open Source Center, "Public Polls About China," *Donga Ilbo*, May 4, 2004, http://www.opensource.gov.

5 Jae-ho Chung, "Dragon in the Eyes of South Korea: Analyzing Korean Perceptions of China," in *Korea: The East Asian Pivot*, ed. Jonathan D. Pollack (Newport, RI: Naval War College Press, 2004), 253–67.

6 Pew Global Attitudes Project, http://pewglobal.org/reports/pdf/260.pdf, 92.

7 "South Korea Seizes Chinese Boats for Violating Territorial Waters," *Yonhap News Agency*, January 11, 1992.

8 "Chinese Boats 'Increasingly Violating' South Korean Waters—Police," *Yonhap News Agency*, November 7, 2005.

9 "Illegal Chinese Fishing," *Korea Times*, September 28, 2008, and "Chinese Envoy to South Korea Expresses Regret over Officer's Death," *Yonhap News Agency*, September 29, 2008.

10 "Korean Embassy in China Hit by Metal Ball," *Korea Times*, December 14, 2011; and "Violent Protest Outside Chinese Embassy in South Korea after Coast Guard death," *JoongAng Daily*, December 14, 2011.

11 "S. Korea to use Special Forces in Crackdown," *The Nation*, December 27, 2011, and "South Korea Toughens Measures against Illegal Chinese Fishing Boats," *Yonhap News Agency*, December 26, 2011.

12 "South Korea Clarifies Status of Disputed ROK in East China Sea—Agency," *The Korea Herald*, July 28, 2011; and Jung Ha-won, "Another Territorial Dispute for Seoul?," *JoongAng Ilbo* (English edition), August 9, 2008.

13 Tokdo/Takeshima is an island in the East Sea/Sea of Japan that is occupied by South Korea but continues to be subject to Japanese sovereignty claims.

14 The *Cheonan* incident involved the March 2010 sinking of a South Korean naval vessel in the West/Yellow Sea. A South Korean–led international investigation attributed responsibility for the sinking to North Korea. The Yeonpyeong incident on November 23, 2010, involved North Korean shelling of the South Korean island of Yeonpyeong near North Korea. That incident resulted in four casualties, including the deaths of two South Korean civilians.

15 "Closer Alliance," *Korea Times*, July 21, 2010.

16 Author conversations in Seoul, December 2010.

17 Bonnie Glaser and Scott Snyder with David Szerlip and See-Won Byun, *Responding to Change on the Korean Peninsula: Impediments to U.S.-South Korea-China Coordination* (Washington, D.C.: Center for Strategic and International Studies, May 2010).

18 "Joint Vision for the Alliance of the United States of America and the Republic of Korea," Office of the Press Secretary, White House, Washington, DC, June 16, 2009, http://www.whitehouse.gov/the-press-office/joint-vision-alliance-united-statesamerica -and-republic-korea.

19 Nicholas Eberstadt, *The North Korean Economy: Between Crisis and Catastrophe* (New Brunswick, NJ: Transaction, 2007), 99–126.

20 "Declaration on the Advancement of South-North Relations, Peace and Prosperity," *Korea.net*, October 4, 2007, http://www.korea.net/news/news/newsView.asp?serial_ no=20071004023.

21 Foreign ministry spokesperson Liu Jianchao's regular press conference, October 9, 2007.

22 Ren Xiao, "Korea's New Administration and Challenges for China's Relations with the Korean Peninsula," *Asian Perspective* 32, no. 2 (2008), http://www.asianperspective .org/articles/v32n2-h.pdf.

23 Shi Yinhong, "China and the North Korean Nuclear Issue: Competing Interests and Persistent Policy Dilemmas," *Korean Journal of Defense Analyses* 21, no. 1 (March 2009): 33–47.

24 Xiaoxiong Yi, "A Neutralized Korea: The North-South Rapprochement and China's Korean Policy," *Korean Journal of Defense Analysis* 12, no. 2 (2000): 71–118.

25 Jing-dong Yuan, "China and the North Korean Nuclear Crisis," Monterey Institute of International Studies, January 2003, http://cns.miis.edu/north_korea/chidprk.htm.

26 Foreign ministry spokesperson Qin Gang's regular press conference, May 27, 2008.

27 Jae-Jung Suh, *Power, Interest, and Identity in Military Alliances* (New York: Palgrave MacMillan, 2007).

28 Author's interview in Seoul, October 2008.

4 How Experience and Identity Shape Vietnam's Relations with China and the United States

Alexander L. Vuving

If great powers are defined as states capable of holding their own against others, East Asia has two. After the United States, only China, with its large economic and military capabilities, its nuclear weapons arsenal, and the strategic depth of its considerable territory and large population, can hold its own. In this regional environment, navigating a course between China and the United States has become the common business that all other governments in the region have to pursue.

Vietnam has much in common with South Korea in this respect.[1] No other modern peoples have more experience in dealing with China than the Mongolians, the Koreans, and the Vietnamese. The Japanese, too, have interacted with China for thousands of years, but—except at certain key moments—geographic distance has lessened the intensity of that encounter. Mongolia's experience with China may be the world's richest if one considers the tribes that occupied the Mongolian steppe, but it is poorer than Vietnam's and Korea's in terms of interstate relations. Both Korea and Vietnam, as member states of the past Chinese world order, developed peculiar approaches to China. While Korea's ruling elites practiced *sadae* ("serving, revering the great"), their Vietnamese counterparts followed the principle of *trong de ngoai vuong* (literally, "inside emperor, outside king"). These two policies, while similar, have important differences. Both stress paying deference to China to maintain good if unequal relations with a powerful neighbor, but the Vietnamese principle balances the acceptance of asymmetry with an emphasis on autonomy. Their similarities stem from the obvious: an insurmountable power asymmetry in favor of China, and the adoption—with twists and tweaks—of Chinese perspectives and culture by both Korean and Vietnamese elites. The differences between *sadae* and *trong de ngoai vuong*, meanwhile, reflect the different geopolitical settings of Korea and Vietnam. After the unification of the Korean Peninsula in the tenth century, there was no scope for further Korean expansion. The same millennium that saw the Koreans sustain their state within the peninsula witnessed the Vietnamese southern and western expansions, halted only by the French colonial conquests of the late nineteenth century.

Korea and Vietnam also share a similar history of relations with the United States. In both, Washington allied with half the nation to combat the other half. These are the only two places where the United States fought direct, hot wars during the Cold War. And yet this shared history cemented two different identities, expressed in different responses to the same "rise" of China and the same U.S. primacy. While South Korea is a close American ally, Vietnam defines itself as the defeater of the United States.

Assuming that states behave similarly under similar conditions, comparing their behaviors is reducible to analyzing contexts and conditions. Yet such analysis quickly reveals that states, while responding to material (and thus more objective) conditions, are also informed by ideational (and, thus, more subjective) factors such as experience, learning, ambition, and identity.[2] Identity derives from various sources, including traumatic experiences of war and crisis; military, economic, and cultural achievements; and perceptions of relative size, capacity, and strategic location. South Korea began to see itself as a "middle power" after the country became one of the major economies in the world in the 1990s. In 2006 the question, "Is Vietnam a small country or not?" spurred a nationwide debate in Vietnam that went on for several months.[3] Most of the participants explicitly or implicitly agreed that Vietnam was small in terms of its economic wealth, level of development, and governance, but not in terms of its population, geography, and history. Most focused on the root causes of Vietnam's contemporary stature and the requisites for achieving greatness. Nearly all expressed the attitudes of a small country trying to get bigger, not those of a self-conscious middle power. Echoing several others, one participant noted that the question "touched on a deep sentiment" shared by all Vietnamese.[4] The debate revealed a nation struggling with two conflicting identities, one rooted in past greatness and another derived from present smallness.

As will be seen in this chapter, the unsettling confluence of these two identities can explain much of Vietnam's strategic behavior. How Vietnam steers its course between China and the United States is decided to a significant extent by its dual identities, which were formed by conflicting historical memories, national ambitions, and learning processes. Needless to say, material conditions and power also play a large part in determining Vietnam's behavior. However, my intent here is to highlight the role of experience, perception, worldview, and ambition in making sense of material conditions. These intangibles are the filters that transmit the effects of material conditions and power relations to state behavior.

In this chapter I examine Vietnam's policies toward China and the United States after the Cold War. I argue that these policies are informed and guided by a two-headed grand strategy that combines two separately coherent but mutually offsetting priorities whose central thrusts are (1) anti-Westernism and (2) modernization. Both were affected by two traumatic experiences in Vietnam's recent history: the collapse of Vietnam's economy in the decade after reunification (1976) and the collapse of communism as a world system (in the late 1980s). I show how the ideas and experiences of these defining times shaped Vietnam's perceptions of China and the United States, and in turn, how these perceptions influenced Vietnam's relations with the two great powers. In addition to outlining the contents and trajectories of Hanoi's policies, I look at the gap between rhetoric and reality.

A Two-Headed Grand Strategy

Despite its outward appearance as a monolithic state, Vietnam's politics is informed and guided by two competing grand strategies based on two contradicting worldviews and national ambitions. Vietnamese politics in the post–Cold War era is characterized by the conflicts and temporary truces made between these two strategies.[5] Both trace their roots back to the Vietnamese anticolonial movement of the early twentieth century and are heavily influenced by ideas from abroad, but their rise to the commanding heights of Vietnamese politics in the post–Cold War era was spurred by developments in the 1980s.

Barely four years after peace returned and the country reunified in 1975, Vietnam found itself plunged into a severe crisis. On the economic front, shortages of all goods became the norm after the country's leadership forced private producers and traders to collectivize and prohibited free markets. On the defense front, invasion came from unexpected sources—the Khmer Rouge and China, who until then had been perceived by the Communist Party of Vietnam (CPV) as comrades. As a result of a joint Sino-Western policy to punish Vietnam's invasion of Cambodia and its alliance with the Soviet Union, the country found itself isolated in the international arena; an economic embargo imposed by the United States after the Vietnam War worsened the hardship.

This situation set off an intense debate about the causes of the hardship and the way to get out of it. Opinions were divided into two major groups. One stressed defects in the system and pointed to the need for reform. The other emphasized enemy sabotage and advocated upholding the system while stepping up countermeasures. As shortages and famine intensified, major changes to liberalize production were adopted as early as 1979, but reforms soon suffered setbacks when conservatives in the government were alarmed by the conspicuous wealth of some who benefited from the reforms. By the mid-1980s, however, Vietnam's economy had virtually collapsed; millions of people were starving, another million had fled the country, and inflation rates soared to triple digits. A decisive blow came in 1985–86, when Vietnam's major ally, the Soviet Union, itself struggling with its own stagnation and shortages, introduced a sea change in its foreign policy and indicated to Vietnamese leaders that it would not be able to sustain the same high level of aid, which at that time amounted to a quarter of Vietnam's gross domestic product (GDP). Hanoi had to look elsewhere for sources of funding and new markets. Against this backdrop, advocates for reform prevailed over critics, and at the CPV Sixth Congress in December 1986, the government launched a massive reform program, *Doi Moi* ("renovation"), that would set the stage for Vietnam's politics in the decades to follow.

What set *Doi Moi* apart from previous reforms was that it included a "renovation of thinking" (*doi moi tu duy*), a new worldview. This was heavily influenced by the Soviet *novoye myshleniye* ("new thinking") that informed *perestroika* ("restructuring"),[6] but it also borrowed ideas from the contemporaneous reforms in China, whose initial success certainly served as an inspiration to Vietnam's reform-minded communists. The new worldview contradicted the incumbent orthodoxy on all major points.

In the old orthodoxy, the world was divided into two opposing camps along the ideological line separating socialism on the one side from capitalism, liberalism, and imperialism on the other. Liberalism is the ideology of capitalism, which turns imperialist in its highest stage of development. The embodiment and power center of this liberal-capitalist-imperialist complex is the West, led by the United States. Since its inception, the CPV embraced Lenin's thesis that capitalism turned imperialism is the main source of war, and socialism on a global scale is the only way to preserve peace. Thus, the highest priority of progressive mankind is to combat imperialism. Originally a Russian-Soviet thought, this Leninist variant of anti-Westernism found keen followers among the left-leaning Vietnamese anticolonialists of the early twentieth century and subsequently served as a basis for the policies of Communist-led Vietnam since its foundation in 1945.[7]

While the old worldview identifies class antagonism as the motive force of world politics, the new worldview stresses national interests and globalization in their stead. It contends that since the 1970s, driven by a new technological revolution, globalization ("internationalization," as it was called in the 1980s) defines the times. This trend has brought the countries of the world into a single market and transformed the central dynamic of world politics from a military confrontation between two ideological blocs to an economic competition among nation-states, at the same time making them increasingly interdependent. In August 1989 a key proponent of the new worldview, Foreign Minister Nguyen Co Thach, wrote, "peace, cooperation, and development have become the supreme interests of the people of the world and the common trend in international relations." In an article in a CPV theoretical journal, he argued that the new technological revolution, a high level of internationalization, and the resulting international division of labor were restructuring the world and opening up unprecedented opportunities for underdeveloped societies to reach high levels of development far more rapidly than previously possible. The rapid road to high development, Thach concluded, runs through the world market. Discussing the implications of these "new historic conditions" for Vietnamese foreign policy, Thach made a plea for the normalization of relations with China and the United States and an appeal for "turning Indochina from a battlefield to a marketplace."[8]

In the same month as Thach's article appeared in the CPV journal, the Party Central Committee convened its Seventh Plenum in Ho Chi Minh City. At this meeting, which was shadowed by news of socialist Poland electing its first non-communist government, CPV general secretary Nguyen Van Linh, who just a year before had been a leading reformer, resurrected the Leninist "two-camp" theory in an effort to revive anti-Western sentiment. In an unmistakable attack on Thach and other proponents of the new worldview, Linh claimed that the recent neglect of Leninist teachings "has led certain individuals to believe mistakenly that the nature of imperialism has changed" and declared that "we do not nurture the illusion that the imperialist forces are willing to achieve peaceful coexistence with us." Linh marshaled a long list of evidence to show that the fundamental conflicts between socialism and imperialism remained vivid and highly relevant, while only their manifestations had undergone change. Against the backdrop of this conflict, Linh drew two major implications for Vietnam, one being to "join hands with other socialist forces, revolutionary forces, and progressive and peace-loving people world-wide in creating a combined strength to oppose the imperialist and reaction-ary forces" and the other to "sharpen the determination to protect the socialist fatherland, effectively cope with all dark plots and acts detrimental to our country's security and territorial integrity, and frustrate the imperialists' and other reactionary forces' schemes aimed at causing our nation and other so-cialist countries to break away from the socialist path."[9]

The contradiction between the old and the new world outlooks cannot be overstated. Whereas the old implies that Vietnam must oppose the Western order, the new suggests that the country must integrate with the Western-led world system if it is to modernize. The binary implications of this divide are felt not only at the level of strategy, but also at the deeper levels of identity and ambition. The old view appeals to those who stress that Vietnam is a socialist country whose primary objective is to save socialism and resist the West. The new view appeals to those who emphasize that Vietnam is a backward coun-try whose primary objective is to further economic development. Choosing between the two may be easy for ordinary people, but for the Communists, the distinctions are more subtle and the choices more painful. At stake for the Communists is the fundamental question of their party's relation to the larger nation. In theory as in practice, those who put the party before the na-tion tend to endorse anti-Westernism, while those who believe that the nation should stand above the party are modernizers. It is when this choice became unavoidable that the once-eager reformer Nguyen Van Linh turned into an ardent anti-Westerner. Linh's case makes it even more remarkable that not a few top-ranking CPV leaders insisted on their own party's subordination to the nation.[10]

While grand strategies remain an elite product, the aspirations they draw upon and the perceptions they shape are more broadly shared among the larger population. Support for both anti-Westernism and modernization arises from a large reservoir of experiences and sentiments that have been molded by history, education, the media, and other forms of national discourse. Ordinary people may not be aware of the details of policy, but they share policymakers' underly-ing identities and even general worldviews. This was evident in the debate over Vietnam's stature, the participants of which were not confined to the elite.

Vietnam's Perceptions of the United States and China

Hanoi's perceptions of U.S. and Chinese capabilities and intentions in large part guide Vietnamese foreign policy. The second half of the 1980s, when the new worldview was born, was a time of hot, polarizing debate among the highest echelons of Vietnamese society. Questions about the nature of the United States were front and center. Then, in 1989–91, intense debate over the nature of China further deepened the divide between anti-Westerners and modernizers.[11]

Perceptions of the United States

Anti-Westerners see the United States as the world's leading capitalist and imperialist force, whose constant ambition is to exterminate communism. The fall of communism in Eastern Europe reinforced the anti-Westerners' perception that the United States poses the most dangerous threat to Vietnam. As CPV general secretary Nguyen Van Linh asserted at the Seventh Plenum of the Sixth CPV Central Committee, the fundamental antagonisms between socialism and capitalism/imperialism continue to exist "as long as imperialism exists and as long as the socialist revolution has not yet achieved victory on a world scale."[12] For anti-Westerners, therefore, the United States is Vietnam's long-term, strategic enemy. Anti-Westerners have identified the West's and the United States' "strategy of peaceful evolution," the use of cultural and economic influence as a means to change the nature of the socialist system, as the major cause of the fall of communism in Eastern Europe and a key part of U.S. policy toward Vietnam. An important concept paper issued by the CPV Central Propaganda Department in June 2010 singled out the United States and the West as the main "hostile forces" faced by Vietnam. It asserted that since 2006 these "hostile forces" had stepped up a strategy of "peaceful evolution" and "cultural invasion" to "eliminate the socialist regime and the Vietnamese cultural identity." The document's authors expressed alarm at U.S. cooperation with Vietnam, identifying the U.S. Peace Corps as an organization specializing in propaganda and subversive activities and U.S. programs of educational cooperation with Vietnam as means of Westernizing the country.[13] Anti-Westerners' perception of the nature of the United States did not change even after Washington formally conveyed its ambition to develop a strategic partnership with Hanoi in 2010.[14] For example, an editorial in a column titled "Frustrating the Strategy of Peaceful Evolution," printed in the military's mouthpiece, *Quan doi Nhan dan,* included the following comment on the nature of U.S. politics: "Whether the Democratic Party or the Republican Party controls Congress, both are one in terms of politics; that is, both are loyal to capitalism and the bourgeois political institutions, support the United States' scheme of 'global leadership,' sabotage socialism, and ultimately, are all loyal representatives of the monopoly capitalist forces."[15]

Modernizers may agree with anti-Westerners that the United States is anti-communist and has imperial ambitions, but unlike anti-Westerners, they focus on its status as an advanced, industrialized nation. Modernizers believe that socialist countries have lagged behind the West on the social, economic, and technological fronts because they have failed to promote technological innovation and economic restructuring. This perception was articulated, for instance, by State President Vo Chi Cong in a speech before the head delegates to the National Assembly in December 1989:

> It should be realized that the crises in the socialist countries lie in the general crisis of the world since the '70s. That was the time when the scientific and technological revolution as well as the international exchange and cooperation developed vigorously toward a high degree of internationalization, when the political consciousness of the people in the socialist countries had reached an ever higher level and when the information explosion began in the world. The imperialist and developed capitalist countries were faced with no other alternative than to vigorously promote the scientific and technological revolution and restructure their economic mechanism. Thanks to this, since 1982 they have gradually come out of the crisis. Meanwhile, the socialist countries were slow to adapt to the situation and to correct their mistakes. Not until the late '70s and mid-'80s had only a few countries embarked on restructuring.[16]

In sum, Vietnam's two political camps see the United States in sharply distinct ways. For anti-Westerners, the United States is first and foremost an adversary; for modernizers, it is foremost a pioneer. These differing perceptions of the nature of the United States have tremendous implications for perceptions of U.S. capabilities and intentions. Anti-Westerners are more suspicious of U.S. intentions and tend to underappreciate U.S. capabilities. In contrast, modernizers are more receptive to U.S. goodwill and often admire U.S. power.

Perceptions of China

For Vietnam's ruling elites, China has four main identities. It is a socialist country, a "big power," a fountain of East Asian culture, and an expansionist and hegemonic force. Debates over the "true nature" of China have occasionally flared up between anti-Westerners and modernizers. They both agree that China's policy has two major thrusts—one socialist, the other expansionist and hegemonic—but they disagree on which is the dominant. Anti-Westerners, impressed by China's bloody crackdown on the Tiananmen Square protests and driven by their search for a great power ally in combating the West, believe that the socialist face of China is dominant. In contrast, modernizers think that although China has a socialist regime led by the Communist Party, its deeper nature is "Great Han nationalism," which entails expansionism and "big power mentality," as expressed in Beijing's excessive claims to territories in the South China Sea, its war against Vietnam in 1979, and its bullying of Vietnam over various issues since.[17]

Vietnam's conflicting perceptions of identity—both its own and China's—put China in the place of both a threat and a model. Anti-Westerners and modernizers agree that China poses a threat to Vietnam, but they differ in their appraisal of this threat. For example, anti-Westerners see China's territorial claims in the South China Sea as secondary to the larger and more dangerous menace of "peaceful evolution" coming from the West. China, after all, covets only a few pieces of Vietnamese territory, and most importantly for anti-Westerners, it does not wish to change the Communist regime; it may even come to the rescue if the CPV is in danger of collapse. Modernizers perceive a far larger Chinese threat. For them Vietnam has a vital interest in the South China Sea, which is of immense importance to the country's economic development. A Vietnam without the Communist regime may still be wealthy and strong, but a Vietnam without the South China Sea can hardly be so. China's territorial and maritime claims in the South China Sea, if fully realized, would reduce Vietnam to a semi-landlocked country, taking away enormous economic opportunities and values. Lacking the focus on "peaceful evolution," modernizers are in general more sensitive to Chinese power than are anti-Westerners. Most recently, some modernizers have expressed alarm at China's increasing economic, cultural, and political influence in Vietnam.[18]

As a world power, China serves as a model for both anti-Westerners and modernizers. Apart from geographic proximity and a habit of looking to China for ideas, both camps see China as a country that pursues similar goals and faces similar conditions. There is a striking similarity between the goals of China's and Vietnam's modernizers. In the 1980s and 1990s, both identified "peace and development" as their highest objectives. Vietnam's modernizers aspire toward a "rich people, a strong country, a democratic, equitable, and civilized society," while China's goal is a "wealthy, strong, democratic, civilized, and modernized socialist country."[19] It is likely that Vietnam borrowed these ideas from China, but it is more important that both are under the influence of the same *zeitgeist*, which traces its roots to the Japanese modernization of the late nineteenth and early twentieth century. China, however, is not the only or even the main model for Vietnam's modernizers. They look to the advanced industrialized countries in the West and the newly industrialized countries in Asia as guides. Vietnam's ambition to develop large state-owned conglomerates (*tong cong ty 91*, later *tap doan*) was, for example, inspired by the success of the South Korean *chaebol*.

Perhaps the most influential of all the ideas that Vietnam's anti-Westerners have borrowed from China since the 1980s is that of "peaceful evolution." It is a highly flexible and inclusive concept that subsumes anything that can undermine Communist Party power short of open war. It has served as the central rallying cry for anti-Westerners throughout the years since 1989. Under the tutelage of General Le Duc Anh, who was state president from 1992 to 1996, the General Department II (intelligence) of the Vietnam People's Army was most instrumental in propagating the concept of peaceful evolution. Its translations of Chinese works on the topic were used as key references in political and defense education, which every upper-middle- to high-ranking Vietnamese official had to undergo. Prior to the midterm party conference in 1994, where the CPV formally coded the primary threats facing Vietnam, delegates were given a required reading list that contained four works dealing with the threat of peaceful evolution. One of the books was a translation of a Chinese account justifying the suppression of pro-democracy demonstrators in Beijing in 1989.[20]

Strategy and Trajectory of Vietnam's Relations with China and the United States

Anti-Westerners believe that as a socialist country, China shares Vietnam's vital interest in promoting the common cause of socialism. In the aftermath of the fall of communism in Eastern Europe, Vietnam's anti-Westerners actively sought to form a new alliance of socialist countries to oppose the West.[21] As the Soviet Union, in their eyes, was breaking away from the socialist path, CPV leaders such as Nguyen Van Linh and Le Duc Anh tried, unsuccessfully, to convince China to assume leadership of the socialist camp and engage in a strategic alliance with Vietnam.[22]

A strategic alliance with China on the basis of a shared ideology and a common enemy is the foreign policy linchpin of Vietnam's anti-Westerners in the post–Cold War era. Although the first attempts by Linh and Anh in 1990 received a cold response, every succeeding anti-Western CPV chief renewed the appeal to Beijing. When the newly elected CPV general secretary Do Muoi did so in 1991, China responded that the two nations could be "comrades but not allies."[23] In 1999 Muoi's successor, Le Kha Phieu, resurrected the idea of an alliance with President Jiang Zemin on Phieu's maiden trip to Beijing in December 1997. Although China maintained its cool stance, Hanoi has continued to regard Beijing as a strategic ally. When Nong Duc Manh, Phieu's successor as CPV general secretary, made his inaugural visit to China in 2001, he defined the Sino-Vietnamese relationship as one of "comrades plus brothers." The joint statement issued on the occasion of that visit vowed, unprecedentedly, to oppose "hegemony," thus formally though somewhat stealthily declaring Vietnam's alignment with China against U.S. power.[24]

The alliance with China, which remains tacit and somewhat unilateral, is also the main hope of those anti-Westerners seeking a peaceful solution to the South China Sea dispute. In an interview on December 22, 2009, General Le Van Dung, head of the General Political Directorate of the Vietnam People's Army, said: "As concerned our issue with China in the East Sea [the South China Sea], we are trying our best to solve it, and in the near future we [Vietnam] will discuss, negotiate, and demarcate the maritime borders with our friend [China]. So the situation would be gradually stabilized and we keep strengthening our relations with China in order to fight plots of the common enemy [the West and the United States]."[25]

Anti-Westerners seek solidarity with China. Their efforts have met with China's equal persistence to give a hierarchical nature to the relationship. Although Vietnam's entreaties for alliance have been politely rebuffed, China has always rewarded the Vietnamese leaders' appeals with some gestures of goodwill. As a result, Hanoi has ended up bowing to Chinese pressure. One example of this deference is Hanoi's effort to erase memories of the 1979 war with China. This short but bloody war is now mentioned in only a few sentences in Vietnamese history textbooks—compared with several chapters devoted to the war with America. Books, songs, films, and other cultural works related to the Sino-Vietnamese war have been blacklisted, while cemeteries of soldiers fallen in that war are left largely neglected.[26] The official name of the war itself has been changed from the "war against the invading Chinese expansionists" to the "war of fatherland defense," while, for comparison's sake, there has been no attempt to change the name of the "war against America."

Unlike anti-Westerners, modernizers think that China cares about the fate of socialism in its own country but not so much outside. Driven primarily by nationalism, China seeks to be the hegemon of Asia; thus, its relations with other socialist countries are subordinate to the highest political objective of modernization.[27] The modernizers' strategy toward China consists of two main principles, balancing and enmeshment, whose combined effect is to interlock China in various networks of power and interests in the region.[28]

Following the pathway of enmeshment, Vietnam engages in various regional mechanisms such as the Association of Southeast Asian Nations (ASEAN), the Asean Regional Forum (ARF) and the Asia-Pacific Economic Cooperation (APEC), just to name a few. ASEAN stands out from the other forums for its tight organizational structure and for the leverage it gives Vietnam. Ten years after its accession to the group (in 1995), Vietnam had developed an ASEAN identity and considered ASEAN its "family."[29] For the first time since the 1989 revolutions, Vietnam felt at home in the world. The idea of joining ASEAN was floated by modernizers as early as 1988,[30] but it met with strong opposition from Singapore and Vietnam's anti-Westerners. If there is any cooperation between Vietnam and South Korea on managing their relations with the United States and China, it takes place mainly within the framework of regional multilateralism.[31]

Following the principle of balancing, modernizers seek to develop strategic partnerships with the great powers of the Asia-Pacific region, including the United States, Russia, Japan, and India. The United States stands out from this group for its preponderant power. If anti-Westerners were persistent in their effort to form an anti-Western alliance with China, modernizers have been equally persistent in their effort to develop a strategic partnership with the United States. Thus far both have been unsuccessful; the anti-Westerners because of China's indifference, and the modernizers because of the anti-Westerners' resistance and—prior to a change in U.S. policy toward Asia in the 2000s—also because of a lack of U.S. interest.

Beginning in the late 1980s, after years of hostility, Vietnam intensified its efforts to seek the renormalization of relations with both China and the United States. Relations with China were normalized in 1991 and with the United States in 1995. Why did normalization with the United States lag far behind that with China? One reason is that Vietnam was more willing to make concessions to China than to the United States, but another is U.S. reticence.[32] The lifting of an economic embargo that had been in effect since 1975 and the normalization of relations with Vietnam were unilateral U.S. decisions. Had the United States wanted to step ahead of China in engaging Vietnam, it might have met with a receptive Vietnam as early as 1988, and the long-term benefits might have been far larger for Washington. After all, it was in April 1988 that Vietnam, on the initiative of Foreign Minister Nguyen Co Thach and other modernizers, and after years of leaning to one side, committed to "diversify and multidirectionalize" its foreign relations.[33]

Two years later, in March 1990, a modernizer and democracy advocate, Tran Xuan Bach, was dismissed from the Politburo, marking a turning point in Vietnamese politics. Now anti-Westerners prevailed over modernizers. Throughout the 1990s, anti-Westerners were in a position to obstruct progress in Vietnam's relations with ASEAN, the United States, and U.S. allies. The landmark U.S.-Vietnam bilateral trade agreement was delayed for two years because General Secretary Le Kha Phieu was upset by Secretary of State Madeleine Albright's lecture on democracy during their September 1999 meeting. Anti-Western leaders in the party and the military also blocked military-to-military relations between the two countries. As former U.S. ambassador to Vietnam Raymond Burghardt recalled, until mid-2003 Vietnam refused to talk about strategic issues with the United States.[34]

July 2003 marked a third turning point in the evolution of Vietnam's foreign policy. Then, the Eighth Plenum of the Ninth CPV Central Committee passed a new national security strategy that removed ideology as a criterion for selecting international friends and foes. This opened the door for strategic engagement with the United States, which had been identified as a strategic enemy by the preceding national security strategy (adopted in July 1992, though unpublicized).[35] Since then U.S.-Vietnam relations have developed far more rapidly than in the preceding decade. Beginning in late 2003, U.S. Navy vessels have visited Vietnamese ports annually, and since 2009 U.S. Navy ships have been sent for repairs to Vietnamese ports. The two countries agreed to exchange visits at the defense minister's level every three years. Since 2008 annual strategic talks have been held at the vice-ministerial level. In July 2010 Prime Minister Nguyen Tan Dung responded positively to a suggestion by Secretary of State Hillary Clinton to raise relations between the two countries to a strategic partnership. These developments were made possible by a new balance between anti-Westernism and modernization in Vietnam's foreign policy.

Vietnam's Relations with the United States and China: Rhetoric versus Reality

Since the mid-2000s, the rhetoric in Hanoi can be summed up as: "there is a convergence and no divergence in the strategic interests of the United States and Vietnam." This is true if Vietnam's interests are seen from the modernizers' perspective. From the anti-Western perspective, however, the United States remains a principal adversary, as the June 2010 concept paper of the CPV Propaganda Department attests. Anti-Westerners continue to be able to impede advances in U.S.-Vietnam relations. A large conflict in the strategic interests of the United States and Vietnam lies in the area of human rights and democracy. The United States has made it clear that, in Hillary Clinton's words, "our ambition to develop a strategic partnership requires that [Vietnam] take steps to further protect human rights and advance political freedoms."[36] This was a bold but risky move. Although the influence of anti-Westerners has been in decline since the moderate Nguyen Phu Trong replaced the anti-Western

Nong Duc Manh as general secretary of the CPV, the balance between anti-Westerners and modernizers in Vietnamese politics remains precarious. It should be noted that U.S.-Vietnam relations cannot be modeled as a two-player game; four players are involved. Anti-Westerners can spoil the game, and China can step in anytime and upset the balance.

The gap between rhetoric and reality in Sino-Vietnamese relations is far wider than that in U.S.-Vietnam relations. In the post–Cold War era, Vietnam's relationship to China is rhetorically defined by several formulations agreed upon by top leaders of the two countries. The first of these is a sixteen-word guideline given by President Jiang Zemin at the inaugural visit of General Secretary Le Kha Phieu to China in 1999. It reads "long-term stability, future orientation, good-neighborly friendship, comprehensive cooperation" in Chinese, but in the Vietnamese version the order is reversed to put friendly neighbors and comprehensive cooperation ahead of long-term stability and future orientation. This change is telling; it reflects a subtle but significant difference in the Chinese and Vietnamese views of their mutual relationship. The second of these formulations is the designation "comrades plus brothers," which used to be that of the China–North Vietnam relationship in the solidarity period of the 1950s and 1960s. It was resurrected unilaterally by General Secretary Nong Duc Manh on the eve of his inaugural trip to China in 2001. But this statement did not find immediate resonance in China. During Jiang Zemin's return visit in 2002, he proposed in response a "four-good spirit," describing the two countries as "good neighbors, good friends, good comrades, good partners." It is noteworthy that Jiang excluded the word "brothers" from the list. Vietnam's state-controlled media kept silent about this "four-good spirit" until Manh's next visit to China in April 2003.

The nature of the China-Vietnam relationship is codified in numerous joint statements made on the occasion of summit meetings. In 2000 a summit meeting of state presidents from China and Vietnam issued a Joint Statement for Comprehensive Cooperation in the New Century, which would serve as the framework for long-term relations between the two countries. In 2008, following a summit meeting between President Hu Jintao and General Secretary Nong Duc Manh, China and Vietnam agreed to raise their bilateral relationship to a "comprehensive strategic cooperative partnership." Chinese officials told Vietnamese visitors that this was the first of its kind for China's foreign relations. Since then China has formally declared a "comprehensive strategic cooperative partnership" with Laos (2009), Cambodia (2010), Myanmar (2011), Russia (2011), and Thailand (2012). The latest joint statement issued on the occasion of General Secretary Nguyen Phu Trong's visit to China in

2011 featured the sixteen-word guideline, the four-good spirit, and the title of "comprehensive strategic cooperative partnership" as the major epithets of the China-Vietnam relationship.

In the post-Cold War era, China has developed a complex of epithets, of which those mentioned above are but some examples, to codify its partnerships with foreign countries. The main titles range from cooperative partnership and comprehensive partnership at a lower rank to strategic partnership and strategic cooperative partnership at a higher rank, and finally to comprehensive strategic cooperative partnership at the highest rank. Although Vietnam was the first to be bestowed this highest title, its relations with China are far from the best among either country's foreign relations. Sino-Vietnamese relations are fraught with issues of contention, the thorniest and largest of which is the South China Sea dispute.

Conclusion

Hardly a middle power in terms of capabilities, Vietnam is somewhere in the middle between China and the United States. In this respect, Hanoi should be compared with Seoul and Pyongyang. Like North Korea and unlike the South, Vietnam harbors strong anti-Western sentiment; like South Korea but unlike the North, Vietnam is on a quest for Western-style modernization. Vietnam's divided identities in the *Doi Moi* era have produced polarized perceptions of the world, and particularly of China and the United States. Hanoi's polarized worldviews entail mutually contradicting appraisals of Beijing's and Washington's core interests and primary objectives, which in turn lead to mutually offsetting policy strategies. While separately coherent, the competing camps of anti-Westerners and modernizers often clash as each seeks to guide Vietnam's foreign policy. The result may well appear as a cleverly designed hedging strategy, but it must be noted that this reflects an agonized identity rather than the tactical adaptation of a unitary identity.

Vietnam's strategies toward China and the United States in the post–Cold War era reflect an ever-shifting balance between anti-Westernism and modernization. The international balance of power, Vietnam's historical experiences, and the constant quest for security, wealth, and status, appear to shape these strategies and shift their balance. In the past three decades, Vietnam has changed course three times, in 1986/1988, 1990, and 2003. As China is rising and a Sino-U.S. competition for regional primacy is emerging, we must expect new turning points to come in the trajectory of Vietnam's foreign policy. Given its preponderant power, the United States is well placed to decide this trajectory. It must, however, bear in mind that its game with Vietnam is complex and involves more than the apparent two actors. There are two major interests vying for influence in Vietnam. Meanwhile, China, as it has been for thousands of years, is an invisible hand shaping Vietnamese politics.

Notes

1 It should be interesting to compare Vietnam with North Korea as well. In chapter 9 of this volume, Tuong Vu suggests that Hanoi is more comparable to Pyongyang than Seoul when it comes to identity and domestic politics.

2 In a similar vein, Leif-Eric Easley, in chapter 8 of this volume, observes that the interests and policies of state leaders are "informed not only by material incentives and constraints, but also by national grievances and international reputational ambitions."

3 The debate was initiated by *Thanh Nien*, a reform-minded newspaper, and Duong Trung Quoc, a renowned historian. The backdrop of this debate included an official review of two decades of reform, Vietnam's imminent membership in the World Trade Organization, and the expectation that the Tenth Congress of the ruling Communist Party of Vietnam in the same year would bring major changes.

4 See Dien dan bao Thanh Nien [Thanh Nien Forum], *Nuoc Viet Nam nho hay khong nho?* [Is Vietnam a small country or not?] (Hanoi: Nha xuat ban Thong tan, 2006).

5 I made this argument more fully in Alexander L. Vuving, "The Two-Headed Grand Strategy: Vietnamese Foreign Policy since Doi Moi," paper at the conference "Vietnam Update 2004: Strategic and Foreign Relations," Singapore, November 25–26, 2004; Vuving, "Strategy and Evolution of Vietnam's China Policy: A Changing Mixture of Pathways," *Asian Survey* 46, no. 6 (November 2006): 805–24; and Vuving, "Vietnam: A Tale of Four Players," in Daljit Singh, ed., *Southeast Asian Affairs 2010* (Singapore: Institute of Southeast Asian Studies, 2010), 367–91.

6 Eero Palmujoki, *Vietnam and the World: Marxist-Leninist Doctrine and the Change in International Relations, 1975–1993* (London: Macmillan, 1997).

7 Major texts articulating this orthodoxy in the late 1980s include "Phat bieu cua dong chi Tong bi thu Nguyen Van Linh be mac Hoi nghi 7 cua Ban chap hanh Trung uong Dang" [Remarks by Comrade General Secretary Nguyen Van Linh concluding the Seventh Plenum of the Party Central Committee], *Tap chi Cong san* (September 1989), 6–16; Bui Ngoc Chuong, "Ban chat, dac diem va dia vi lich su cua chu nghia de quoc" [The nature, characteristics, and historical status of imperialism], *Tap chi Cong san* [Communist Review] (March 1987), 99–106; Le Duc Anh, "Nang cao canh giac, cung co quoc phong va an ninh cua dat nuoc" [Heighten vigilance, strengthen national defense and national security], *Tap chi Cong san* (April 1988), 5–10. For a discussion of this orthodoxy, see Palmujoki, *Vietnam and the World*; Gareth Porter, "The Transformation of Vietnam's World-view: From Two Camps to Interdependence," *Contemporary Southeast Asia* 12, no. 1 (June 1990): 1–19.

8 Nguyen Co Thach, "Tat ca vi hoa binh, doc lap dan toc va phat trien" [All for peace, national independence, and development], *Tap chi Cong san* (August 1989): 5, 8. Other major texts by CPV leaders articulating the modernizers' worldview and grand strategy include Vo Nguyen Giap, "De cho khoa hoc ky thuat thuc su tro thanh dong luc phat trien kinh te-xa hoi" [For science and technology to really become a driving force of

socioeconomic development], *Tap chi Cong san* (January 1989), 7–15; Vo Chi Cong, "Speech on the continued renovation of the party's leadership towards the activities of the National Assembly and the renovation of the latter's work at a meeting of the head delegates to the sixth session of the 8th National Assembly," December 18, 1989, Vietnam News Agency, December 19, 1989, FBIS-EAS-89-243, pp. 67–69; Vo Van Kiet, "Thu gui Bo chinh tri" [Memo to the Politburo], August 9, 1995, *Dien Dan* [Forum], No. 48 (January 1996), 16–19; Nguyen Co Thach, *The gioi trong 50 nam qua (1945–1995) va the gioi trong 25 nam toi (1995–2020)* [The world in the last 50 years (1945–1995) and the coming 25 years (1995–2020)] (Hanoi: Chinh tri Quoc gia, 1998); Vo Van Kiet, "Mot so van de ve tong ket ly luan va thuc tien 20 nam doi moi trong linh vuc kinh te" [Some issues on the review of theory and practice of twenty years of Doi Moi in economics], in *Vo Van Kiet: Nguoi thap lua* (Ho Chi Minh City: Tre, 2010), 514–31.

9 "Phat bieu cua dong chi Tong bi thu Nguyen Van Linh be mac Hoi nghi 7 cua Ban chap hanh Trung uong Dang" [Remarks by Comrade General Secretary Nguyen Van Linh concluding the Seventh Plenum of the Party Central Committee], *Tap chi Cong san* (September 1989), 6–8.

10 Most prominent among the latter are State President Vo Chi Cong, Prime Minister Vo Van Kiet, Foreign Minister Nguyen Co Thach, National Assembly Chairman Nguyen Van An, and most forcefully but most unfortunately, Tran Xuan Bach, the Politburo member in charge of foreign affairs during 1987–89.

11 See Tran Quang Co, *Hoi uc va Suy nghi* [Recollections and reflections], unpublished manuscript (2003).

12 Phat bieu cua dong chi Tong bi thu Nguyen Van Linh be mac Hoi nghi 7 cua Ban chap hanh Trung uong Dang [Remarks by Comrade General Secretary Nguyen Van Linh concluding the Seventh Plenum of the Party Central Committee], *Tap chi Cong san* (September 1989), 6.

13 Vuving, "Vietnam: A Tale of Four Players," 381.

14 The message was formally conveyed by Secretary of State Hillary Clinton to Prime Minister Nguyen Tan Dung in July 2010 and again by Clinton in a major outline of U.S. foreign policy in November 2011.

15 Hong Hai, "Vach tran nhung 'loi keu goi'" [Unmasking "Entreaties"], *Quan doi Nhan dan* [People's Army], July 3, 2011, http://www.qdnd.vn/qdndsite/vi-VN/61/43/5/5/5/153111/Default.aspx

16 Vo Chi Cong, speech on the continued renovation of the party's leadership towards the activities of the National Assembly and the renovation of the latter's work at a meeting of the head delegates to the sixth session of the 8th National Assembly, December 18, 1989, Vietnam News Agency, December 19, 1989, FBIS-EAS-89-243, p. 67.

17 For example, see reports of the debate in the CPV Politburo in Tran Quang Co, *Hoi uc va Suy nghi*.

18 Concerns about China's influence in Vietnam have since 2007 become a major narrative in the reform-minded and commercially oriented press and the blogosphere. For some recent examples, see Dang Tan, "Vinh Cam Ranh; Chuyen that nhu bia!" *Tuan Viet Nam*, June 4, 2012; Bui Van Bong, "Loi ich ca nhan va van menh dan toc," June 30, 2012; Tong Van Cong, "Nguoi Viet Nam uu tien dung hang … nuoc nao?" *viet-studies*, August 14,

2012; Thanh Quang, "Viet Nam khong the thoat gong kim Trung Quoc?" *Radio Free Asia*, August 20, 2012; "Chuyen gia kinh te Pham Chi Lan; Doanh nghiep con thieu lien ket va hay nghi ky nhau," *Thanh Nien*, December 12, 2012.

19 The goal of "a rich people, a strong country, and an equitable, democratic, and civilized society" was adopted at the 9th Congress of the Communist Party of Vietnam in 2001. The word "democratic" was moved ahead of "equitable" at the 10th CPV congress in 2006. It was CPV modernizers who advocated the adoption of these formulations and interpreted the goal of "a rich people and strong country" and democracy as the "nature of socialism." See Prime Minister Vo Van Kiet's August 1995 letter to the Politburo. "A wealthy, strong, democratic, civilized and modernized socialist country" is identified as China's goal in the Constitution of the Chinese Communist Party. For an early use of it, see, "Speech by Jiang Zemin, CPC General Secretary and President of China at the Meeting at the Great Hall of the People in Beijing to Commemorate the 100th Anniversary of Mao Zedong's Birth on 26 December 1993," *China Report* 31, no. 1 (February 1995): 153.

20 Carlyle A. Thayer, "Vietnam's Relations with China and the United States," paper at the conference on the Role of Vietnam in the Asia-Pacific, Vietnam National University, Hanoi, December 10, 2010.

21 Thanh Tin [Bui Tin], *Hoa xuyen tuyet* [The snow-breaking flower] (Irvine, Cal.: Nhan Quyen, 1991); Tran Quang Co, *Hoi uc va Suy nghi*; Carlyle A. Thayer, "Comrade Plus Brother: The New Sino-Vietnamese Relations," *Pacific Review* 5, no. 4 (September 1992).

22 Tran Quang Co, *Hoi uc va Suy nghi*.

23 Carlyle A. Thayer, "Sino-Vietnamese Relations: The Interplay of Ideology and National Interest," *Asian Survey* 34, no. 6 (June 1994): 523.

24 Vuving, "Strategy and Evolution of Vietnam's China Policy," 816–17.

25 "Tim moi cach giai quyet van de Bien Dong" [Making every effort to solve the South China Sea issue] (Interview with General Le Van Dung), *Tuoi Tre*, December 22, 2009, http://tuoitre.vn/Chinh-tri-Xa-hoi/354571/%E2%80%9CTim-moi-cach-giai-quyet-van-de-bien-Dong%E2%80%9D.html.

26 Some changes to this policy started to be seen in 2012, after more Chinese assertiveness in the South China Sea.

27 See, for example, debates among CPV leaders in Tran Quang Co, *Hoi uc va Suy nghi*.

28 Vuving, "Strategy and Evolution of Vietnam's China Policy." See Vo Van Kiet, "Tong ket ly luan va thuc tien 20 nam doi moi," for the strategy of interlocking.

29 See also Brantly Womack, chapter 7 in this volume.

30 The idea came originally from the Foreign Ministry, and party chief Nguyen Van Linh publicly suggested it for the first time to a visiting Philippine foreign minister in 1988, in the aftermath of a bloody naval clash between Vietnam and China in the Spratly Islands and after the adoption of Politburo Resolution No. 13, a key document stipulating the "diversification and multidirectionalization" of Vietnam's foreign relations.

31 See also Pham Quang Minh, chapter 5 in this volume.

32 I make this argument more fully in Alexander L. Vuving, "Grand Strategic Fit and Power Shift: Explaining Turning Points in China-Vietnam Relations," in *Living with China:*

Regional States and China through Crises and Turning Points, ed. Shiping Tang, Mingjiang Li and Amitav Acharya, (New York: Palgrave Macmillan, 2009), 229–45.

33 Nguyen Co Thach, "Nhung chuyen bien moi tren the gioi va tu duy moi cua chung ta" [New changes in the world and our new thinking], *Quan he Quoc te,* no. 3 (January 1990): 2–7; Porter, "Transformation of Vietnam's World-view."

34 Raymond Burghardt, "Old Enemies Become Friends: U.S. and Vietnam," *Brookings Northeast Asia Commentary,* November 2006.

35 Vuving, "Strategy and Evolution of Vietnam's China Policy," 817–18; Vuving, "Grand Strategic Fit and Power Shift," 239–40.

36 Hillary Clinton, "America's Pacific Century," *Foreign Policy,* November 2011, http://www.foreignpolicy.com/articles/2011/10/11/americas_pacific_century?page=0,5.

5 East Asia and the Pacific: The Regional Roles of Vietnam and South Korea

Pham Quang Minh

In 2012 the Socialist Republic of Vietnam and the Republic of Korea (ROK) celebrated twenty years of diplomatic relations. On December 22, 1992, Vietnam and South Korea had made a historic decision to establish relations— a notable sign of progress in overcoming the legacy of the Vietnam War, ideological differences, and emerging obstacles. Since then Vietnam-ROK relations have developed rapidly, beyond any expectation. Vietnam's former deputy premier Vu Khoan recently compared this diplomatic progress to that of an endless line of water that starts from a shallow stream, grows into a big river, then flows into the ocean. The growth of Vietnam-ROK relations over the past two decades could be considered "the Pacific miracle."[1]

How did these two countries develop such an eye-catching relationship? The majority of analysts in Vietnam have paid most attention to historical and cultural factors, judging these as the foundation of bilateral relations.[2] In this chapter, I argue that the decisive factor prompting both sides to transform past rivalry and mutual distrust into friendly, cooperative, strategic ties was not their cultural commonalities but instead the mutual recognition of shared interests in the context of a post–Cold War global and regional environment. From the early 1990s onward, this recognition fostered a willingness on both sides to establish and expand cooperation in both domestic and external policy goals.

The main objective of this chapter is to analyze the dynamics of expanding Vietnam-ROK cooperation as it relates to East Asian and Pacific regionalism. To this end, I shall first provide some historical background to illuminate why the establishment of diplomatic relations was considered to be such a profound turning point. Second, I will compare the roles of Vietnam and South Korea in the newly emerging East Asian security environment. As Michael Mullen and the Joint Chiefs of Staff have described, in the new context of a "multi-nodal world—characterized more by shifting interest-driven coalitions based on diplomatic, military, and economic power than by rigid security competition between opposing blocs,"[3] Hanoi recognizes that big powers continue to play an important role but also believes that "the middle and small powers will actively participate in the effort to build regional institutions having a more balanced and diversified orientation."[4] In this framework Vietnam and South Korea would do well to use multilateral regional mechanisms to advance their common interests. In the third part of the chapter I will examine Vietnamese foreign policy toward the region by looking at key moments since 1986 that illustrate Vietnam's attitude toward, and perception of, regional organizations. I conclude that Vietnam and South Korea, faced with similar security challenges in the new strategic environment, share the same point of view on the building of an emerging Asia-Pacific security architecture in which each plays an active and constructive role.

A Brief History of Relations between Vietnam and South Korea

Vietnam-ROK relations date back to the thirteenth century, when Vietnam (Dai Viet) witnessed a power transition from the Ly dynasty to the Tran dynasty. The Ly dynasty was founded in 1009 by Ly Cong Uan, a former temple orphan who had risen to commander under the early Le (Le Hoan) dynasty, and who adopted the title Ly Thai To. The Ly dynasty was the first Vietnamese dynasty that managed to hold onto power for more than two centuries (1009–1225), allowing it to secure and expand its territory. Internally the Ly created a centralized administrative system by choosing Dai La as the capital (later renamed Thang Long, Hanoi today) and establishing the first University of Vietnam (Temple of Literature) in 1070. Externally the Ly had to deal with the Confucian state of China (Song dynasty) in the north and two Indian-ized states in the south, Chenla and Champa. As the Ly dynasty's territory expanded as the result of its Southward March (Nam tien), the Ly dynasty kings looked to China as a model for organizing a strong centralized state while maintaining the devout Buddhism of northeast Asian countries. After a decade of stability, civil wars followed among various rival warlords and ended with the victory of the imperial force led by Tran Thu Do, the head of the Tran clan. In 1225 Ly Chieu Hoang, the last empress regnant of the Ly dynasty, was forced to cede the throne to her consort, Tran Canh, one of the nephews of

Tran Thu Do. However, worried that the Ly dynasty might seek to restore itself to the throne, Tran Thu Do brutally killed all Ly dynasty members. In order to eradicate all knowledge of the Ly dynasty in future generations, Tran Thu Do went so far as to force all Vietnamese bearing the surname Ly to change it to Nguyen.[5] Facing such a threat, Prince Ly Long Tuong, together with some subordinates and his ancestors' altar, escaped in 1226 from Thang Long. He built a ship, crossed the sea, and arrived in Korea, seeking asylum.[6] The specific motivation for Prince Ly Long Tuong's decision to seek asylum in Korea remains unclear to this day.[7] Historical records establish that the prince played a decisive role in the defeat of Mongolian aggression in Korea in 1253, making a great contribution to the independence of Korea in the thirteenth century. The Vietnamese Ly clan became one of the most successful clans in Korean history.[8]

Later, the relationship between the two countries took the form of exchanges between Vietnamese and Korean poets (who served as ambassadors of their respective countries) on tributary missions to Beijing. From the end of the sixteenth century to the middle of the nineteenth century, dozens of such meetings took place. The first occurred in 1597 between Phung Khac Khoan from Vietnam and Ly Toi Quang (Lee Suk Wan, with the pseudonym Taibon) from Korea; the two exchanged poems in an atmosphere of cordiality and mutual respect. In their poems they pointed to their cultural similarities, even as they described unique historical and cultural characteristics.[9]

Sharing a long history, rich culture, and a passion for freedom, Vietnam and Korea became more closely aligned during the "Waking Up Asia" (Chau A thuc tinh) movement against imperialism. Phan Boi Chau (1876–1940), leader of the "Go East" movement (Dong Du), played an important role in strengthening the relationship between the two countries. A Vietnamese, he facilitated meetings and discussions with Korean friends on a variety of issues relating to the two peoples' common challenges and fate. Nguyen Ai Quoc (1890–1969) also had intensive relations with Korean revolutionaries in the course of his revolutionary work.[10]

In contemporary times, the relationship between the two countries was adversely influenced by the bipolar international system that drew South Korea into the Vietnam War as a U.S. ally. Between 1965 and 1973, 325,517 South Korean soldiers (including 288,656 army, 36,246 navy, and 615 air force) fought in South Vietnam.[11] This fact in particular made the process of normalization between the two countries difficult. However, the end of the Cold War and the dynamics of development in the two countries fostered the possibility of overcoming historical obstacles. According to former deputy premier Vu Khoan, at the outset of the 1990s Vietnam launched a reform and opening policy aimed at expanding cooperative relations with all countries around the world, with particular attention on the Asia-Pacific region, including South Korea. At the same time South Korea, through its embassy in Bangkok, signaled a wish to establish relations with Vietnam. To this end, South Korea invited a Vietnamese delegation led by Vu Khoan to attend a meeting of the Economic and Social Commission for Asia and Pacific (ESCAP) in Seoul. Seoul wanted to establish relations at the ambassadorial level, while Hanoi initially indicated a preference to launch ties at the consular level. At the root of these differing views were unresolved issues stemming from the war. The outcome was the establishment of a liaison office. After several rounds of discussions, by the end of 1992 both sides agreed to establish relations at the ambassadorial level.[12]

Vietnam had many reasons for establishing diplomatic relations with South Korea: it sought a means of escape from a socioeconomic crisis, hoped to accelerate its domestic reform process, and saw in South Korea a successful development model of direct relevance to Vietnam's ambitions.

Despite the continued U.S. imposition of an embargo on Vietnam, South Korea proceeded to establish diplomatic ties with Vietnam. Besides the historical and cultural factors mentioned above, South Korea's principal interest in establishing relations with Vietnam was to develop a new market for its exports. In addition, South Korea had taken note of the inclination of major powers—China, Japan, the European Union (EU), and the United States—to gradually move toward normalizing relations with Vietnam. Last but not least, an interest in peaceful cooperation toward development was starting to dominate the regional politics of the Asia-Pacific.

In 2011 South Korea was the number-one foreign investor in Vietnam, with more than 3,000 projects valued at $23.5 billion. South Korean foreign direct investment (FDI) projects provided jobs for more than 400,000 Vietnamese. South Korea was ranked number two among foreign official development assistance (ODA) providers, and Vietnam became South Korea's leading ODA receiver, with 34 projects having a cumulative value of $1.2 billion. During the previous twenty years, the bilateral foreign trade turnover increased from $500 million to $12.9 billion. South Korea ranked as Vietnam's fourth-largest trade partner, while Vietnam was South Korea's ninth-ranking export market. In addition, South Korea had become the world's third-ranking host of Vietnamese workers, who in 2011 numbered more than 65,000 persons.[13] In addition to the intensive two-way flow of tourists and visitors participating in commercial and political discussions, there are about 100,000 Vietnamese residents in South Korea and roughly the same number of South Koreans in Vietnam. The relationship between the two countries is being further deepened by the existence of 45,000 Vietnamese-Korean families. In parallel with this rapid expansion of economic and cultural relations, the South Korean interest in and demand for Vietnamese studies has accelerated, as has the corresponding Vietnamese interest in Korean studies. Accordingly the ROK government has allowed South Korean students to choose the Vietnamese language as an official subject for higher education entrance examinations from the year 2014 onwards.[14]

In short, contemporary Vietnam-ROK relations are rooted in the distant past and have undergone many changes over the years, including the rapid and positive development seen in the past two decades. The main explanation for their current closeness is that the two countries, which share many common features of history and culture, have now identified common interests to motivate a partnership in meeting the new circumstances and challenges in the region. In the next part of this chapter I will examine the underlying dynamics of the East Asian security environment that have significantly influenced both Vietnam and Korea.

Vietnam and South Korea in the New Security Environment of East Asia

A number of factors account for the complicated conditions observed in the East Asian region (including Northeast and Southeast Asia).[15] Among other things, the region has historically been an arena for competition between two leading states, namely China and Japan.[16] According to the institutionalist school's theory of hegemony, based on the European and American experience, leading states in a given region set the parameters for the actions and ambitions of medium to small states. The case of Germany and France in Europe represents one convincing example.[17] While the China-Japan relationship is somewhat analogous to that of Germany and France in Europe, in recent years China and Japan did not find a way to overcome their historical baggage and individual ambitions to cooperate in providing the structural leadership necessary for smooth regional integration. There are three major obstacles to the building of a constructive new China-Japan relationship akin to the post-World War II (WWII) ties between France and Germany: first, Beijing and Tokyo hold very different perceptions of Japan's invasion of China during WWII; second, the two still face territorial disputes over the Senkaku (Diaoyu) Islands; and third, Japan's alliance with the United States, which implicates China's unfulfilled national goal to achieve unification with Taiwan and otherwise, serves to counter and contain China's pursuit of its regional ambitions. Absent Sino-Japanese cooperation, East Asian regional integration is unlikely to be feasible in the near future.

In this case, a third party—the United States—as a Pacific nation more powerful than either China or Japan has played the primary role of regional facilitator. The United States not only played this role vis-à-vis Germany and France in the 1950s and '60s, but also to some extent with Japan and Korea in 1960–70.[18] However, the United States cannot accomplish the same mission vis-à-vis China and Japan, for several reasons. First, there is distrust between China and the United States; second, it is not clear whether the United States even wishes to promote Sino-Japanese reconciliation and cooperation; and third, China threatens the U.S. position in East Asia. Under these circumstances, the question is whether any other state or group of states can achieve what neither the leading states of the region nor the United States has been willing or able to do.

Uniquely, East Asia has shown that small and middle powers—in this case Vietnam and other Association of Southeast Asian Nations (ASEAN) member countries—can take the lead in fostering regional cooperation, here through such regional mechanisms as the ASEAN Regional Forum (ARF), ASEAN+3, and ASEAN+1. The possibility is promising: small and middle powers can rarely abuse power. Through ASEAN+3, the involvement of China, Japan, and South Korea is also present. As South Korea and Vietnam work closely with ASEAN, they have nothing to lose and much to gain; they can only strengthen their regional position and increase their influence in power bargaining. Vietnam-ROK cooperation is especially important if it is indeed true that—as Shiping Tang, deputy director of the Center for Regional Security Studies, Chinese Academy of Social Sciences, Beijing, words it—"East Asia is a region with simply too much external presence for a single regional power to be able to achieve dominance."[19]

Last, but not least, South Korea has embraced an approach to regional politics that "is not focused on criticizing the existing Japan- or China-centered belief and establishing a new center," but instead on "how to maintain a balanced perception between them."[20]

Prior to the end of the Cold War era, two factors had great influence on Vietnamese and South Korean perceptions and attitudes toward regional integration. The first factor was colonialism: the French attack on Vietnam in 1858 and the subsequent occupation from 1885 until 1945, and the Japanese annexation of Korea from 1910 until 1945. Even as Vietnam was part of the *Union l'Indochine française*, Korea was incorporated into the Japanese empire. Within such a framework, there was obviously no place for regional integration motivated by either Vietnam or Korea.

The second factor was ideology. The First Indochina War (1946–54) and the Korean War (1950–53) divided the two countries at the 17th parallel and 38th parallel, respectively. In both cases, the southern part of the divided country allied with the United States, while the northern part opted for socialism. While Vietnam was unified in 1975, Korea remains divided. Perhaps owing largely to their strategic geographic locations, both Vietnam and South Korea have sought to maintain a delicate balance among their allies and neighbors. For Vietnam, the Soviet Union and China were key; for South Korea, it was the United States, Japan, and China. Both Vietnam and South Korea have proven adroit at managing complex political relations through skillful diplomacy.

The end of the Cold War marked the beginning of a regional integration that had been blocked by the old bipolar system. The new regional context requires that both Vietnam and South Korea fundamentally change their foreign policy. If during the Cold War both Vietnam and South Korea had tended to play major powers off against one another to maintain a balance among them, now they needed to take on a new role: facilitating cooperation between big powers such as the United States, China, and Japan. The goal was to induce them to cooperate for the common regional interest.

The ASEAN offers a mechanism for both Vietnam and South Korea to play an active and constructive regional role. In 1994, not long after the Cold War's end, the ASEAN succeeded in bringing all major powers into the ARF, a forum on regional security. The ARF soon proved its utility in the regional security environment developing since the collapse of the Soviet Union, the fall of Eastern European communist governments, the "rise" of China, and the settlement of the Cambodia conflict. The role of Vietnam increased alongside these changes; Rodolfo points out that "discussion of regional political and security matters would not [have been] effective without the participation of China, Russia or Vietnam, none of which was at that time an ASEAN member or Dialogue Partner."[21] For North and South Korea, according to Rodolfo, "it [was] only in the ARF [that] they [could] consult, hold dialogues, network and discuss regional-security issues comprehensively and in a broad setting."[22]

Realizing the goal of an integrated East Asia requires not only political and financial capital from each country, but also the devotion of creative individuals supported by public intellectuals. It is unlikely that the present EU could have formed without leaders such as Jean Monnet, Robert Schuman, and Konrad Adenauer or the commitment to an integrated Europe shown by

France and Germany. Vietnam's reform policy (*Doi Moi*) and the "New Korea" policy within the "Globalization Strategy"[23] of the administration of President Kim Young Sam could together be the locomotive driving the process of regional integration.

In December 1997, at the very first unofficial summit between leaders of the ASEAN countries and the three major Northeast Asian states—convened to commemorate the ASEAN's 30th anniversary—the South Korean leader outlined his nation's point of view on the future of East Asia in the twenty-first century, the current financial crisis, and the strengthening of regional economic linkages. Despite the fact that Vietnam was a new member, it participated actively from the beginning of the process. In 1998 Vietnam hosted and successfully convened the 6th ASEAN Summit in Hanoi, and together with other members issued the Hanoi Action Program to fill the development gap between ASEAN members. Although the summit adjourned without any formal agreements, it was a highly meaningful event that marked the beginning of East Asian integration. As the first de facto East Asian summit, the event laid the foundation for the subsequent development of a framework for East Asian cooperation.

Realizing the enhanced possibilities for East Asia cooperation, South Korea exhibited an activist bent and offered concrete proposals when it participated, the following year, in the second summit of the ASEAN+3, held in Vietnam. South Korean president Kim Dae-jung suggested the establishment of an East Asia Vision Group (EAVG) to carry out research and make specific proposals to push forward the regional cooperation process. South Korea's former foreign minister, Han Sung-Joo, was tapped to be chief of the EAVG. In 1999, at the third ASEAN+3 summit, held in Manila, South Korea signed "The Joint Statement on East Asia Cooperation," which was the first declaration on the need for cooperation between the ten ASEAN members and the three Northeast Asian countries. The statement identified several fields for potential cooperation in the ASEAN+3 process, including economic development, cooperation on finance and currency, social and human resources development, science and technology, information and cultural exchange, regional security, and the addressing of transnational problems within the region.[24]

At the fourth ASEAN+3 summit, held November 2000 in Singapore, South Korea cooperated with other member states in solving problems of trade, currency, financial training, human resources, and infrastructure development for the countries located in the lower Mekong basin. Korea also supported Malaysia's initiative to transform the ASEAN+3 into the East Asia Summit (EAS), and it backed Thailand's suggestion to negotiate free trade agreements

(FTAs) among the ASEAN+3 members. When the next summit was convened a year later (November 2001) in Brunei, under the shadow of the September 11 events in the United States and the threat of terrorism, South Korea and other members negotiated and published a "Resolution of Cooperation in the Struggle against Terrorism." South Korea also proposed assigning the East Asia Studies Groups (EASGs) to assist in the drafting of an FTA agreement among the ASEAN+3 states. From 2001–07 South Korea fully participated in all East Asian cooperation summits. At the second EAS in January 2007, held in Cebu (the Philippines), South Korean president Roh Moo-hyun focused on the necessity of concrete measures for signing FTAs in the region.

In the political-security field, South Korea became an ASEAN Dialogue Partner in 1991, and a year later, in Jakarta, South Korea and the ASEAN agreed to establish a Joint Cooperation Committee. The actual ROK-ASEAN dialogue was launched officially in 1993, and since 1997, a ROK-ASEAN summit has taken place annually. In 2005 Korea became the fourth country—after China and India (in 2003) and Japan (in 2004)—to sign the Treaty of Amity and Cooperation (TAC). With respect to economic relations, South Korea and the ASEAN signed an FTA in August 2006, a high-water mark in the relationship between the two parties.

In short, facing the Asian financial crisis in 1997 and cognizant of the deleterious consequences of competition and mutual distrust among the United States, China, and Japan, South Korea focused on East Asian regionalism as a key to future peace and progress. For its part, it increasingly played an active and constructive regional role, designing concrete proposals for mechanisms to foster regional cooperation and integration.

Vietnam's Foreign Policy since *Doi Moi*[25]

The end of the Cold War in 1989 and the collapse of the Soviet Union in 1991 brought about tremendous structural changes for world politics as well as for Vietnam and South Korea. From a Cold War outpost of the communist bloc engaged in a struggle between big powers to achieve national independence and unification, Vietnam has shifted to a more balanced position emphasizing regional cooperation. During the Cold War, official documents of the Communist Party of Vietnam (CPV) defined its *raison d'être* as ideological confrontation. Today, by contrast, Vietnam explains its foreign policy goals in terms of pursuing national interests including the fostering of a peaceful environment through independence, self-strengthening, diversification, and multilateralism in foreign relations. The transformation of Vietnam's foreign policy occurred gradually over time, shaped by a combination of external and internal factors and reflecting the CPV's perception of and attitudes toward the regional environment in which Vietnam finds itself.

Despite its location in the heart of Southeast Asia, Vietnam only joined the ASEAN in the middle of the 1990s. Vietnam's membership in the ASEAN could be considered a turning point both in the nation's perception of the world and its stance toward the region. During a very short period of time, Vietnam made timely and logical readjustments in its policies so as to meet an array of domestic and external challenges. This was preceded by the evolution of both how Vietnam perceived the region and the world—and how it was perceived.

During the Vietnam War, Vietnam identified itself as a member of the communist bloc, and its foreign policy was determined by a Marxist-Leninist ideological point of view. According to this, the world was divided into two poles, capitalist and communist, representing two diametrically opposed camps of "enemies and friends" (*địch và ta*). Compromise between the two camps was inconceivable and impossible because of their antagonistic contradictions. In general, the CPV based its foreign policy outlook and practice on the theory of "three revolutionary waves" (*ba dòng thác cách mạng*) and "four fundamental contradictions" (*bốn mâu thuẫn cơ bản*).[26]

There was no place even for the "peaceful coexistence" (*cùng tồn tại hòa bình*) theory enunciated by Nikita Khrushchev, general secretary of the Communist Party of the Soviet Union (CPSU) during the period 1956–64. In fact, Vietnam was strongly influenced by the Sino-Soviet dispute over leadership of the communist bloc. China denounced the Soviet Union as a supporter of "revisionism" (*chủ nghĩa xét lại*), while the latter in its turn claimed that China adhered to "dogmatism" (*chủ nghĩa giáo điều*). Each of the "big brothers" tried to pull Vietnam to its side by supporting the nation's liberation struggle. Understanding well the complexities and implications of the Sino-Soviet split, and being in any case focused on obtaining maximum support for its paramount goals—liberation and national unification—Vietnam pursued a foreign policy of limited independence and balance that sought to avoid friction with either side. Vietnam's "close-as-lips-and-teeth" relationship with China began to fray only toward the end of the Vietnam War when China occupied the Paracel Islands in 1974.[27] Sino-Vietnamese relations deteriorated sharply by the end of that decade owing to what Vietnam terms the "Chinese incident"[28] and by Vietnam's direct involvement[29] in the Cambodia conflict. These events put an end to Vietnam's long-standing friendly relations with its giant northern neighbor. Instead, Vietnam took the side of the Soviet

Union and in November 1978 signed a bilateral agreement on cooperation and friendship with Moscow that guaranteed Vietnam's security for the next twenty-five years. However, the international situation changed rapidly before the bilateral agreement had even been in force for half the specified period. By the end of the 1970s and early 1980s Vietnam faced a comprehensive crisis. On the Soviet side, the CPSU general secretary Mikhail Gorbachev[30] enunciated new political thinking featuring *perestroika* and *glasnost* that in effect pushed Vietnam into carrying out a series of reforms.

Vietnam's foreign policy toward the region and international organizations underwent a complex set of conceptual policy shifts, with many twists and turns, over the ensuing decades. The conceptual turning points in Vietnam's changing worldview were documented in Politburo Resolution No. 32 (1986), Politburo Resolution No. 13 (1988), the Resolutions of the Seventh National Congress (1991) and the Ninth National Congress (2001), and the Resolution of the Eighth Plenum of the Party Central Committee (2003).

Until 1986, when Vietnam officially launched *Doi Moi*, the resolutions of the Sixth National Congress of the CPV still defined Vietnam as a member of the communist camp led by the Soviet Union and portrayed the relationship with the Soviet Union as the cornerstone of its foreign policy. However, very soon after the Sixth Congress, the Politburo issued Resolution No. 32, which outlined new opportunities and possibilities for Vietnam to consolidate and develop its economy.[31] Faced with an internal economic crisis and external isolation due to the Cambodian involvement, Resolution No. 32 identified peace and development as the highest national priority. Resolution No. 32 laid the foundation for "new thinking" (*Tư duy mới*) in Vietnam's conceptualization of its foreign and security policy. This so-called new thinking proclaimed that Vietnam's foreign relations should be based on the internal strength of the Vietnamese people and the nation's external strength in the era. It explicitly pointed to favorable international conditions for stability and economic construction. In regard to regional organization, Resolution No. 32 stressed the importance of pursuing peaceful coexistence with China, the ASEAN, and the United States, and helping Southeast Asia become a region characterized by peace, stability, and cooperation.[32] However, due to internal ideological conflict, former deputy premier Vu Khoan observed that "in these circumstances it was not easy to recognize correctly the dynamics of trends and development of the world."[33]

Resolution No. 32 was considered the first important step in renovating Vietnamese foreign policy, but proved somewhat irrelevant in the face of strong opposition to Vietnam's ongoing role in the Cambodian conflict. According to vice foreign minister Tran Quang Co: "The period of struggle aimed at a total victory of the Cambodian revolution, under the illusion that the 'situation is irreversible,' had come to an end, and we had to acknowledge the reality of a step-by-step struggle to achieve a political solution for the Cambodian question."[34]

On May 20, 1988, the CPV Politburo adopted an extremely important document on foreign policy, Resolution No. 13 "On the External Mission and Policy in the New Situation."[35] Resolution No. 13 laid out the serious and comprehensive crisis that the country faced toward the end of the 1980s. Internally, the political, social, and economic socialist transformation that Vietnam had carried out since unification had not brought success, but had instead prompted wide distrust and even protests among citizens, especially in South Vietnam.[36] Externally, the long involvement in the Cambodian crisis had resulted in foreign pressure, isolation, and embargos. The main architect of Resolution No. 13 was Nguyen Co Thach, minister of foreign affairs.[37] He was the first Politburo member to realize the importance of economic development as the main trend of world politics, and the necessity of Vietnam's making use of this trend for the good of its own domestic economy. Nguyen Co Thach explained: "The global production force has developed very highly, and the world has become an integrated market. We have the chance to make use of the global production force and we have to do so. As Resolution No. 13 mentioned on international issues, we have to take full advantage of the world market in order to bring our developing economy to an average level of world development in the relatively short time of 20 to 25 years."[38]

Resolution No. 13 had multifaceted meanings. First, it identified for the first time Vietnam's foreign policy in terms of promoting the "national interest" (*lợi ích dân tộc*) instead of pursuing ideological objectives such as "proletarian internationalism" (*chủ nghĩa quốc tế vô sản*) and "the struggle of who wins over whom" (*cuộc đấu tranh ai thắng ai*). Second, with the adoption of Resolution No. 13, the CPV formally departed from the Marxist theory that dominated during the Cold War, and the old competition between two poles; it embraced in its place the concept of an interdependent world.[39] In such a world, the appropriate external approach should be accommodation instead of confrontation. Third, and as a result, Resolution No. 13 called for a "multidirectional foreign policy" orientation that would help Vietnam to reduce the pressure resulting from embargo and isolation. In order to achieve those goals, Resolution No. 13 set as Vietnam's main task "to maintain peace [and] take advantage of favorable world conditions" in order to stabilize the domestic situation and lay the foundation for economic development over the next ten to fifteen years. For the first time, the CPV presented a new concept of security that departed from the orthodox one. According to Resolution No. 13, "the weak economy, the political siege and economic isolation are the main threats to the security and independence of our country."[40] Therefore, it stressed: "With a strong economy, with a sufficiently strengthened national defense and with an expansion of international relations we will have more power to maintain our independence and successfully construct socialism."[41] In short, Resolution No. 13 served as the guide for Vietnam's strategic development by charting a new approach that combined the respective strengths of economic health, military power, and diplomacy.

Three years after Resolution No. 13, the Seventh National Congress convened in June 1991 and officially adopted a multidirectional foreign policy, which represented the next important evolution in Vietnam's worldview.[42] Still facing international isolation despite having withdrawn all military forces from Cambodia, Vietnam aimed to diversify and multilateralize economic relations with all countries and economic organizations. The main slogan of the Seventh National Congress was: "Vietnam wants to become a friend of all countries in the world community, and to struggle for peace, independence and development." In the new circumstances, ideology ceased to pose a barrier to Vietnam's foreign policy: "We stand for equal and mutually beneficial co-operation with all countries regardless of different socio-political systems and on the basis of the principle of peaceful co-existence."[43]

In the context of the collapse of Eastern European countries and the complicated situation in the Soviet Union, the Seventh National Congress hesitantly decided to turn toward neighboring countries in East Asia and Southeast Asia and toward capitalist countries outside the region. The document stressed that Vietnam wished "to develop friendly relations with other countries in Southeast Asia and the Asia-Pacific region, and to strive for peace, friendship and co-operation within Southeast Asia; to expand equal and mutually beneficial co-operation with Northern and Western European countries, Japan and other developed countries; and to promote the process of normalization of relations with the United States."[44]

In the years following the Seventh National Congress, Vietnam successfully implemented its resolution by diversifying its foreign relations with other countries, first focusing on those in the region. After years of distrust and rivalry Vietnam was able to normalize its relations with all members of the ASEAN during 1991. Then, in November 1991, Vietnam achieved its most important foreign policy success: the restoration of normal relations with

China. Vietnam decided to accede to the 1976 ASEAN Treaty of Amity and Cooperation; in November 1992, Vietnam won Japan's agreement to resume its ODA, which had been cut off following Vietnam's intervention in Cambodia. In another major foreign policy achievement, Vietnam established diplomatic relations at the ambassadorial level with South Korea on December 22, 1992. Finally, the year 1995 represented the culmination of Vietnam's foreign policy shift. In that year Vietnam normalized relations with the United States, became the seventh member of the ASEAN, and signed a Framework Agreement with the EU.

Among all of these events, ASEAN membership was perhaps most significant in terms of changing Vietnam's outlook on the region. According to Donald S. Zagoria, senior vice president of the National Committee on American Foreign Policy, Vietnam's decision to join the ASEAN served its national security and economic reform aims in the context of the collapse of the Soviet Union and, with it, Soviet-Vietnamese security arrangements. Vietnam's accession to the ASEAN also bolstered the organization when it was already becoming wary of a rising, increasingly assertive China, as illustrated by that nation's occupation of the contested Mischief Reef—opposed by the Philippines—in early 1995.[45] From the Vietnamese perspective, Foreign Minister Nguyen Manh Cam observed that joining the ASEAN was mainly dictated by Vietnam's need to secure a peaceful environment for economic development, especially at a moment when it was transforming its centrally planned economic model into a market economy. In addition, Vietnam judged that ASEAN membership could strengthen its voice in international negotiations and meetings. Especially in the context of the collapse of the Soviet Union and the communist camp, ASEAN membership helped Vietnam to overcome its identity crisis and its isolation from the regional and international community.[46]

Whatever the precise combination of factors, the decision had been a long time in coming, and it was by no means an easy one for either Vietnam or the ASEAN. Vietnam's reputation had suffered and its intentions were regarded skeptically by a region still inclined to view the nation in terms of the Vietnam War, the postwar refugee problem, and especially Vietnam's intervention in Cambodia. Hostility and distrust characterized the region's attitude toward Vietnam until that nation decided to draw back all its military forces from Cambodia in November 1989. This action opened the door for multilateral discussions among Vietnam and the ASEAN member states, the Cambodian parties, and the major powers, including the United States, Soviet Union, and China. Then the November 1991 Paris conference brought to an end the Cambodian conflict and laid the foundation for enduring peace in Southeast Asia.

As a result of the increased awareness of Vietnamese and ASEAN mutual interests, new initiatives followed in rapid succession. During his October 1993 visit to Singapore, CPV general secretary Do Muoi enunciated a new four-point policy toward Southeast Asia: (1) Vietnam follows an independent, self-reliant, and multilateral foreign policy; (2) it attaches much importance to broadening friendly relations with countries in the Asia-Pacific region including with the ASEAN, and it aims to join the ASEAN at an appropriate moment; (3) Vietnam is ready to participate in bilateral and multilateral political and security dialogue with regional states; and (4) Vietnam supports peaceful negotiation as the basis for resolutions of conflict including the dispute in the East Sea.[47] In comparison with the old four-point policy toward Southeast Asia that the Vietnamese government had proclaimed in 1976, the new policy showed that Vietnam was ready to cooperate with the ASEAN on a new basis of mutual trust and confidence. On its side, the ASEAN welcomed the Vietnamese application, considering this an important step toward strengthening the association.

Therefore, the year 1995 marked a turning point both in Vietnamese foreign policy and in the history of the ASEAN. In a word, the Vietnam-ASEAN relationship had been transformed from one of mutual suspicion and distrust into one of mutual cooperation. For Vietnam this ended the long hostility dating back to the Cold War era and corresponded to the realities of the post–Cold War environment in a region where ideological confrontation had been replaced by cooperation in the common interest. Along with the reorientation of its policy, which the Sixth National Congress had officially announced in 1986, Vietnam expressed its will to become a friend and reliable partner to all countries in the world community striving for peace, cooperation, and friendship. The ASEAN membership also meant a new national identity for Vietnam, which had suddenly ceased to be a member of the communist bloc upon the Soviet Union's collapse in 1991. During the era of a bipolar world order, Southeast Asia had been divided between Indochina's communist countries on one side, and the rest of Southeast Asia on the other. The logic of such a division ended concomitantly with the end of the Cold War, opening the door for the ASEAN to structure itself as an inclusive regional organization. For Vietnam, then, joining the ASEAN could be regarded as a homecoming.

It is therefore difficult to quarrel with the following analysis, from a senior assistant in international relations at the University of Tampere: "Thus regionalism can perhaps be said to have become a part of Vietnam's identity building. I therefore emphasize the political nature of identity building in contrast to those views that emphasize the common cultural values behind regional identity.[48] For Vietnam, the commitment to regional identity is a result of the political search for a state identity after the Cold war."[49]

Vietnam not only gained tangible benefits from its ASEAN membership, the association's loose political structure offered Vietnam a flexible instrument to help mold its relationship with the region as well as to express its new identity. At the same time, Vietnamese officials were cognizant of the problems arising from the ASEAN's structure, including an ongoing tendency among member nations to place their national interests above regional ones. Such dynamics have constrained Vietnam's pursuit of certain goals through the ASEAN, for example, its relationship with the World Trade Organization (WTO) and its negotiation of terms for accession to that organization.[50]

There is room for debate over how well suited ASEAN membership has in fact been to Vietnam's foreign policy goals. Does the ASEAN indeed represent an ideal forum through which Vietnam can pursue its aims, or would it be more realistic to view the association as a golden cage that offers an inviting arena for the management of the regional order but that also conspicuously restricts Vietnam's foreign policy options?

In many ways, Vietnam has become one of the region's strongest supporters of the traditional approach to intergovernmental cooperation, which is characterized by a strict adherence to consensus building based on the lowest common denominator, nonbinding decision making, and noninterference.[51] Frankly speaking, however, Vietnam's regional participation during this period remained very limited. The CPV Eighth National Congress, held in 1996 on the first anniversary of Vietnam's ASEAN membership, reserved only one sentence in its official resolution for this event: "to make every effort for strengthening the relationship with neighboring countries and the member countries of ASEAN."[52] Further, in Communiqué No. 17-TB/TU issued on October 30, 1996, the CPV Politburo insisted on the following principles to govern its relations with the ASEAN countries. On the one hand, Vietnam has "to solidify its independent, self-reliant foreign policy, and to pursue multilateral and diversified external relations," but on the other hand it must "gather all forces for maintaining independence, sovereignty and a peaceful environment to build up the country."[53] A careful analysis of the CPV Politburo communiqué helps to understand how opaque and passive Vietnam's position and attitudes toward the ASEAN really were. Touching on the challenges of Vietnam's relations with the ASEAN countries during this period, the communiqué used the phrase "to fall in line with" (hòa nhập)—which tacitly acknowledged its passivity—instead of "to integrate" (*hội nhập*) with the regional market, which would have denoted Vietnam's readiness to seize the initiative as an active player.

Following an initial period of integration that coincided with the 1997–98 Asian financial crisis and the September 11, 2001, terrorist attacks on the United States, the CPV took stock of its foreign policy and set its strategy for the years ahead. In contrast to the earlier period, the beginning of the twenty-first century marked a significant strengthening of Vietnam's position and capacity. Vietnam called for a strengthening of friendly relations with neighboring countries along with ASEAN unity and coherence. In his July 23, 2001, opening remarks delivered during the 34th ASEAN foreign ministerial meeting in Hanoi, Vietnamese premier Phan Van Khai confirmed that Vietnam considered the ASEAN to be an important component of Vietnam's foreign policy and international cooperation. He explained that active efforts to promote international economic integration can be decisive, and that Vietnam's motto is to be a friend and reliable partner of all countries of the world that are striving for peace, independence, and development.[54] This fundamental principle was strongly reaffirmed in a series of meetings, in the remarks of Vietnamese government and party leaders, and explicitly in Resolution No. 07-NQ/TW, dated November 27, 2001, "On International Economic Integration."

Whereas international economic integration is a long-term strategy, the CPV has been obliged to make frequent adjustments appropriate to changing circumstances and new challenges. This is to be expected given that the Asia-Pacific region is one of the most dynamic and complex in the world. A new contest for influence in the region arose among major powers upon the end of the Cold War; this has intensified since the beginning of the new millennium. On the central court of the competition is China on one side and the United States on the other. While the former seeks to build a new multilateral regional order opposed to "the enlargement of the existing bilateral military alliances in Asia-Pacific, which were left over from the Cold War,"[55] the latter aims to consolidate its bilateral military alliances using a hub-and-spokes model.

This contest has influenced how events have recently unfolded in the South China Sea. The relationship between China's rise and increasing tension in the South China Sea is broadly acknowledged. At the same time, scholars inside and outside China hold to differing interpretations on the origin of the tensions. While most non-Chinese scholars link the increase in tensions to China's more assertive policy,[56] the Chinese view typically holds that the root of the tensions can be found in collusion between the United States and regional claimant states against China.[57] "China's rise" was the crucial factor impelling America's "pivot" or "rebalancing" toward Asia and its active reengagement with Southeast Asia, although this has never been openly stated by Washington. China's assertive policy especially after 2007[58] pushed the United States into increased engagement with the region. Secretary of State Hilary Clinton clearly stated this on July 23, 2010, at the 17th ARF meeting in Hanoi: "The United States, like every nation, has a national interest in freedom of navigation, open access to Asia's maritime commons, and respect for international law in the South China Sea. . . . The U.S. supports the 2002 ASEAN-China declaration on the conduct of parties in the South China Sea. We encourage the parties to reach agreement on a full code of conduct. The United States is prepared to facilitate initiatives and confidence building measures consistent with the declaration."[59]

Facing a new and uncertain constellation of forces in its immediate security environment, the CPV in July 2003 issued Resolution No. 8 of the Central Committee (Section IX), "On strategy for fatherland defense in the new context." This resolution provided new definitions that sharply differed from previous ones in Vietnamese foreign policy. For example, relating to the question of partner (*doi tac*) and opponent (*doi tuong*), the resolution explained: "Everyone who advocates respect for our independence and sovereignty along with promotion of a relationship based on friendship, equality, mutual interests and cooperation is considered our partner; everyone who conspires or takes action against our country's objectives to build up and to defend the fatherland is an opponent that must be fought."[60]

It is necessary here to remind the reader that the previous delineation of "ours and yours" in Vietnamese policy was based mainly on the assumption of Marxist class struggle and ideology, and influenced deeply by the division of the world into two poles and camps. However, Resolution No. 8 also maintained: "It is necessary to have a dialectical point of view: in every opponent there may be some elements that (we) could cooperate with and take advantage of; in some partners there may be differences and conflicts. Based on these facts, it is necessary to overcome both trends, namely being vague and lacking vigilance or being inflexible in perception, guideline and in dealing with concrete situation."[61]

It was previously mentioned that after the 1986 launching of *Doi Moi* (reform), CPV Resolution No. 8 (Section IX) was the second strategically important document after Resolution No. 13 (Section VII). It determined the main principles and guidelines of Vietnamese foreign policy toward other countries that may have different political systems and levels of economic development.

In an interview on January 8, 2011, for *Vietnam Net*—the most popular online newspaper in Vietnam—Vietnamese deputy defense minister Lt. Gen. Nguyen Chi Vinh stated: "I believe that Resolution No. 8 became a historical document in the history of the Fatherland defense akin to (the role played by) Resolution No. 15 during the war against America."[62]

Conclusion

For a variety of reasons the process of East Asian and Pacific regional integration and cooperation began in earnest only after the end of the Cold War, but soon became both very dynamic and very complex. The region became a central focus of global politics owing to the "rise" of China, Sino-Japanese competition, and U.S. hub-and-spokes bilateral alliances, the evolution of an emerging security architecture initiated by the ASEAN, and the persistence of traditional security issues along with the appearance of nontraditional ones.

Vietnam and South Korea—finding themselves in a broadly comparable geopolitical strategic position; sharing many historical, cultural, and political similarities; and emerging as two recognized middle powers—decided to establish diplomatic ties in 1992 right after the end of the Cold War. Since then, both nations have worked actively and intensively in multilateral regional mechanisms, sometimes separately and sometimes in concert, to pursue their own and common interests.

It would be hard to imagine that regional mechanisms such as the ARF, ASEAN+3, and EAS could work effectively without the participation of Vietnam and South Korea. Both South Korea and Vietnam strongly supported the initiative to establish the East Asia Vision Group (EAVG), East Asia Study Group (EASG), and East Asia Summit (EAS). In order to strengthen regional cooperation, in 2004 South Korea signed an ASEAN-ROK Free Trade Agreement, which Vietnam considered as a first step toward an East Asian free trade area. Despite their limitations and inefficiency, these mechanisms have provided a good chance for both countries to promote their positions in the international arena, and have served as instruments for them to pursue their policies. Both Vietnam and South Korea seem well positioned and politically committed to making both individual and joint contributions to peace, stability, and prosperity of the region.

For South Korea, the 1997–98 Asian financial crisis encouraged its participation in the newly established ASEAN+1 and ASEAN+3 institutions. This helped Seoul to lay the foundation for a "New Korea" and to strike a balance in its diplomacy between Sinocentrism and Japanocentrism.

Vietnam, due to its previous membership in the communist bloc and the mistakes it committed after national unification in 1975, had a longer and more difficult path toward participating actively in efforts toward regional integration. It only became an ASEAN member in 1995. One exciting result of this gradual process was that Vietnam reconceptualized its foreign policy from a model heavily based on ideology to a model centering on *realpolitik*. Vietnam's increasing regional role can best be understood in terms of its geopolitical position, the success of its domestic reform policies, and the diversification and multilateralization of its foreign affairs.

The success of both Vietnam and South Korea has demonstrated two aspects of regionalism: (1) the important role that regional cooperation and formal institutions can play in fostering economic development of individual nations in the region, and (2) the increased opportunities for middle powers to play a more significant role within and beyond the region. There is no doubt that both South Korea and Vietnam will be active in regional cooperation due to their similar perception on the role of middle powers, their position on regional integration, and their common interest in fostering a peaceful environment for development. The foundation for cooperation is the bilateral, comprehensive relationship that the two countries have built over the past two decades.

Notes

1 Vũ Khoan, "Từ thù địch đến đối tác chiến lược" [From enemy to strategic partner], Báo cáo trình bày tại Hội thảo Quan hệ đối tác chiến lược Việt Nam-Hàn Quốc lần 2 Chia sẻ tầm nhìn, hướng tới thịnh vượng [Speech delivered on the Second Conference of Vietnam-Korea Strategic Relations Sharing Vision, Looking Toward Prosperity], Hanoi, December 21, 2011, 3.

2 Trường Đại học Khoa học Xã hội và Nhân văn [University of Social Sciences and Humanities], *Tương đồng văn hóa Việt Nam-Hàn Quốc* [The cultural similarities of Vietnam and Korea] (Hanoi: The Culture and Information Publishing House, 1996); see also Nguyễn Văn Ánh, Đỗ Đình Hãng, Lê Đình Chỉnh, *Hàn Quốc Lịch sử-Văn hóa* [Korean history and culture] (Hanoi: The Culture and Information Publishing House, 1996), 5–8.

3 Michael Mullen and Joint Chiefs of Staff, *The National Military Strategy of the United States of America 2011: Redefining America's Military Leadership* (Washington, DC: Joint Chiefs of Staff, 2011), 4.

4 Viện Nghiên cứu Chiến lược Bộ Ngoại giao [Institute of Strategic Studies MOFA], *Đề án nâng cao hơn nữa hiệu quả tham gia của Việt Nam tại các tổ chức, diễn đàn đa phương* [Project to promote the efficiency of Vietnam's participation in the international multilateral organization and forums] (Hanoi: Institute of Strategic Studies MOFA, 2012).

5 Trần Trọng Kim, *Việt Nam sử lược* [A brief history of Vietnam] (Saigon: Khai Trí Publishing House, 1962), 121.

6 Kinh Bắc, "Di duệ Vua Lý Thái Tổ ở Nam Triều Tiên" [Descendents of King Ly Thai To in South Korea], *Newspaper Lao Động*, Spring 1991. See also: Sở Văn hóa Thông tin Thể thao Hà Bắc [Department for Culture, Information and Sport of Ha Bac Province], *Xung quanh sự tích Hoàng tử Lý Long Tường ở nước ngoài* [*Around the Legend of Prince Ly Long Tuong Abroad*] (Habac: Department for Culture, Information and Sport of Ha Bac Province, 1994),12.

7 Bắc, "Di duệ Vua Lý Thái Tổ ở Nam Triều Tiên," 11.

8 Cho Jae Hyon, "Quan hệ Hàn Quốc-Việt Nam: Quá khứ, hiện tại và tương lai" [Korea-Vietnam relations: past, present and prospect], in *Tương đồng văn hóa Việt Nam-Hàn Quốc* [The cultural similarities of Vietnam and Korea], ed. Trường Đại học Khoa học Xã hội và Nhân văn [University of Social Sciences and Humanities] (Hanoi: The Culture and Information Publishing House, 1996), 27–28.

9 Bùi Duy Tân, "Tứ hải giai huynh đệ-Những cuộc tạo ngộ sứ giả-nhà thơ Việt-Triều trên đất nước Trung Hoa thời trung đại" [People in four oceans are brothers—the meetings between ambassadors-poets from Vietnam and Korea in China in the mediaeval period], in *Tương đồng văn hóa Việt Nam-Hàn Quốc* [The cultural similarities of Vietnam and Korea], ed. Trường Đại học Khoa học Xã hội và Nhân văn [University of Social Sciences and Humanities] (Hanoi: The Culture and Information Publishing House, 1996), 56–59.

10 Đỗ Quang Hưng, "Quan hệ Việt-Hàn, phác thảo lịch sử" [Vietnam-Korea relations—a brief history] (paper presented during the seminar organized by the National Center of Social Sciences and Humanities, Hanoi, April 1994), 2–4.

11 http://www.imhc.mil.kr/imhcroot/data/vetnam_view.jsp?seq=7&page=1.

12 Khoan, "Từ thù địch đến đối tác chiến lược," 2.

13 Viện Nghiên cứu Chiến lược Bộ Ngoại giao [Institute of Strategic Studies MOFA], *Báo cáo về Hội thảo Quan hệ đối tác chiến lược Việt Nam-Hàn Quốc lần 2 Chia sẻ tầm nhìn, hướng tới thịnh vượng* [Report on the Second Conference of Vietnam-Korea Strategic Relations Sharing Vision, Looking Toward Prosperity] (Hanoi: Institute of Strategic Studies MOFA, December 21, 2011).

14 Lee Kang Woo, "Tình hình đào tạo tiếng Việt tại Hàn Quốc" [The situation of Vietnamese language training in Korea], paper presented to the 13th Korea Forum at the University of Social Sciences and Humanities, Vietnam National University-Hanoi, January 13, 2012.

15 John Ikenberry and Michael Mastanduno, eds., *International Relations Theory and the Asia-Pacific* (New York: Columbia University Press, 2003).

16 Lezsek Buszynski, "Sino-Japanese Relations: Interdependence, Rivalry and Regional Security," *Contemporary Southeast Asia* 31, No.1 (April 2009): 143–71; June Teufel Dreyer, "Sino-Japanese Rivalry and its Implications for Developing Nations," *Asian Survey* 46, No.4 (July/August 2006): 538–57; Jin Yang, "Sino-Japanese Relations and Implications for Southeast Asia," *Contemporary Southeast Asia* 25, No. 2 (August 2003): 306–27.

17 Douglas Webber, "Regional Integration in Europe and Asia: A Historical Perspective," in *Regional Integration in East Asia and Europe Convergence or Divergence*, eds. Bertrand Fort and Douglas Webber (London and New York: Routledge Taylor and Francis Group, 2006), 289–311.

18 Ann L. Phillips, "The Politics of Reconciliation Revisited: Germany and East Central Europe," *World Affairs* 163, No. 4 (Spring): 171–91.

19 Shiping Tang, "Leadership in Institution Building the Case of ASEAN+3," in *Regional Integration in East Asia and Europe Convergence or Divergence*, eds. Bertrand Fort and Douglas Webber (London and New York: Routledge Taylor and Francis Group, 2006), 80.

20 Choi Wonsik, "A Korea-Based Alternative or an East Asia-Based Alternative? Korea and East Asia," in *East Asia as a Discovery*, eds. Chung Moongil, Wonsik Choi, Youngseo Baik, and Hyungjun Jeon (Seoul: Northeast Asian History Foundation, 2009), 37.

21 Rodolfo Severino, *The ASEAN Regional Forum* (Singapore: ISEAS Singapore 2009), 21.

22 Ibid., 30.

23 Byung Nak Song, *Kinh tế Hàn Quốc đang trỗi dậy* [*The Rising Economy of Korea*] (Hanoi: Statistics Publishing House, 1998), 80.

24 http://www.aseansec.org.

25 Excerpted from the author's own article, "The East Asia Security Environment in the Beginning of the Twenty-first Century and the Adjustment in Vietnam Foreign Policy," *Asia-Pacific Review* 18, no. 1 (May 2011): 98–108.

26 Đảng Cộng sản Việt Nam [Vietnamese Congress Party], "Nghị quyết của Hội nghị lần thứ chín Ban chấp hành Trung ương Đảng Lao động Việt Nam về tình hình thế giới và nhiệm vụ quốc tế của Đảng ta tháng 12 năm 1963" [Resolution of the Ninth Meeting of Central Committee of Vietnam's Labour Party on the World's Situation and International Task of Our Party, December 1963], in *The Party's Completed Documents, Volume 24 (1963)* (Hanoi: National Political Publishing House, 2003), 729. The three waves were: the wave of communist countries; the national liberation movement in Asia, Africa, and Latin America; and the struggle of the working class and laboring masses in capitalist countries. The four contradictions were: between the socialist camp and the imperialist camp, between the proletariat and the capitalist class within capitalist countries, between oppressed peoples and imperialism and colonialism, and both between imperialist countries and between capitalist corporations within imperialist countries.

27 In 1974, taking advantage of Vietnam's weakness during civil war (in which North Vietnam was supported by China, while the United States—South Vietnam's ally—was prevented from involvement in the war by its signing of the Paris agreement in 1973), China militarily attacked the Paracels, then still under South Vietnam's control. Despite South Vietnam's defense of the islands and unified Vietnam's protests to Beijing after 1975, China has continued to occupy the Paracels and assert its sovereignty over them.

28 The so-called "Chinese incident" occurred very soon after the fall of Saigon, during the socialist transformation in South Vietnam. The government of the recently unified Socialist Republic of Vietnam (SRV) intended to construct a communist society through a comprehensive campaign to transform capitalist owners who were mostly overseas Chinese (*Hoa kiều*) or Vietnamese with Chinese origins (*người Việt gốc Hoa*) through national confiscation or collectivization of their ownership. The Government of the People's Republic of China (PRC) reacted by asserting that the SRV had discriminated against its citizens and effectively forced them to leave Vietnam for China. The socialist transformation campaign in Vietnam in fact resulted in the departure of hundreds of thousands of overseas Chinese

from Vietnam. This produced major losses for the Vietnamese economy, caused widespread distrust within Vietnamese society, and exacerbated existing frictions and rivalry in the Sino-Vietnamese bilateral relationship. The flow of overseas Chinese from Vietnam in the following years also resulted in the phenomenon of the so-called "boat people" (*thuyền nhân*).

29 In the first week of January 1979, Vietnamese military forces decided to help the Cambodian people overthrow the Khmer Rouge regime of Pol Pot. Vietnamese troops marched into Cambodia, deposed the Khmer Rouge, and sponsored establishment of the new Democratic Republic of Kampuchea. Vietnamese forces remained in Cambodia until 1989.

30 Leszek Buszynski, *Gorbachev and Southeast Asia* (London: Routledge, 1992).

31 Cục Lưu trữ Văn phòng Trung ương Đảng [Department of Archive of VCP Central Committee], *Tình hình thế giới và chính sách đối ngoại của Đảng và Nhà nước ta* [The world's situation and foreign policy of our party and state] (Hanoi: Department of Archive of VCP Central Committee, 1986).

32 Cục Lưu trữ Văn phòng Trung ương Đảng [Department of Archive of VCP Central Committee], Nghị quyết 32 Bộ chính trị khóa 6 [Resolution No. 32 of Politburo (Section VI)] (Hanoi: Department of Archive of VCP Central Committee, 1986).

33 Vũ Khoan, "Thành tựu trong lĩnh vực đối ngoại qua 20 năm đổi mới" [Achievements in the field of external relations after 20 years of renovation], *Nhan dan Newspaper*, November 14, 2005.

34 Trần Quang Cơ, "Hồi Ký Trần Quang Cơ" [Memoir of Tran Quang Co], http://www.ykien.net/tqco1.html.

35 Nguyễn Cơ Thạch, "Những chuyển biến trên thế giới và tư duy mới của chúng ta [The changes in the world and our new thinking], *Tạp chí Quan hệ quốc tế tháng 1 năm 1990* [*Journal of International Relations*, January 1990]; Phan Doãn Nam, "Ngoai Giao Viet Nam Sau 20 Nam Doi Moi" [Vietnam's diplomacy 20 years after renovation], *Tạp chí Cộng sản số 14* (760) tháng 7 năm 2006 [*Communist Review* 14, no. 760 (July 2006): 26–30].

36 W. Duiker, *Vietnam since the Fall of Saigon* (Athens: Ohio University Center for International Studies, 1985), 31–51; M. Beresford, *National Unification and Economic Development in Vietnam* (New York: St. Martin's Press, 1989).

37 Đinh Nho Liêm, "Nguyễn Cơ Thạch-Nhà ngoại giao xuất sắc" [Nguyen Co Thach—an excellent diplomat], in *Nhà Ngoại giao Nguyễn Cơ Thạch* [Diplomat Nguyen Co Thach] (Hanoi: National Political Publishing House, 2003), 80–81; Nguyễn Tuấn Liêu, "Nét đặc sắc, tiêu biểu ở anh Nguyễn Cơ Thạch" [The unusual excellent character of Nguyen Co Thach] in *Nhà Ngoại giao Nguyễn Cơ Thạch* [Diplomat Nguyen Co Thach] (Hanoi: National Political Publishing House, 2003), 116.

38 Nguyễn Cơ Thạch, "Trả lời phỏng vấn của Tạp chí Quan hệ Quốc tế" [Answers to Interview of Journal International Relations], Hanoi, January 1990, 6.

39 Thạch, "Những chuyển biến trên thế giới và tư duy mới của chúng ta."

40 Cục lưu trữ Văn phòng Trung ương Đảng, Nghị quyết 13/BCT ngày 20/5/1988 [Department of Archive of CPV Central Committee, Resolution No. 13/BCT, May 20, 1988].

41 Thạch, "Những chuyển biến trên thế giới và tư duy mới của chúng ta."

42 Vũ Khoan, "Một số vấn đề quốc tế của Đại hội VII" [Some international issues of the Seventh National Congress] trong: Bộ Ngoại giao, Hội nhập quốc tế và giữ vững bản sắc

[in *International Integration and firmly maintain identity*, ed. Ministry of Foreign Affairs] (Hanoi: National Political Publishing House, 1995), 75.

43 CPV (Communist Party of Vietnam), *The Documents of the Seventh National Congress* (Hanoi: Vietnam Foreign Languages Publishing House, 1991), 134.

44 Ibid., 135.

45 Donald S. Zagoria, "Joining ASEAN," in *Vietnam Joins the World*, eds. James Morley and Masashi Nishihara (London: M. E. Sharpe, 1997).

46 Nguyễn Mạnh Cầm, "Phát biểu tại Lễ kỷ niệm một năm gia nhập ASEAN" [The speech delivered on the ceremony of one year of joining the ASEAN], Hanoi, August 1996.

47 Đỗ Mười, "Lập trường bốn điểm về ASEAN" [The four stand points on the ASEAN], *Báo Quân đội Nhân dân ngày* 17 tháng 10 năm 1993 [*People's Army Newspaper*, October 17, 1993].

48 Aero Palmujoki, "Vietnam's Integration into the World: National and Global Interfaces," in *Vietnam's New Order: International Perspectives on the State and Reform in Vietnam*, eds. Stephanie Balme and Mark Sidel (NY: Palgrave Macmillan, 2007), 122.

49 Nguyen Vu Tung, "Vietnam-ASEAN Cooperation after the Cold War and the Continued Search for a Theoretical Framework," *Contemporary Southeast Asia* 24, no. 1 (2002): 106–20.

50 Tran Phuong Lan, "Vietnam with the Idea of ASEAN Economic Community," *The Communist Review* 65 (2004).

51 Joern Dosch, "Vietnam's ASEAN Membership: Golden Opportunity or Golden Cage?" *Contemporary Southeast Asia* 28, No. 2 (2006): 236–37.

52 CPV (Communist Party of Vietnam), *The Documents of the Eighth National Congress* (Hanoi: Vietnam Foreign Languages Publishing House, 1996), 121.

53 Cục lưu trữ Văn phòng Trung ương Đảng, Thông báo số 17-TB/TW ngày 30/6/1996 ý kiến của Bộ chính trị về những mặt công tác cần thiết để nâng cao hiệu quả hợp tác với các nước trong Hiệu hội ASEAN. [Department of Archive of VCP Central Committee, Communiqué No.17-TB/TW on October 30, 1996, of Politburo's points of view on the necessary works to promote efficiency in cooperation with the ASEAN countries].

54 Viện Quan hệ Quốc tế [Institute of International Relations], *Chính sách đối ngoại Việt Nam* [Vietnam's foreign policy] (Hanoi: Institute of International Relations, 2002), 91.

55 Ma Xiaotien, "Promote Security Cooperation for a Harmonious Asia-Pacific Region," Shangri-La Dialogue, Singapore, May 30, 2009.

56 Ian Storey, "China's Missteps in Southeast Asia: Less Charm, More Offensive," *China Brief*, December 17, 2010; Michael D. Swaine, "Perceptions of an Assertive China," *China Leadership Monitor* 32 (2010); Sarah Raine, "Beijing's South China Sea Debate," *Survival* 53, no. 5 (2011): 69–88; Edward Wong, "China Navy Reaches Far, Unsettling the Region," *New York Times*, June 14, 2011; Mingjiang Li, "Reconciling Assertiveness and Cooperation? China's Changing Approach to the South China Sea Dispute," in *Security Challenges* 6, no. 2 (Winter 2010): 46–98.

57 Ji Peijuan, "China Needs to Accelerate Development in the South China Sea," *National Defense Times*, June 29, 2011; Wang Xi, "China Smartly Fights Back at American "Soft Containment," *National Defense Times*, August 5, 2011; Ding Gang, "Why the South China

Sea Issue Has Become So Hot," *People's Daily*, August 2, 2011; Zhou Biao and Jiao Dongyu, "The Next Step in the South China Sea Game," *National Defense Time*, August 17, 2011; Li Xiaokun, "Navigation in South China Sea 'Not a Problem,'" *China Daily*, October 23, 2010.

58 In 2007–08 China protested against British Petroleum and American Exxon Mobil cooperation with Vietnam to explore oil and gas fields in the South China Sea, eventually prompting both to suspend their work. In March 2010 some Beijing officials even stated that the South China Sea was a "core national interest" equivalent to Taiwan and Tibet.

59 H. Clinton, Statement made during the 17th ARF Meeting, Hanoi, July 23, 2010.

60 Cục Lưu trữ Văn phòng Trung ương Đảng [Department of Archive of CPV Central Committee], Nghị quyết Trung ương 8 [Khóa IX] về chiến lược bảo vệ Tổ quốc trong tình hình mới [Resolution No.8 (Section IX) on Strategy for Fatherland Defense in the New Context], Hanoi, 2003, 17.

61 Ibid., 18.

62 Nguyễn Chí Vịnh, "Không để nước khác thỏa hiệp trên lưng mình" [Do not let other country making compromise behind us], 2011, http://www.vietnamnet.vn.

6 South Korea's Middle-Power Diplomacy[1]

Su-Hoon Lee

Is South Korea a "middle power" in the international system? In other words, does it exhibit foreign policy behaviors appropriate to middle-power status? These are relatively fresh questions in the Korean political science community. Until recently, becoming an advanced state had been the national vision. Political leaders aspired to develop their country as such. While the term "middle power" may have been uttered loosely in reference to the country's place in the global order, no political leader ever promoted a vision of Korea as a middle power.

The objective of this chapter is to revisit the Roh Moo-hyun administration (2003–08) and its key foreign policy stances. I argue that South Korea's foreign policy behavior during the Roh administration closely reflects that of a middle power. Looking at the administration's regional community building in Northeast Asia (NEA)[2]—specifically, the NEA Cooperation Initiative—I see a high-water mark in the evolution of South Korea's middle-power diplomacy. To support my argument, I look at three implications of the initiative; that is, inherent strategies toward (1) China, (2) the alliance of the Republic of Korea (ROK) with the United States, and (3) a regional environment conducive to improving inter-Korean relations in the midst of the second North Korean nuclear crisis.

South Korea and Middle-Power Activism

There is no widely accepted definition of what constitutes a middle-power state. Generally, middle states have relatively less political, economic, and military power and size than great powers—but are less vulnerable than small powers—and have more diplomatic options at their disposal.[3] Regarding this last point, middle powers may be best identified by their international behavior, or "middle-power diplomacy." They tend to pursue multilateral solutions to international problems, seek compromise in international disputes, and embrace notions of good international citizenship. They favor the existing international order, strive to maintain peace through coalition building, and largely support international conflict management and resolution activities. They also try to avoid direct confrontation with great powers, in many cases working to support the global hegemon, and yet often seek to clarify their own nuanced stance on specific issues.[4]

In their analysis of middle powers, scholars have sought to distinguish between traditional and emerging ones,[5] with recent focus on the latter category.[6] South Korea is most often called an emerging middle power,[7] although some have argued its evolution into a traditional middle power[8] while others have classified it more specifically as a "pivotal middle power."[9]

South Korea is indeed unique among middle powers. In terms of capacity, South Korea's gross domestic product (GDP) and purchasing parity power (PPP) per capita hover just below the average level of the European Union (EU), and its population of 50 million is relatively large, although it is estimated to decline in the decades ahead. The country serves as an example to other middle powers striving to catch up with the developed countries of the West via a strategy of robust economic growth and rapid modernization. A member of the Group of Twenty (G-20),[10] and one of the biggest of the middle powers based on the size of its economy, some argue that with its successful emergence, South Korea could even be considered "an ideal type or the 20th century anticipation of the 21st century phenomenon."[11]

However, as Adam Balcer notes, "From the perspective of international order, the most important is the classification which divides the middle powers into those playing an important regional role, and those which despite a big potential, are not able to completely stretch out their wings because their geopolitical environment or serious internal weaknesses make it hard for them to achieve that goal."[12] This is particularly true of the South Korean experience (especially during the Cold War), as Northeast Asia's geopolitics, bilateral alliances, and security situation—rocked by the division of Korea—constrained South Korea's ability to stretch its foreign policy "wings." However, the advent of the Roh Moo-hyun government and its execution of the NEA Cooperation Initiative mark a significant step forward. Now South Korea plays a much more substantive role in the region, one that substantiates its classification as an emerging middle power.

A Brief Look at Korea's Middle-Power Evolution

As mentioned, middle powers tend to exercise influence on the international system through coalition building, especially through promotion of and active involvement in multilateral institutions. South Korea has long been a proponent of building multilateral security architecture in the region. At the United Nations (UN) General Assembly in 1988 President Roh Tae-woo recommended the creation of a "Consultative Conference for Peace in Northeast Asia." Then, at the Asia Regional Forum Senior Officials' Meeting in Bangkok in 1994, South Korea proposed a Northeast Asia Security Dialogue (NEASED). These are two early examples of advocacy, despite the fact that both proposals were seen as supplements to and bounded by the existing bilateral security alliance with the United States.

Earlier in the post–Cold War era, ROK foreign policy (even as it promoted multilateralism) did not reflect its middle-power capacity—at least not until the Kim Dae-jung government came to power, a watershed event in South Korea's middle-power evolution.[13] The Kim administration's Sunshine Policy helped transform South Korea from a capacity-based middle power into a behavior-based one. By emphasizing the principle of coexistence with its estranged "other"—North Korea—the policy demonstrated a qualitative departure from past administrations' hard-line policies against the Democratic People's Republic of Korea (DPRK). As the former Australian foreign minister Gareth Evans describes, middle-power diplomacy, in method and motivation, is characterized by coalition building and good international citizenship, respectfully, its effectiveness contingent primarily on opportunity, capacity, creativity, and credibility.[14] While the method and motivation of South Korea's diplomacy prior to the late 1990s falls short in this regard, the Sunshine Policy was a brilliant example. Reversing a decades-long policy of enmity in favor of peaceful engagement, it seized upon an opportunity created by a relative thaw in DPRK-U.S. relations to then show a foreign policy choice independent of its longtime patron, the United States, that simultaneously drew in other major and middle powers. In depth, conviction, and the garnering of public support, the policy was a prime example of middle-power activism as it encouraged various countries, including other middle powers, to engage with North Korea.[15]

The succeeding Roh Moo-hyun government both embraced Kim's engagement policy and creatively expanded it in form and scope. Throughout the Roh administration's tenure, South Korea demonstrated greater consistency in middle-power behavior than during any previous administration. During this time foreign policy actions increased Korea's capability to act independently, using the methods of compromise, cooperation, and coordination.

One aspect of the Roh government's foreign policy was the NEA Cooperation Initiative, which in hindsight serves as a prime example of Korea's attempt to demonstrate middle-power behavior. Through the initiative South Korea took a more independent foreign policy, yet not without seeking the support of its alliance partner and global hegemon, the United States. Seoul sought a multilateral solution to specific problems that had plagued the Northeast Asian region for decades: the division of the Korean Peninsula and the security threats posed by North Korea, including its infamous nuclear capacity. (An in-depth discussion of the NEA Cooperation Initiative will follow in the next section.)

Under the Lee Myung-bak government, one could argue that South Korea achieved a level of capacity and behavior consistent with its middle-power status. Throughout the past years South Korea has demonstrated significant diplomatic activism, niche diplomacy, coalition building, and good international citizenship, especially through its active support of international institutions and summits: for example, (1) it actively supported the G-20 as the international body to address the global financial crisis, and even cohosted the G-20 summit in 2010 with another middle power, Canada; and (2) it organized and held the Second Nuclear Security Summit in March 2012, to discuss international cooperative measures to protect nuclear materials and facilities from terrorist groups. The Lee administration's New Asia Initiative—which incorporates Korea's entering into free trade agreements (FTAs) with Asian nations and the creation of a low-carbon, "green" growth strategy in the Asia-Pacific region to tackle global economic and environmental challenges—would also seem to confirm South Korea's expanding role as a middle power. South Korea's capacity, as a good international citizen, to provide significant financial support to other economies has also grown, as evidenced by South Korea's ability to contribute rescue funds to the International Monetary Fund (IMF), one of the lending agencies involved in bailing out Greece during the ongoing European sovereign debt crisis.[16] Furthermore, South Korea has maintained membership in nearly every multilateral forum, hosted many key diplomatic events over President Lee's term in office, and maintained a significant number of Korean nationals in key positions in various international multilateral organizations. In sum, South Korea has positioned itself closer to the core of international society,[17] further bolstering its position as a middle power.

However, while doing much that would suggest Korea's continuing forward movement in its middle-power evolution—at least in terms of behavior—in another sense President Lee's policies can be seen as a step backward; many of his policies were widely viewed as "pro-American" rather than putting Korea's interests first. The previous administration had attempted to devise an independent foreign policy and seek a more distinct, mediator's role in the multilateral effort to deal with the security situation on the Korean Peninsula and in the region, one embracing both antagonists and allies. Lee, meanwhile, went to great lengths to make the ROK-U.S. alliance once again central to South Korea's foreign policy, often ignoring public discontent in the process. Such an approach is rather anachronistic, and in effect retightened one strap of the bridle that has restricted Korea's foreign policy decision-making for decades.

The NEA Cooperation Initiative and Its Strategic Implications

How can we conceive of the Roh government's NEA Cooperation Initiative? For the most part, it was an initiative that sought "to accelerate economic, security, and sociocultural cooperation among regional and concerned nations to build a peaceful and prosperous Northeast Asia."[18] Contrary to conventional thinking, the NEA Cooperation Initiative had strategic implications for South Korea and regional community building, including how to address (1) China, both in the short and long term, (2) the United States and the transforming ROK-U.S. alliance, and (3) regional attitudes toward relations between the two Koreas.

China Strategy

During the Cold War, South Korea's relationship with China was characterized by mutual distrust. This antagonism prevailed for decades until it was turned around in 1992, when the two countries established diplomatic relations soon after the end of the Cold War in 1989. At the time, China was already undergoing serious reforms and opening, claiming socialism while promoting rapid economic growth in the world capitalist market system—rising as a "global factory" aggressively hosting foreign investment.

Since the establishment of diplomatic relations between China and the ROK, their bilateral relations have advanced at an incredible speed. Economic relations strengthened alongside an increase in mutual trade and investment, and political and security relations were put on a more cooperative track. Also, thanks to the countries' geographical proximity, sociocultural exchanges increased remarkably. Yet even today, scholars and policymakers debate how South Korea should perceive China[19]—whether as a threat or an opportunity.

And further groundwork needs to be laid before Sino-Korean relations can promote peace on the Korean Peninsula. Such concerns, however, have not stopped business. Even as fears of a Chinese threat gained popularity in the late 1990s, domestic companies in South Korea continued to expand their business into China. China soon became South Korea's largest trading partner, surpassing the United States and Japan as of 2010.

Back in 2005, I argued the significance of China "in the NEA era," calling for deepening cooperation with China and suggesting the importance of a "balanced foreign policy without excluding China and Russia, who have made progress with the U.S. and Japan in developing friendly and future-oriented relations."[20] Other China experts seemed to agree with this argument.[21] President Roh Moo-Hyun himself regularly underscored the emergence of China in Northeast Asia, a fact that influenced the NEA Cooperation Initiative.[22] It was Roh's hope to build an integrative and community-like order in Northeast Asia similar to that seen in Europe. To do so, it was clear that the powers surrounding the Korean Peninsula needed to cooperate. Elsewhere I have explained how the NEA Cooperation Initiative incorporated the theories of cooperation among countries in the region.[23]

President Roh later introduced the NEA Cooperation Initiative as a part of his strategy to accommodate the regional shifts stemming from the increasing role of Northeast Asia in the new world order. Indeed, the administration felt the need to use this strategic initiative to deal with the various ripple effects associated with the "rise" of China. For example, there was a need to manage the implicit rivalry between a rapidly growing China and the United States and Japan, with the intent of guarding against conflicts between these major continental and sea powers—a dynamic that was feared to usher in a new Cold War system. Also, the NEA Cooperation Initiative was introduced to both contemplate and explore various options for South Korea's security and diplomatic strategies. The controversial notion of South Korea as a "balancer of Northeast Asia"—introduced in spring 2005—was also a by-product of this effort. At the time, President Roh argued that "it is not the matter of which side to take between the competition of major powers,"[24] but rather for South Korea to push forward to try and augment its role as a regional mediator. He noted that "without leaning on China or Japan, South Korea needs to rise to the level of balancing on its own, to take the path with its own strength."[25]

Regardless, the Roh administration began advancing a "comprehensive and cooperative partnership" with China, all the while strategically bolstering cooperation through the principles of the NEA Cooperation Initiative. This

bespoke a perceived need to cooperate in order to overcome discord and foster common interests. At that time, Sino-ROK relations faced conflicts that
included China's *dongbukgongjeong* ("Northeast Asia Project"), historical
memories, and issues of maritime sovereignty, among others. Despite these
problems, leaders from both nations were enthusiastic and motivated to cooperate, building trust through bilateral dialogue and negotiations.

Also included in South Korea's approach to China, as envisioned in the
NEA Cooperation Initiative, were strategic considerations for the resolution
of the nuclear issue on the Korean Peninsula. Soon after the Roh administration took office in 2003, the new nuclear crisis posed serious security and
foreign policy concerns, making China's cooperation both inevitable and indispensable for a peaceful diplomatic resolution of the North Korean nuclear
crisis. As neoconservatives were leading the George W. Bush administration,
Washington and Seoul seemed unable to find a common perspective and approach in their policies toward North Korea. China's role thus became critical
as a means of providing a mid- to long-term approach to North Korea, including the nuclear crisis. During the years of the Roh administration, China's policy toward the Korean Peninsula did not waver. Its aims were to ensure North
Korean regime stability, encourage reform and opening, safeguard peace and
stability on the Korean Peninsula, maintain a comprehensive cooperative partnership with South Korea, and sustain a constructive role in the reunification
process of the two Koreas.

Today an increasing number of analysts are concerned that a possible new
Cold War environment may be taking shape in Northeast Asia. Cooperation
between China and South Korea is elusive; instead, discord prevails over several issues. Political trust that had been built during the Roh Moo-hyun government has severely eroded. It is imperative to realize the risk South Korea
is taking by strengthening the ROK-U.S. alliance for the alliance's sake while
"thrashing" China, at a time when a strategic approach to China is sorely
needed.

South Korea faces a huge dilemma as it simultaneously deepens economic
relations with China and buttresses political and security relations with the
United States. Instigating—or witnessing—conflict between China and the
United States on and over the Korean Peninsula will bring no conceivable
benefit to South Korea; it is, in fact, the worst-case scenario from the South
Korean perspective, as Seoul weighs its foreign policy strategy and options.
During the Roh administration, this possibility was anticipated—which brings
us back to the NEA Cooperation Initiative.

Supplementing the ROK-U.S. Alliance

The NEA Cooperation Initiative had two strategic concerns in regard to the ROK-U.S. alliance. One was the Korean people's perception of the alliance. The NEA Cooperation Initiative was aimed to douse domestic fears of a Cold War, which have tended to occur alongside changes in the ROK-U.S. alliance. The second was a plan to restructure the ROK-U.S. military alliance, an inescapable requirement at a time when reduction and relocation of U.S. troops in South Korea were under discussion. The concerns of the time still apply today; if they are not properly dealt with, any changes in the alliance might spur real security threats or stir a highly negative public reaction.

During his administration, President Roh had a keen interest in a self-reliant national defense policy. He was also concerned about the asymmetry in ROK-U.S. relations. Consequently, what evolved was a severe and palpable discord between Seoul and Washington. Some even conjectured that the reduction and relocation of U.S. troops in South Korea were part of a scheme to "tame" Roh Moo-hyun (he had come to power with the help of anti-American sentiments).[26] The reduction of U.S. troops as well as the deployment of ROK troops to Iraq were two of the most sensitive issues creating turbulence in the domestic political and social climate. Koreans emphatically did not see these developments as part of normal alliance politics, but immediately inferred that the ROK-U.S. alliance was in jeopardy, linking it to a political and ideological battle.[27] The South Korean people have been inclined to see the United States in subjective terms. This tendency is reflected in the following statements by specialists in the field:

> ROK-U.S. relations have never been so frail for the past 50 years. The Korean frustration with America's unilateralism matched with American frustration with Korea's ungratefulness is dominating the atmosphere of the current relations between the two nations. . . . Symptoms of fatigue with the alliance [are] creeping up to the surface on both sides.[28]

> Recent events suggest that ROK-U.S. relations are facing their ugliest atmosphere in the past 50 years. Scenes of anti-American Korean mobs ripping up the American flag are being broadcast live on American televisions and the Americans too are going ahead with relocation and general policy changes in regards to American troops in Korea, with no consideration for Korea. It is clear that a problem has emerged for the ROK-U.S. alliance.[29]

Whatever the conditions may have been domestically, most analysts agreed that external conditions, especially the changes occurring across the globe, were pressing both the ROK and U.S. governments to review and adjust their alliance.[30] These external conditions included changes in global security affairs, the U.S. policy toward the rest of the world, the geopolitical transformation of East Asia (most notably China's "rise"), and changes in the dynamics of the Korean Peninsula. Both Seoul and Washington saw that restructuring the alliance to correspond to the changing security environment of the times was of utmost importance, and therefore placed it as a priority among the pending issues relevant to the security field. This resulted in an ROK-U.S. alliance realignment policy.

As a result of pursuing this policy, changes such as reduction and relocation of U.S. troops, transfer of military responsibilities to the ROK, and planning for the transfer of wartime command (that is, operational control) took place. Although the transfer of wartime command was completed in 2006, the reduction and relocation of U.S. troops were issues decided at the beginning of the government's term. From a military standpoint, these adjustments could be seen as a weakening of the alliance. How the ROK would fill the vacuum left after the removal of the American "tripwire" defense was one of the biggest concerns. In the end, it became inevitable that ROK pursue a self-reliant national defense policy *and* the ROK-U.S. alliance, simultaneously.

However, a self-reliant national defense policy is both time-consuming and resource intensive, requiring a medium- to long-term approach. As such, complementary efforts were needed to secure the ROK-U.S. alliance in the face of change. One factor is Northeast Asia security cooperation, discussions of which have been fairly common of late. As Roh took office, however, his foreign policy and security team wondered how the South Korean populace and media would respond to the idea. There were deeply rooted worries that the pursuit of regional security cooperation would clash with the ROK-U.S. alliance. Many people assumed any cooperative efforts in Northeast Asia would be inevitably "pro-China." Despite these doubts, the government pursued discussions of building such a regional cooperative mechanism with academics and specialists. Such conceptual explorations were formally overlooked by a consultative body, the Presidential Committee on the Northeast Asia Cooperation Initiative, an organ directly under the president.[31] Reports from specialists, events to increase and expand discussions, and strategic discussions between Korean and foreign specialists were enthusiastically carried out.

In September 2005 a joint statement was issued following the fourth session of discussions at the Six-Party Talks (a forum created to resolve the North Korean nuclear issue) in Beijing. The joint statement, aimed at resolving the

North Korean nuclear crisis, stated that "the six parties agreed to explore ways and means for promoting security cooperation in NEA." This created a foundation for discussing a security cooperation mechanism within the region. The ROK government was determined to make it clear to the United States that such a venture would not conflict with the ROK-U.S. alliance. At the November 2005 ROK-U.S. summit in Gyeongju, the two nations came to a mutual understanding that a security cooperation mechanism in Northeast Asia did not contradict or conflict with the alliance but was complementary and could be pursued simultaneously.[32] Only after the ROK government reached a consensus with the United States on this topic, did it begin to actively pursue the building of a regional security cooperation mechanism.

Although it is difficult to attribute it solely to the Roh government's efforts, the United States seemed surprisingly enthusiastic about a security cooperation mechanism in Northeast Asia. The fact that this mechanism was to be a significant agenda item at the Six-Party Talks in December 2008 reflected the positive atmosphere. It is important to note that it was the smaller nations that played the role of catalysts as Europe pursued the Helsinki Process in the early 1970s. On the heels of the U.S. financial crisis in 2008, a Korea-China-Japan trilateral summit meeting was held in Fukuoka in December. The agenda for that meeting included discussions of regional security cooperation and, as a related topic, nontraditional security threats. Also discussed were possible joint measures in response to pollution such as "yellow dust"; cooperation against natural disasters such as earthquakes, typhoons, and floods; and an increase in the capacity of joint management of climate change. Although these topics were commonly acknowledged as legitimate threats in the region, the accomplishment of such a formal discussion was a result of South Korea's consistent efforts toward pursuing cooperation in Northeast Asia.

Redefining the Environment for Improved Inter-Korean Relations

The Roh administration sought to continue the previous engagement policy of the Kim Dae-jung government by taking the goals of reconciliation and cooperation to the next level of peace and prosperity. Kim's engagement policy was pursued with an emphasis on close ROK-U.S.-Japan collaboration, while Roh's peace and prosperity policy was implemented under the bigger umbrella of the NEA Cooperation Initiative. In other words, inter-Korean relations were approached under the larger context of regional cooperation. The backdrop of this occurrence was the understanding that the geopolitical structures of the Korean Peninsula and the Northeast Asian region were mutually influenced.

The NEA Cooperation Initiative was initiated on the premise that the North Korea policy would not be fruitful without changes to the regional order. In his inaugural address in February 2003, President Roh elucidated that peace on the Korean Peninsula and his notion of the NEA Cooperation Initiative were interdependent, and he emphasized that the North Korean nuclear crisis and unstable inter-Korean relations were acting as obstacles to greater cooperation in the region.[33] Furthermore, he explained that to achieve a peaceful settlement to the Korean question, various conflicts and disputes existing in the NEA region had to be resolved. He also emphasized that problems on the Korean Peninsula could be the source of confrontations and conflicts in the broader regional context.

At the launch of the Roh administration, the second North Korean nuclear crisis was already in full swing. The Bush administration named North Korea, along with Iran and Iraq, as members of an "axis of evil," which elicited predictable vituperation from Pyongyang. Such a North Korean policy driven by hard-liners in Washington pushed DPRK-U.S. relations into their worst phase. The Roh administration, which advocated a solid ROK-U.S. alliance, needed close coordination with the United States to push ahead with its peace and prosperity policy. However, Washington remained unyielding and inflexible toward Seoul's preferred policy toward North Korea—at least until the autumn of 2006, when the Bush administration finally modified its rhetoric toward North Korea. Seoul, for its part, could not ignore Washington to conduct a peace and prosperity policy toward North Korea unilaterally. The nuclear issue was serious and of utmost importance for both the United States and South Korea, which made implementing the policy toward North Korea extremely difficult.

The Six-Party Talks had a profound influence on the Roh administration's NEA Cooperation Initiative. A key principle of the Six-Party Talks was that the North Korean nuclear issue should be resolved through peaceful means and dialogue, by arriving at common goals and serving mutual interests while incorporating the principles of the NEA Cooperation Initiative. Ameliorating withered inter-Korean relations and weakened bilateral dialogue required cooperation and policy coordination among countries of the Northeast Asia region. The Six-Party Talks represented a considerable step forward for this purpose.

Despite the usual inefficiency of multilateral dialogue frameworks, the Six-Party Talks proved successful in drawing up several agreements concerning North Korea, including the nuclear problem. The September 2005 joint statement could be called a comprehensive peace charter for building a foundation in the symbiotic order between Northeast Asia and the Korean Peninsula for the resolution of the North Korean nuclear issue. This joint statement addressed such items as the resolution of the North Korean nuclear problem, energy and economic assistance for reconstruction of the North Korean economy, normalization of DPRK-Japan and DPRK-U.S. relations, the building of an NEA peace and security regime, and the establishment of a separate forum for promoting peace on the Korean Peninsula. Of course, this joint statement suffered difficulties almost immediately after it was signed due to U.S. financial sanctions against North Korea stemming from the Banco Delta Asia (BDA) incident. Eventually the February 13 Agreement was signed in 2007 as an implementation road map to resolve the nuclear crisis. The positive outcome of the Six-Party Talks was possible because of the Roh government's cooperative initiative and active and creative diplomacy.

The Roh government was under immense domestic pressure to hold an inter-Korean summit after it took office, and so it continued with an engagement policy toward North Korea. But confusion arose within the public after it was brought to light that former President Kim Dae-jung had paid North Korea to hold the first ever inter-Korean summit back in June 2000. Without any meaningful progress on the nuclear issue, President Roh felt that a summit with North Korean leader Kim Jong-il would be difficult, even with significant consensus between Seoul and Pyongyang.

Only after the February 2007 agreement was signed did a summit seem possible. Right before the September 2007 Asia-Pacific Economic Cooperation (APEC) Summit in Sydney, President Bush confirmed his support for ending tensions on the Korean Peninsula and for building peace in the region. After such an exchange and agreement between Seoul and Washington, the second inter-Korean summit was held in October 2007 in Pyongyang. Its outcome was the October 4 joint statement: "The South and the North have also agreed to work together to advance the matter of having the leaders of the three or four parties directly concerned to convene on the peninsula and declare an end to the war." ROK-DPRK relations were no longer an independent, domestic matter but had evolved to a point where they could be dealt with jointly among the relevant actors in Northeast Asia.

For progress to be made in inter-Korean relations, the spirit of cooperation envisioned in the NEA Cooperation Initiative was needed. Under the Roh government, the nuclear issue and inter-Korean relations were dealt with simultaneously. The task posed difficulties in implementing an assertive engagement with Pyongyang. In actuality, the former Roh administration did not neglect trying to improve inter-Korean relations; rather it pushed forward with a firm belief that inter-Korean relations were closely associated with the geopolitics of the region, and thus maintained an active role in this endeavor. To illustrate this, at the time when the Six-Party Talks were at a deadlock because of the BDA scandal, the Roh administration moved forward to hold bilateral, ministerial-level talks between the South and the North. In other words, there was a clear understanding that inter-Korean relations consisted of a virtuous—not vicious—circle consisting of multiple actors in Northeast Asia operating in a reciprocal way.

Conclusion

Caught by history and surrounded by great powers in an often tension-filled geopolitical regional environment, South Korea admirably established itself as a middle power in Northeast Asia, both in terms of capacity and, more recently, foreign policy behavior. The Roh Moo-hyun government's NEA Cooperation Initiative helped demonstrate that despite historical legacies and a restrictive geopolitical environment, Seoul could stretch its foreign policy "wings" to play a bigger and more active role in the region; manage the ROK-U.S. alliance, the "rise" of China, and inter-Korean relations; and promote multilateral designs for a regional security cooperation architecture.

This does not mean that the middle-power status South Korea has achieved cannot be reversed. To keep what it has gained, in the years ahead Seoul will need to be cautious yet creative, treading lightly yet affirmatively in its diplomacy with its allies and neighbors—if it is to induce positive change in the security situation on the peninsula, whittle down the strategic distrust between great powers and rivals, and prevent the onset of confrontation in Northeast Asia. South Korea will need to promote coalition building and multilateral approaches; find and encourage compromise when called for; remain a dependable partner with its ally, the United States (the declining hegemon); and ensure that it is a strategic partner with China (the region's "rising" power). Seoul must stretch its foreign policy wings cautiously, building upon the confidence and spirit of cooperation exhibited by the Roh government's middle-power diplomacy and embodied in its NEA Cooperation Initiative.

Notes

1 Parts of this chapter are taken from an earlier published article: Su-Hoon Lee, "Strategic Implications of Regional Community Discourse: Northeast Asia Cooperation Initiative," *Journal of Northeast Asia Development* 12 (2010): 69–92.

2 I hold as a premise that the Northeast Asian region is comprised of state participants in the Six-Party Talks (South Korea, North Korea, China, the United States, Japan, and Russia), and that, despite having been in hiatus for several years, the talks still exist as the only Track-I multilateral security dialogue in the region, which influences and impacts South Korea's domestic politics and foreign policies.

3 Margaret P. Karns and Karen A. Mingst, *International Organizations: The Politics and Processes of Global Governance*, 2nd ed. (Boulder, CO: Lynne Rienner, 2010), 271.

4 Eduard Jordaan, "The Concept of a Middle Power in International Relations: Distinguishing between Emerging and Traditional Middle Powers," *Politikon* 30, no. 2 (November 2003): 165–81; Gareth Evans, "Middle Power Diplomacy," Inaugural Edgardo Boeninger Memorial Lecture, Chile Pacific Foundation, Santiago, Chile, June 29, 2011. For discussion in Korean, see Kim Chi Wook, "Middle Power as a Unit of Analysis of International Relations: Its Conceptualization and Implications," *Korean Journal of International Studies* (in Korean) 49, no. 1 (2009): 7–36; Soo Hyung Lee, "Pivotal Middle Power Theory and Balanced and Pragmatic Diplomacy in the Participatory Government," *Korea and World Politics* (in Korean) 24, no. 1 (Spring 2008): 217–49.

5 For example, see Jordaan, "The Concept of a Middle Power."

6 Global banking and investment firms and experts themselves have created new terms to categorize the emerging middle-sized powers: for example, CIVETS (Colombia, Indonesia, Vietnam, Egypt, Turkey, and South Africa), MIST (Mexico, Indonesia, South Korea, and Turkey), and Next-11 (Bangladesh, Egypt, the Philippines, Indonesia, Iran, South Korea, Mexico, Nigeria, Pakistan, Turkey, and Vietnam). Adam Balcer, "Golden Age of Middle Powers?" (policy paper, *demos Europa* [Center for European Strategy], January 2012), 2.

7 Surrounded by three major powers—China, Japan, and Russia—Korea could be conceived of as a small power buffer state in Northeast Asia, but a middle-power ally of the United States. See Woosang Kim, "Korea as a Middle Power in the Northeast Asian Security Environment," in *The United States and Northeast Asia: Debates, Issues, and New Order*, ed. G. John Ikenberry and Chung-in Moon (Lanham, MD: Rowman & Littlefield, 2008), 123–41; Kim, "Middle Power as a Unit of Analysis"; Balcer, "Golden Age of Middle Powers?"

8 Jeffrey Robertson, "South Korea as a Middle Power: Capacity, Behavior, and Now Opportunity," *International Journal of Korean Unification Studies* 16, no. 1 (2007): 151–174.

9 Lee, "Pivotal Middle Power Theory."

10 Argentina, Australia, Brazil, Canada, China, the European Union, France, Germany, India, Indonesia, Italy, Japan, Mexico, Russia, Saudi Arabia, South Africa, South Korea, Turkey, United Kingdom, and the United States.

11 Balcer, "Golden Age of Middle Powers?" 2.

12 Ibid., 3–4.

13 Robertson, "South Korea as a Middle Power," 157–58.

14 Evans, "Middle Power Diplomacy."

15 Robertson, "South Korea as a Middle Power," 157–60.

16 Chang Jae-soon, "Lee Calls for Excruciating Restructuring Efforts in Eurozone," *Yonhap*, June 19, 2012.

17 Jeffrey Robertson, "Time to Start Debate on Korea's Role as a Middle-Power," *Korea Herald* (Seoul), March 22, 2012.

18 Su-Hoon Lee, ed., *Security and Foreign Policy of the ROK Government* (Seoul: Happy Reading, 2007), 16.

19 Lee Hee-Ok, "The Characteristic of a Rising China in Korea: Perspective and Evidence," *Korea and World Politics* (in Korean) 25, no. 4 (2009).

20 Su-Hoon Lee, ed., *China and the Northeast Asian Cooperation* (Seoul: Arche Publishing House, 2005), 6.

21 Hee-Ok Lee, "Korea-China Relations: Present Conditions and Future Prospects," in *Security and Foreign Policy of the ROK Government*, ed. Lee Su-Hoon (Seoul: Happy Reading, 2007).

22 Bae Ki-Chan, "Reality and Future of the 'Northeast Asian Cooperation Initiative,'" *Korea and World Politics* (in Korean) 24, no. 1 (2008).

23 Lee Su-Hoon, "New Concept of Northeast Asian Cooperation Initiative," in Paik Nak-Chung et al., *The 21st Century Model for the Korean Peninsula* (in Korean) (Seoul: Changbi Publishers, 2004).

24 Roh Moo-hyun, "National Independence Day Celebration Speech," August 15, 2003.

25 Roh Moo-hyun, "Speech Records of Advisory Consultants Meeting related with Unification, Diplomacy and Security," July 22, 2005.

26 Kim Il-Young, "Readjustment of U.S. Armed Forces in Korea: Why, How Far, and Where To," in *50 years of ROK-U.S. Alliance* (in Korean), ed. Shim Ji-Yeon and Kim Il-Young (Seoul: Baek San Seodang Publishers, 2004), 169.

27 Gi-Wook Shin, *One Alliance and Two Lenses: U.S.-Korea Relations in a New Era* (Stanford: Stanford University Press, 2010), chapter 4.

28 See Kim, "Readjustment of U.S. Armed Forces in Korea," 161.

29 Lee Choon-Geun, "Diagnosis of ROK-U.S. Alliance and Logic of Its Reinforcement," *National Strategy* 9, no. 3 (2003): 40.

30 Kim Ki-Jung, "U.S.-ROK Alliance in Transition: Theories and Practices" (in Korean), in *Adjustments of the ROK-U.S. Alliance: 2003–2008*, ed. Su-Hoon Lee (Seoul: Kyungnam University Press, 2009), 357–94

31 Presidential Committee on Northeast Asian Cooperation Initiative, *Presidential Committee on Northeast Asia Cooperation Initiative White Paper* (Seoul: Presidential Committee on Northeast Asian Cooperation Initiative, 2008).

32 Cheong Wa Dae, "Outcome of ROK-U.S. Summit" Press Release, November 17, 2005.

33 Roh Moo-hyun, "Inaugural Speech," February 25, 2003.

7 Identity in Motion: Vietnam since 1976[1]

Brantly Womack

Any discussion of identity usually involves interpreting conflicting narratives about the collective self, of its essence, as well as of its relationship to others.[2] Those sharing a national identity are assumed to be in the same boat, and, not surprisingly, the exploration of the content of national identity usually concentrates on continuities. The common (though sometimes disputed) accounts of the boat's dimensions, memories of travels thus far, attitudes toward other boats, and outlooks on the future provide rich material for analysis. This chapter takes a somewhat different approach. I examine the changing perspectives of those in the Vietnamese boat as they have progressed through the remarkable rapids of the past thirty years. The focus here is on motion rather than continuity—how unexpected contextual changes have shaped and reshaped the Vietnamese outlook. Material life, politics, external relations, and ideology have undergone profound and sometimes sudden changes. While Vietnam's turbulent waters did not begin in 1976, an examination of the phases of Vietnam's recent past—1976 to 1985, 1986 to 1995, 1996 to 2008, and 2008 to the present—does much to reveal its internal situation and its relations to other nation-states.

Modern Korea and Vietnam are particularly interesting when seen as identities in motion. Their turbulent recent histories have reshaped both their national common ground and their relationships to others. From the late nineteenth to the late twentieth century their experiences diverged even as both nations were subjected to forces of imperialism, the Cold War, and modernization. Since 1990, and especially since 2008, their contexts have become more similar, historically novel in their degree of globalization and at the same time resonant with the China-centered history (and present) of East Asia. Although I concentrate on Vietnam in this chapter, I conclude by offering some points of comparison with South Korea.

The post–Cold War era has been one of tremendous change for Vietnam, and I divide the development of contemporary Vietnamese identity and its domestic and international contexts into several distinct phases. I first examine the various changes resulting from the reunification of Vietnam in 1976. Then I turn to the years 1986–95, when Vietnam abandoned the socialist triumphalism of the immediate postwar period and reexamined its traditional friends and enemies, choosing a path of reform (*Doi Moi*) and global openness. From 1996 to 2008 its new policy framework was confirmed by success. From 2008 the global economic crisis and China's peaceful leap forward have sharpened Vietnam's difficult choice: express pragmatic deference to the world's great powers, or preserve autonomy? In each of these phases, the nation's identity has been shaped and reshaped by developments in the spheres of economics, politics, international policy, and ideology.

1976–86: Post-Victory Illusions

The defeat of the Saigon government in April 1975 and the reunification of Vietnam in 1976 were historic accomplishments that transformed not only Vietnam but the entire region of Southeast Asia. Success, however, is a poor teacher of feasible limits and of the need to redirect policies. Vietnam faced the new challenges of peace with the overconfidence of a victor.

In order to appreciate Vietnam's overconfidence in the mid-1970s, it is worth reflecting on the magnitude of Vietnam's struggle for national reunification. The Vietnamese people, led by the Communist Party of Vietnam (CPV), displayed extraordinary solidarity and tenacity in their resistance to Japanese occupation, French colonialism, American support for a separate government in the south, and direct American military intervention. In the north commitment to a desperate and terrible fight was universal. The situation was more complicated in the south, where the National Liberation Front could rightly claim the popular banner of national liberation while the Saigon regime was compromised by its continuity with French colonialism and by its American patronage. Below the high ground of ideology, the land reform initiated by the Viet Minh against the French—and continued by the National Liberation Front—provided substance in rural areas to the general patriotic appeal of the Communists.[3] After American military withdrawal in 1973 the Nguyen Van Thieu regime became more and more isolated, and thus the final campaign of 1975 was easier than expected.[4]

The international consequences of Vietnam's victory were profound. If we define colonialism as the forcible occupation and control of territory by an outside power, Vietnam's victory marked the end of colonialism in Southeast Asia. When it became clear that no further dominos would fall, American attention turned elsewhere. Meanwhile European countries that had been critical of the American war were ready to become involved in Vietnam's reconstruction, and the Soviet Union and Eastern Europe continued their support. With Southeast Asia no longer a global front line, the region's nations had to adjust their policies toward both China and Vietnam. As tensions appeared between China and Vietnam, many moved to improve relations with China, even while continuing to worry about Vietnam. Meanwhile the revolutions in Laos and Cambodia—roughly simultaneous to Vietnam's—left the impression that there were now three independent but similar regimes in Indochina, with Vietnam *primus inter pares.*

It is hardly surprising that in this context Vietnam's leaders felt triumphant. The CPV's Fourth National Congress (held December 14–20, 1976) provided the ultimate platform for self-congratulation: "In a world perspective, the victory of our people has smashed the greatest counterattack the chieftain of imperialism has mounted against the revolutionary forces since the Second World War."[5]

The country's name was changed from the Democratic Republic of Vietnam to the Socialist Republic of Vietnam. Its leaders figured that the same ideology and solidarity that had brought an end to decades of struggle could also foster progress. They blamed the exigencies of war for the backtracking seen in the north during its socialist transformation, and emphasized more disciplined cooperation in the countryside and a command economy in the cities.[6] The south was seen as ideologically backward; northern officials were put in charging of helping it catch up. Socialist internationalism remained the core concept of Vietnam's foreign policy. Vietnam expected continued assistance from fraternal socialist countries and despised the weak capitalism of its neighbors. It was willing to normalize relations with nonsocialist states, but the terms of contact were to be strictly controlled. Normalization with the United States was made contingent on the delivery of the reparations promised in 1972 by Henry Kissinger and President Nixon.

Reality, however, was not kind. The United States lost interest in Southeast Asia and could not bring itself to normalize relations even when Vietnam dropped its demand for reparations in 1978.[7] China ceased its wartime aid while increasing support for the Khmer Rouge in Cambodia, and Vietnam reluctantly had to move closer to the Soviet Union for support.[8] The first war between the communist states soon replaced socialist internationalism. The Southeast Asian region was suspicious of Vietnam's ambitions in Indochina. The defeat of the Khmer Rouge was easy, but the occupation of Cambodia led to Vietnam's isolation. By 1980 Vietnam had managed to make its external environment more hostile than it was even during the wars.

Domestic disillusionment was even more profound. Affected by the patterns of U.S. bombing, in 1975 the northern economy was dispersed across the countryside and heavily dependent on subsidies, while the south had developed bloated urban areas to service the American presence. From 1975 to 1977 central leadership tried to incorporate surviving elements of the southern economy into a new pattern, while reducing wartime exceptions to central control in the north.[9] But in 1978 Vietnam began a disastrous attempt to consolidate the economy using a command model. It persecuted the southern business community, predominantly ethnic Chinese (Hoa), and agricultural production collapsed under the weight of cooperatization. Nguyen Van Linh, later a reform leader, was removed in February 1978 from his leading position in southern transformation for being too soft on local capitalism. The crisis induced by consolidation policies, however, led to tactical backtracking by the end of 1979. For the next six years Vietnamese policies fluctuated between attempts to push a socialist agenda and necessary concessions to reality.

Instead of the rapid rise of a united socialist family, continuing hardships, policy failures, and inevitable postwar disorientation contributed to a leaden atmosphere across the nation. The CPV was in charge, but nothing was working out as imagined. Control of Indochina was both a material and a diplomatic burden. There were tensions with the Soviet Union, and China was joining with the Association of Southeast Asian Nations (ASEAN) and the United States in an anti-Vietnam entente. Domestically the seesaw of counterproductive consolidation and pragmatic retreats was dispiriting. Attention drifted from the accomplishments of victory to the wounds of war.[10] Deprivation continued but without credible goals.

Identity Restored, Confused

In 1975–76 Vietnam achieved, through popular struggle, what Koreans in their still-divided nation wish for: reunification and autonomy from external powers. Not only was Vietnam's embedded identity confirmed, but victory resonated with national traditions of patriotic resistance to foreign pressure. However, the aftermath did not match the dream. Vietnamese were now in the same boat, but the differences between north and south were ignored, and the Hoa, Vietnam's most industrious minority, was excluded until 1984. The Vietnamese boat seemed in greater peril when the leaders paddled than when they rested. China became the new enemy, but there were no new friends. After thirty years of war Vietnam did not panic easily, but it was clear to all that a new direction was necessary.

1986–95: Redirection

By 1985 both the leaders and the citizens of Vietnam were thoroughly disillusioned; the rosy forecasts of socialist construction and socialist internationalism expressed at the Fourth Party Congress in 1976 had not come to pass. Continued hardship could no longer be justified by an overarching patriotic objective, and tactical retreats were insufficient. The occupation of Cambodia left Vietnam isolated and dependent on the patronage of the Soviet Union. A fundamental reorientation of domestic and foreign policy was launched in 1986 and began to show results in the early 1990s. By 1995 Vietnam was clearly committed to market reforms as it entered the ASEAN and normalized relations with the United States.

Economy

In 1986, with the adoption of *Doi Moi*, Vietnam changed course. The driving force of *Doi Moi* was economic reform, however, the results were by no means immediate. Annual inflation was 774 percent in 1986, 223 percent the following year, and 394 percent in 1988.[11] It did not settle down to the 5–15 percent range until 1992. A bad harvest produced near-famine conditions in 1987. International isolation strangled trade, but the rate of gross domestic product (GDP) growth increased from an annual 2.6 percent in 1986 to 8.6 percent in 1992. Vietnam faced a looming foreign exchange crisis when the Soviet Union reduced its aid in 1990, but was rescued by foreign donors and the beginning of revenues from offshore oil (from 0 in 1987 to 6 percent of GDP in 1990). Drastic measures were taken to control inflation and to reduce the burden of unprofitable state-owned enterprises (SOEs), and foreign investment regulations were rewritten to attract foreign investment. Goods from China began to creep over the most heavily mined border in the world, relieving both consumers and farmers. By the early 1990s all of these measures had begun to pay off: the wisdom of *Doi Moi* was confirmed by the recovery of the economy from uncertainty and crisis. The GDP had doubled by 1996, exports had risen tenfold, and inflation hovered at 5 percent.

Politics

As in China, the policies of reform and openness were adopted proactively by the Communist Party rather than forced upon it by organized societal forces, and thus the success of *Doi Moi* strengthened the party-state at the same time as it made governance tasks more complex. Importantly, the reform process focused attention on the National Assembly and on local voices and interests. The dilemma of preserving order while promoting reform was rendered more acute by the demise of European communism and revulsion at the Tiananmen Square massacre in 1989. Meanwhile Ho Chi Minh City (and the ethnic Chinese, the Hoa) again emerged as the powerhouse of the modern economy, the national party leadership remained centered in the north, and the military concerned itself with maintaining its stature in a postwar, lean-budget environment. Policy tensions and personnel cuts were inevitable, but *Doi Moi* stayed on track.

International Environment

The first ten years of *Doi Moi* witnessed a remarkable transformation in Vietnam's external relations. Regionally, the nation went from isolation (during the occupation of Cambodia) to membership in the ASEAN. Relations with China were reestablished in 1991, as were relations with other global powers. France led the way; the United States was last on board, in 1995. Meanwhile Vietnam had maintained relations with European post-communist states. With great caution on both sides, visits by overseas Vietnamese (Viet Kieu) commenced. As Tuong Vu suggests in chapter 9, many Viet Kieu felt justified in their anti-communism by the failure of ideological commandism, but they were puzzled by the party's involvement in reform. As with domestic *Doi Moi*, party leaders promoted international openness, though some were more eager than others. An important example of the party's adjustment to a changing international environment was the announcement in August 1985 of a unilateral withdrawal from Cambodia by 1990.

Ideology

The failure of socialist construction and the collapse of the Soviet Union were massive shocks to Vietnam's communist orthodoxy and their vision for the future. But the party-state had the capacity and the pragmatism to adjust to a fundamentally different governance situation. Vietnam was more severely affected than China by the fall of European communism, but it had the advantages of a less rigid and more tolerant system than China's. The "Thought of Ho Chi Minh" could play a progressive role in Vietnam, in contrast to the "Thought of Mao Zedong" in China.

Identity Redirected

The above is necessary background to the profound shift in Vietnamese consciousness in the first decade of *Doi Moi*. The illusions of victory that followed Vietnam's reunification had died by 1985. The south was not catching up with the socialist north, but rather was being dragged down by socialist commandism. The Soviet alliance was an uncertain lifeline in isolation, rather than an anchor for new regional prominence. The overthrow of the Pol Pot regime in 1979 was necessary, but the continuing occupation of Cambodia became a drag on scarce resources and a roadblock to improved international relations.

At this juncture, the example of Mikhail Gorbachev's *perestroika* and sidelong glances at China's first five years of successful reform led Vietnam's intellectuals and party leaders to promote decentralization and to replace the "friends and enemies" framework of socialist internationalism with the "make friends everywhere" mentality of globalized internationalism. As Alexander Vuving details in chapter 4, there were heroes and laggards in the shift. The collapse of the Soviet Union gave strength to conservative worries about stability, but the experience of bankruptcy during the previous course and the gradual success of new domestic and foreign policies confirmed the new direction.

The climb of the economy not only encouraged cautious optimism, it also shifted the legitimacy and governance tasks of the party away from national, ideological vanguardism toward the effective management of an increasingly diversified society. Meanwhile, an increasing number of international partners profoundly changed Vietnam's sense of itself in the world. Even China was no longer an enemy, although managing economic relations with it remained difficult. The continued success of China's reforms was reassuring as Vietnam pursued a similar path. Diplomatic recognition from the United States in 1995 marked an important formal watershed in the relationship, although in practice there was a slow transition in American attitudes from hostility to ambivalence. Most important, entry into the ASEAN in 1995 identified Vietnam as a Southeast Asian nation—for the first time in its history.

1996–2008: Confirmation by Trial and Success

The second decade of *Doi Moi* began with the 1997 Asian financial crisis. Although not as severely affected as Korea, Vietnam was shown the risks of globalization. In response, it focused on its neighborhood, strengthening ties to ASEAN and China. Meanwhile, GDP growth from 2000 to 2007 not only confirmed the wisdom of *Doi Moi*, but fostered complacent optimism.

Economy

Despite the Asian financial crisis, the Vietnamese economy was a regional paragon of success at the turn of the millennium. The GDP growth rate dipped to a respectable low of 4.8 percent in 1999, but rose to above 8 percent in 2005–07. Inflation was brought under control, with the consumer price index actually going negative in 2000–01, though rising to above 7 percent from 2004. The percentage of the population in poverty fell from 58 percent in 1993 to 37 percent in 1998 to 16 percent in 2007. Exports doubled by 1999, redoubled by 2004, and doubled again in 2007. By that time they were ninety times the export levels of 1985 (even as Vietnam wrestled with a chronic trade deficit amplified by wholesale smuggling from China). Underlying the rosy picture was an increase in oil revenues (to more than 10 percent of GDP) and an influx in foreign investment, focused on firms producing goods for export. Along with greater prosperity and societal diversification came a shift in priorities, from getting by to getting ahead.

Politics

The party-state remained the driving force behind reform, both external and internal. The 1992 constitution guaranteed freedom of movement and residence, in contrast to China's *hukou* (household registration) system, thereby avoiding some abuses of migrant labor.[12] Relations between reformers and conservatives were initially tense: a delay in the filling of top leadership posts in 1996 embarrassed both, but there was considerable turnover in the National Assembly and Central Committee and also experimentation with electoral reform within the party. By the end of the decade China's Vietnam experts considered Vietnam more politically progressive than China, to the distress of some of China's leaders. Yet reforms only went so far: progress occurred within the old party-state framework, still intact, and any criticism of the system was controlled. Corruption grew despite public campaigns and prosecution.

International Environment

The major progress in this decade was the strengthening of regional relationships. The signing of a bilateral trade agreement with the United States in 2001 allowed a vast expansion of exports. Then, in 2007, admission to the World Trade Organization (WTO) capped the success of Vietnam's policy of globalized internationalism. But the shock of the Asian financial crisis had demonstrated the urgency of regional solidarity, and so Vietnam took on a prominent role in ASEAN and moved to a fully normalized relationship with China. All ASEAN countries shared similar vulnerabilities to global forces, and strengthening economic cooperation helped to buffer their exposure.[13] Most dramatically, multilateral improvement of relations with China was accomplished in 2002–03 when China joined the ASEAN Treaty of Amity, signed the Declaration of Conduct in the South China Sea, and launched the China-ASEAN Free Trade Area (CAFTA). China's multilateral engagement with the region reduced the pressure on its bilateral relationship with Vietnam. The land border dispute was resolved in principle in 1999, with the Gulf of Tonkin following in 2000.[14] Vietnam continued to run a severe trade deficit with China, but an increasingly favorable balance with the United States and European Union compensated for the deficit and enabled trade to mushroom from 2002 to 2009.

Ideology

By 1996 the role of ideology in Vietnam has shrunk to the maintenance of the party-state system and the prevention of overt challenges to the orthodoxy. As Pham Quang Minh details in chapter 5, Vietnam's outlook on the world evolved from a Marxist analysis of class to one of national interests, and in 2003 to a more complex view of partners and opponents. There has been a comparable relaxation in domestic ideology. In contrast to China, religious believers are admitted into the CPV. Conservatives lean on the old dogma while reformers evade it, but the basic dividing line on the ideological frontier is between caution and adaptation. In Vietnam's citizen-regarding party-state, the residue of socialist values remains despite the market turn of the economy. Also in contrast to China, Vietnam's Gini coefficient (an index of inequality) has held relatively steady during the reform period.

Vietnam's New Regional Identity

Initially under *Doi Moi*, Vietnam's Southeast Asian neighbors were simply the closest recipients of Vietnam's global openness, but the Asian financial crisis demonstrated the region's common vulnerability, even as China emerged as a regional stabilizer. With the admission of Cambodia in 1999, the ASEAN completed its transition from a discussion club of six rather prosperous states to a comprehensive regional organization with a broad agenda. Vietnam acquired a regional identity that it never before had. In contrast to the forums open to Korea, the ASEAN is an organized group of states with more interests in common than differences. China received the appreciation of the region when it held the value of the renminbi (RMB) steady during the financial crisis and dealt multilaterally with the ASEAN, boosting the confidence of each of its bilateral partners, including Vietnam. In early 1999, on the twentieth anniversary of the 1979 border war, China and Vietnam pledged to "long-term, stable, future-oriented, good neighborly and all-round cooperative relations." This so-called Sixteen-Word Guideline has been repeated ever since at meetings of top leaders as the official mantra of the relationship.[15]

Vietnam's new regionalism did not come at the expense of broader global ties. Southeast Asia looks out toward the world, as demonstrated by the Asia-Pacific Economic Cooperation (APEC), ASEAN Regional Forum (ARF), ASEAN plus X, and annual postministerial conferences. Global openness and inclusiveness are basic postulates of Southeast Asian regional diplomacy. Developments after 1997 did not involve protectionism, but rather various sorts of group insurance against global volatility. The motive behind the CAFTA was to stabilize a neighborly trade relationship with China rather than to keep the formidable global competitor at arm's length. It was a particular relief to Vietnam to reach a trade agreement with the United States and then to join the WTO. Its global isolation was finally over, even as it had acquired a new regional identity.

Domestically, confidence in material progress increased. Although still poor, Vietnam was the best-performing growth economy in Southeast Asia. Regional identity enhanced, rather than subordinated, Vietnam's domestic sense of worth. The global framework eased relations with the Viet Kieu and at the same time made possible new international activities for residents. The ethnic Chinese community in Ho Chi Minh City reestablished itself as a major nexus for international modernization. There were the problems common to frontiers of rapid growth—corruption, fraud, environmental degradation, displacement, urbanization—but these were not enough to derail continued development. There was a temptation toward complacency, however, in the expectation that Vietnam was now on the right road and that progress could be projected indefinitely.

2008–12: The Global Crisis and the Shadow of China

The era of global economic uncertainty that began in 2008 was a major shock to Vietnam's global alignment and to its regional situation, although it did not force a major shift in either. The effects felt thus far are more sudden than large, but some will surely last into the long term.

Economy

By mid-2008 the Vietnamese economy was dizzy with success. It picked an inopportune moment to rest on its laurels. Since 2004 inflation had crept up to near the growth rates of 7–8 percent; with the world price increases of early 2008, inflation surged to 23 percent. Vietnam adopted retrenchment policies to cope with the heat, and immediately the financial collapse of the second half of the year required a reversal to stimulus. The overall growth rate slowed to 6.3 percent in 2008, then 5.3 percent in 2009. Growth rose to 6.8 percent in 2010, but with 8.9 percent inflation. In 2011 growth was 5.9 percent, but inflation had reached 18.6 percent.[16]

Reported trade with China approached 10 percent of total trade in 2002 and rose to 14.7 percent in 2007. But even without counting informal trade, Vietnam's import dependence on China was growing, offset by exports to developed countries. By 2010 imports from China had increased almost ten times faster than the average, and four times faster than those from the United States. Vietnam had been receiving roughly one-quarter of its imports from other ASEAN countries, but in 2010 China surpassed the rest of ASEAN as an import source for the first time, and in 2009 exports dropped off to all developed countries except Korea. In stormy weather, the Vietnamese economy is sailing closer to China's lee shore.

Politics

The 11th National Congress of the CPV, held in January 2011, was notable for its democratic innovations in selecting leadership, but the economic message was sobering and the new leadership has been noted more for its caution than for its daring reforms. The complacency of the previous decade has vanished, though the commitment to *Doi Moi* within a party-state framework remains. In contrast to the leading personalities that dominated CPV politics into the nineties, consultative institutional processes and vested interests are stronger.

In foreign policy the leadership made a cautious step forward by replacing its earlier commitment to "international economic integration" with a more general phrase, "international integration." While the policy implications of the shift in terminology are unclear, it opens a broader field of discussion on Vietnam's external interactions. Vietnam faces the difficult task of deepening its asymmetric relationship with China while at the same time maintaining its autonomous interests. This has required controlling popular expressions of anger at China, while at the same time protesting perceived encroachments and expanding military capability to meet the Chinese challenge. A case in point is the 2009 attempt of Chinalco, China's big aluminum company, to invest in a bauxite operation in central Vietnam. Vietnam desperately needs the investment, but there was popular outcry against allowing China in.

International Policy

The shock of 2008 and its repercussions have affected several dimensions of Vietnam's international policy. In the previous decade, globalization was seen to be an overarching priority that required regional solidarity, including closer relations with China. Today's economic uncertainty has underlined the weaknesses and limitations of the globalized, developed country system, even as China rises to yet greater heights. Of all Southeast Asian states, Vietnam is the most sensitive to China, for several reasons. Culturally, the idea of heroic resistance to China runs deep and was reemphasized by the conflict of 1979–91. Also, Vietnam shares the concerns of some neighbors regarding the Spratly Islands and the South China Sea, and it has an additional resentment against China's occupation of the Paracel Islands.[17] Added to this, no other Southeast Asian state is as dependent on trade with China or runs such a chronic trade imbalance. In other words, no other Southeast Asian state is as exposed to China as Vietnam.

Despite the general enthusiasm in Southeast Asia for the American "return" to the region, there are important differences between Vietnam's attitude and those of its neighbors. Vietnam, after all, fought a war with the United States, and the United States was slow to normalize relations and has remained ambivalent if not cold. Full normalcy was not achieved until the last day of the U.S. Congressional session of 2006. Meanwhile, Vietnam has been eager to restore relations since 1979, and so it is delighted to receive greater attention under Obama, both bilaterally and under the umbrella of U.S. policy in the region. The South China Sea has been a focus of attention since 2008—a material symbol of the general anxiety over China's "rise" that is particularly acute in Vietnam.

Identity Shift: From China's Neighbor to China's Backyard?

The amount of increase in China's GDP in 2011 ($556 billion) was five times the size of the entire Vietnamese economy in 2010, and twice the increment of the U.S. economy in 2010. These two facts highlight the complex dilemma facing all of China's neighbors. Not only is China outpacing the capability of its neighbors, it is also closing the gap with the global superpower. China is already the strongest regional power in Asia; soon its regional political primacy may outstrip that of the United States. The prospect of China's neighborhood becoming China's backyard is gratifying to China, but unsettling to everyone else.[18]

Vietnam is especially sensitive to this tectonic shift: its regional identity and its normalization with China are recent, and its ties with the United States problematic. While a working relationship with China remains a sine qua non, Vietnam is eager for regional solidarity and an American presence, including better military-to-military relations. However, it would never side with the United States against China; it once made a mistake of that kind when favoring the Soviet Union in 1978–90. Balancing against China would be an even greater mistake today.

Meanwhile popular identities and pressures pull in all directions, and the Vietnamese economy is at its most stressful point in twenty years. Although the basic commitment to reform and openness has remained intact, crisis has sharpened the differences between reformers and conservatives. Is Vietnam's party-state system at fault? If so, then why is China so successful? Meanwhile, China offers Vietnam the biggest opportunity even as it poses the biggest threat to the nation's autonomy. This is not simply a government dilemma, but, ultimately, the government has to walk the balance while individuals can indulge in righteous indignation or private pursuit of business interests. Domestically, as the priorities of ordinary Vietnamese go beyond survival to reach for success, more sophisticated demands for representation and government accountability are being made. The Vietnamese state is not in crisis, but the populace is looking beyond the status quo.

Vietnam and Korea in an Age of Uncertainty

Comparing the contemporary situations and mentalities of Vietnam and Korea is a task fraught with difficulty. I will offer four different points of comparison. None is a straw man but all have limitations, so for each point I will present the argument and then its limitations as I see them. The four points of comparison are: a shared middle-power status, similar paths of progress, similar relations to China and the United States, and fundamental differences.

Vietnam and Korea as Middle Powers

Keyser and Shin, in their introductory chapter, do an excellent job of explicating the ambiguities of middle-power status in the international relations literature. Indeed, any "middle" category is difficult to define, since it must be dichotomous on both ends of its range. "Middle" lives uncomfortably between "either" and "or." Nevertheless, it is useful to consider the commonalities and differences between Vietnam and Korea as states not strong enough to challenge global and regional powers, yet capable of securing autonomy and exerting resistance. Both endured the hot wars of the Cold War. Boosted by democratization and increasing prosperity, Korea has developed beyond the status of a client state. Vietnam demonstrated its autonomy in successive wars with France, the United States, and China. Both Vietnam and Korea will defer to global and regional powers by choice, not out of fear.

The "middleness" of Vietnam and Korea is, however, quite different in nature. Korea is on a divided peninsula, in a vortex churned by two very different rivals, one of them a global power whose armed presence is felt throughout the nation. Korea's astonishing economic success and enthusiastic globalization have allowed it to punch above its weight on the world stage. It shares with other middle powers, such as Canada, a strong interest in the international rule of law. By contrast, Vietnam's position has been less contingent and more isolated. No one would doubt its capacity to resist outside pressures, but until it joined the ASEAN in 1995 and the WTO in 2007 it was not seriously involved in international forums. Only in the past decade has it moved decisively beyond "friends and enemies" to a more complex concept of "partners" and finally to "international integration." In sum, one could say that Korea is impressive as a global middle power but constrained by its geography, while Vietnam is less advanced on the global scene but stronger in the region.

Vietnam as a Korea-Come-Lately

In the early 1990s I had the pleasure of talking to a Samsung executive during a flight from Ho Chi Minh City to Hanoi. He was most enthusiastic about developing operations in Vietnam, for two reasons. First, it was one of the few places Japan had not gotten to first, giving Korean businesses an equal footing. Second, and more important to him, the Vietnamese reminded him of Koreans twenty years earlier: poor but educated, healthy, and willing to work extra hard to get ahead. He was therefore planning to move much of his Bangkok operations to Ho Chi Minh City. The businessman was right to be optimistic. At that time Vietnam's per capita GDP purchasing power parity (PPP) was at the level of Korea's in 1969–70—a gap of twenty years.[19] But the gap is not so easily reduced. Vietnam in 2010 was at the same level as China in 2003 in per capita terms, and China in 2010 was comparable to Korea in 1984. To the extent that prosperity based on manufacturing has similar prerequisites and similar societal effects, Vietnam could still be viewed as a generation behind Korea.

The limitations of interpreting Vietnam as a budding Korea, however, begin with Vietnam's economic ecology. Both are developmental states in the broadest sense, but Vietnam's SOEs are quite different from Korea's *chaebol*, and export-oriented foreign direct investment (FDI) plays an important role in Vietnam. Moreover, Korea's industries could incubate under American benevolent neglect, while Vietnam has had a more difficult time entering a more saturated global economy. Vis-à-vis China, Korea can trade high-tech components for labor-intensive goods, while Vietnam competes for low-margin products and supplies raw materials. Vietnam will have to work harder and for a longer time to keep pace with Korea's developmental footsteps.

The political consequences of development are more difficult to predict than development itself. Korea's democratic transition in the 1980s was not spontaneously generated by prosperity, but had roots in democratic, broad-based, and organized oppositional traditions dating back to 1948. Martial law and large-scale repression kept a lid on increasing societal pressure. The Vietnamese party-state reaches throughout society and adapts policy to popular needs. Opposition is not permitted, but opposition is neither large-scale nor organized.[20] Moreover, because the CPV has a constitutional monopoly on political leadership, a transition to a multiparty framework would be more traumatic. Post-communist Russia might give a more appropriate picture of what to expect than postmilitary Korea.

Vietnam and Korea as Brothers, Neighbors

Another parallelism between Vietnam and Korea could be drawn on the basis of their common position in a changing East Asia. They have a centuries-old tradition of paying tribute to China, but also more recent memories of war with it. Confucianism has been a continuous influence in both, part of the core heritage that had to be defended against the foreign domination of Japan and France. China is now the largest trading partner of each (for Vietnam since 2010). While their economic prospects have been lifted by access to China, both are alarmed by the implications of China's peaceful leap forward since 2008. As figure 7.1 demonstrates, with the exception of Korea's partial rebound from the Asian financial crisis, China has had a higher growth rate than either since 1991. Korea's GDP was one-third of China's in 1985, and Vietnam's was 5.5 percent. By 2010 the GDPs of all three countries had expanded, but Korea's was 14 percent of China's, and Vietnam's 3 percent. Of course, both will remain China's neighbors whatever else happens. If the relative Chinese growth rate diminishes, they will both feel more at ease; if China collapses, they will be worried about the consequences.

Vietnam and Korea are also interested in better relations with the United States. Ironically, this is not because they trust American power, but because

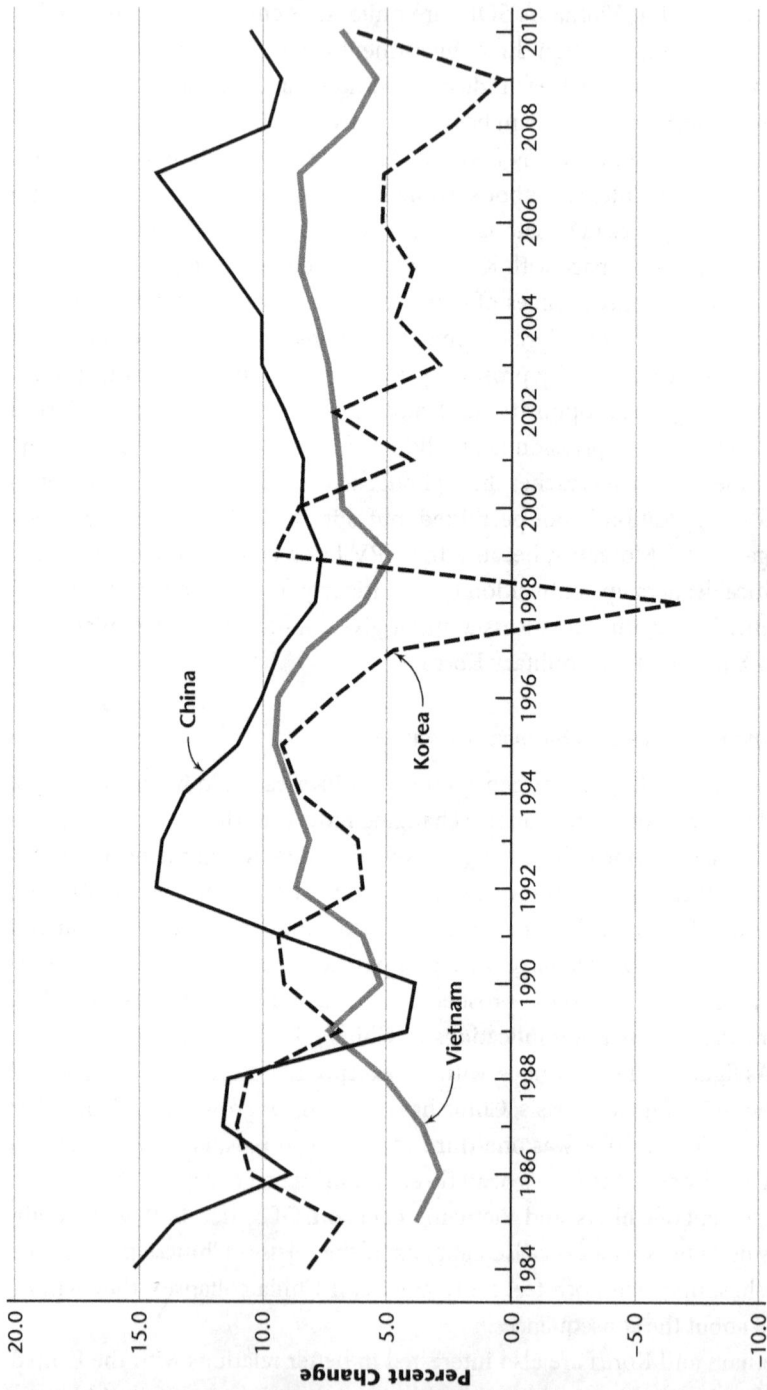

FIGURE 7.1 Annual percentage change in GDP, 1984–2010
Source: World Bank, *World Development Indicators.*

they desire continued American engagement in the Western Pacific. They approach the United States from different directions, however. Vietnam would like to secure and confirm a solid relationship with a hitherto reluctant and distant United States; Korea, like the Philippines, is swinging back from its popular aversion to American domination. Meanwhile, both are interested in buffering their regional asymmetric relationship with China by strengthening their global ties. Both are interested in East Asian regional integration. Nothing would be worse for either than to be forced to choose sides in a bipolar situation.

A closer look at the regional positions of Vietnam and Korea reveals important differences. Vietnam has ASEAN; the Korean Peninsula is in a vortex of rivalry. Vietnam is concerned with China's ambitions in the South China Sea; Korea is concerned about China's relationship with the Democratic People's Republic of Korea (DPRK). Vietnam's national task is development; Korea's is reconciliation and reunification. Vietnam's diaspora is largely composed of former enemies of the regime and expelled ethnic Chinese; Korea's diaspora has a more positive relationship to the culture and politics of the homeland.

Vietnam and Korea as Foils

There are important differences between Vietnam and Korea. They share common Sinitic traditions, but Vietnam is less hierarchical than Korea, perhaps due to the revolutionary solidarity of its recent past. Vietnam's Southeast Asian characteristics include the greater autonomy of women and the location of most ethnic minorities in highlands and on borders. The major urban exception, the ethnic Chinese, is also typical of Southeast Asia. Ethnic Vietnamese are 86 percent of the population, in contrast to the 99+ percent homogeneity in both the Koreas. Catholicism has deeper roots in Vietnam than Christianity in Korea, but these roots were entangled with French colonialism. Vietnam's cosmopolitanism is perhaps more diverse than Korea's, with strong influences from France, the United States, China, Russia and Eastern Europe, and Southeast Asia. However, as a whole Korea is more globalized. While Vietnam is unified, there are inherent challenges in the geography of a long, skinny country with population centers at both ends.

Politically, both were split by the Cold War, but had different winning sides. Vietnam's communist government is rooted in the populist traditions of national liberation and people's war, giving it a broad social base similar to China's. The party-state's successful adaptation of *Doi Moi* has strengthened the path dependency of the regime, as well as raising new challenges. It is an executive regime rather than a legislative one, but it has proven capable of policy change and internal reform.[21] While there is no instance of a developed country with a party-state constitution, there are now two examples of protracted and successful modernization efforts utilizing market forces and international openness handled by party-states. In 1979 the successful course since taken by China and Vietnam was unimaginable to most observers, let alone its possible success.

Although Vietnam has come from a different context and prospered on a different path than Korea, they (and we) exist in a newly horizonless world of connectivity, where attempts to isolate are futile. The cultural referents of youth are more often international than local. Moreover, the connectivity revolution has fatally undermined media control by the establishment and enabled quick and spontaneous public action. All governments are now more vulnerable to base-level volatility, though it poses a special challenge to party-state regimes premised on the illegitimacy of organized opposition. While the party-states of China and Vietnam have been successful thus far and are committed to increasing their governance capabilities, neither has a clear vision of what a modern, democratic party-state would look like. When party leaders and publics talk about democratization in the future, they seem to indicate the generic model of a legislative, oppositional democracy. Ideas do not always take concrete shape, but it is hard to sustain political self-confidence without them. It remains to be seen whether convergence in the policies of modern governance will lead to a convergence of systems.

Perhaps the immediate heuristic utility of comparing the situations of Vietnam and Korea lies in the challenge of rising above the idiosyncratic study of each to confront questions of similarities and differences in context and path. An even more basic utility is that these are two of the most significant countries in East Asia, and both, to their sorrow, were pivots of global Cold War confrontations. In trying to grasp the options of contemporary East Asia and of the United States vis-à-vis Asia it is important to connect conceptual generalizations with regional realities, and two connection points are better than one.

Notes

1 I would like to thank conference participants and also Lew Stern, Myungsik Ham, and Nguyen Tuan Viet for their comments. Unless otherwise indicated, data are taken or derived from the World Bank, *World Development Indicators* (Washington, DC: World Bank, December 2011), http://data.worldbank.org/.

2 See Leif-Eric Easley, chapter 8 in this volume, for a detailed explication and application of these categories to Vietnam and Korea.

3 Frances Fitzgerald, *Fire in the Lake* (Boston: Little Brown, 1972); Jeffrey Race, *War Comes to Long An: Revolutionary Conflict in a Vietnamese Province* (Berkeley: University of California Press, 1972).

4 William Turley, *The Second Indochina War: A Concise Political and Military History*, 2nd ed. (Lanham: Rowman and Littlefield, 2009).

5 Le Duan, *Communist Party of Vietnam 4th National Congress Documents*, Central Committee Political Report (Hanoi: Foreign Languages Publishing House, 1977), 8.

6 Adam Fforde and Suzanne Paine, *The Limits of National Liberation* (London: Croom Helm, 1986).

7 Nayan Chanda, *Brother Enemy* (New York: Macmillan, 1986).

8 Ezra Vogel, *Deng Xiaoping and the Transformation of China* (Cambridge: Harvard University Press, 2012), 270–74.

9 William Turley and Brantly Womack, "Asian Socialism's Open Doors: Guangzhou and Ho Chi Minh City," *China Journal* 40 (July 1998): 95–119.

10 Bao Ninh, *The Sorrow of War*, tr. Phan Thanh Hao (New York: Pantheon, 1995).

11 The World Bank's online data for consumer price inflation begins in 1996. I have supplemented it with data from the Vietnam Statistical Yearbooks of 1992, 1995, and 1998.

12 China's *hukou* system restricts most urban services and rights to registered residence, in effect making the migrant laborers—currently one-third of total urban population—second-class citizens. See Tom Miller, *China's Urban Billion* (London: Zed Books, 2012).

13 Guan-Yi Leu, "Cooperating for Diversification: Partnership Selection in Preferential Trade Agreements in East Asia" (PhD dissertation, University of Virginia, Charlottesville, 2012).

14 Although the border between China and Vietnam had remained basically stable since the Song dynasty and had been demarcated in detail by joint Chinese and French surveyors in the 1880s, there were some disputed areas. In 2000 both sides agreed to a fifty-fifty split of the disputed areas. Zones of control in the Tonkin Gulf were also agreed to.

15 Brantly Womack, *China and Vietnam: The Politics of Asymmetry* (New York: Cambridge University Press, 1986), 212–37.

16 World Bank, *World Development Indicators*, December 2011, http://data.worldbank.org/.

17 The Spratly archipelago is disputed in whole or in part by China (People's Republic of China and Republic of China), Vietnam, Malaysia, Philippines, and Brunei. The Paracels have been occupied by China since 1974 and are disputed between China and Vietnam.

18 Brantly Womack, "The Spratlys: From Dangerous Ground to Apple of Discord," *Contemporary South East Asia* 33, no. 3 (2011): 370–87.

19 Calculated from *World Development Report* (WDR) data. Gross domestic product (GDP) PPP figures before 1980 had to be walked back using gross national product (GNP) growth rates.

20 Ben Kerkvliet, "Workers' Protests in Contemporary Vietnam," *Journal of Vietnamese Studies* 5, no. 1 (2010): 162–204; "State Authorities' Actions toward Regime Dissidents in Contemporary Vietnam," paper presented at "Authoritarianism in East Asia: Vietnam, China, North Korea," City University of Hong Kong, June–July 2010.

21 I make this argument more fully in Brantly Womack, "Modernization and the Sino-Vietnamese Model," *International Journal of China Studies* 2, no. 3 (August–September 2011): 157–75.

8 The Squeezed Middle? Korean and Vietnamese National Identities Navigating Chinese and American Power

Leif-Eric Easley[1]

Post–Cold War studies of international and regional relations show growing interest in the role of so-called middle powers.[2] From a theoretical perspective, this literature often conflates the identity (national self-conception) of middle-power states with their performance (foreign policy) on the international stage.[3] From an empirical perspective, the literature neglects East Asia as a region for generating and testing political theories. Studies of middle powers tend to focus on European countries, Canada, Australia, and South Africa,[4] while research on contemporary East Asian international politics tends to focus on great powers (i.e., China, Japan, and the United States) or the development of regional institutions (e.g., the Association of Southeast Asian Nations, ASEAN).

In this chapter I aim to contribute to the middle-power literature by comparing the post–Cold War national identities and foreign policies of South Korea and Vietnam.[5] The goal is to bring to light the complexities of South Korean and Vietnamese national self-conceptions, and to investigate how these may be informing change in Seoul's and Hanoi's foreign policies.[6] The policy outcomes of interest are not so much within the functional space between stronger and weaker powers,[7] but rather within the geopolitical space between the United States and the People's Republic of China (PRC).

I proceed as follows. First, I introduce a framework for understanding Korean and Vietnamese national identities, followed by a discussion of the events that helped shape them. In the second section I investigate how shared and conflicting identities affect South Korea's and Vietnam's relations with China and with each other.[8] In the third section I discuss how identity trajectories may be influencing South Korea's and Vietnam's positioning in U.S.-China geo-politics. I conclude with prospects for middle-power cooperation in East Asia.

National Identities of South Korea and Vietnam

The end of the Cold War unleashed competing forces in East Asia: the integrating processes of globalization and the often-divisive ambitions of na-tional identity.[9] While globalization and nationalism are understood to be competing phenomena, they are similar in being inherently complex, difficult to define, and even more difficult to measure. The present investigation un-packs various aspects of national identity rather than discussing nationalism as a monolithic force. National identity is defined broadly, to include the wide range of characteristics and beliefs that foreign policy decision-makers con-sider important when distinguishing their nation from others in the realm of international politics.

To ensure that such a broad definition is analytically useful, it is necessary to adopt a framework for making a slippery concept tractable. A recent and comprehensive study of South Korean nationalism by Gi-Wook Shin provides such a framework and has not yet been applied to a comparison of Korean and Vietnamese national identities.[10] Shin examines national identity along three dimensions: how it is embedded, contingent, and contested. National identity is embedded in primordial factors such as geography, race, and cul-tural traditions with ancient (even mythical) roots. It is contingent on histori-cal processes of nation-building and struggles over power and legitimacy.[11] It is contested by competing categories of identity (e.g., class, region, religion, gen-der), as different stakeholders attempt to pull or push the content of national identity in different directions.

Korean and Vietnamese national identities can be compared along these three dimensions. First, in terms of primordial factors, relative ethnic ho-mogeneity is a large part of national identity in Korea and Vietnam; nation, race, and ethnic culture are essentially equivalent in the eyes of the Korean and Vietnamese peoples and states.[12] However, Vietnam includes 54 differ-ent ethnic groups, and while over 85 percent of citizens identify themselves as Vietnamese (Kinh),[13] the historical and cultural influences of ethnic Chinese are significant.[14] In both the Korean and Vietnamese cases, Confucian tradi-tions and legacies are infused in national identity.[15] With this comes a his-torical consciousness that Korea and Vietnam were members of an ancient China-centered regional order.[16]

For hundreds of years, Vietnamese and Korean elites were culturally in-tertwined with China (they wrote with Chinese characters, debated Chinese

philosophy, and so on) and looked to the Chinese emperor to bestow legitimacy on their leaders.[17] The Korean *yangban* were cosmopolitan, closer to
Chinese elites than to the ethnic Korean masses.[18] But the primordial issues
that matter most today seem to be Korea's and Vietnam's ethnic differentia-
tion from China, and their historical struggle to master geography and defend
their autonomy against a larger neighbor.[19] This is evident in the historical
trends upon which the development of contemporary Korean and Vietnamese
national identities are contingent.

The historical processes that shaped Korean and Vietnamese identity
largely involved resisting outside pressure and influence. Even when embedded in the Sinocentric order, the bureaucracies of the Korean kingdoms were
comparatively autonomous and well developed.[20] Meanwhile, Vietnamese national identity was forged over centuries of opposition to Chinese hegemony,
even as Vietnam was part of the Chinese empire.[21] External threats help forge
identity, overriding internal divisions by motivating cohesion for the grand
purpose of autonomous survival.[22]

Such a process was evident in Korea and Vietnam under colonialism.[23]
Japanese and French imperialism and the battles fought against them for
liberation reverberate throughout Korean and Vietnamese institutions and
political cultures.[24] Both countries remain sensitive to issues of sovereignty,
though the colonial era affected them differently.[25] Japanese colonialism (unlike Western colonialism) did not draw many new borders, so in the case of
Korea, rather than many tribes being thrust together within contrived imperial boundaries, a relatively homogenous ethnic group ended up divided into
two states.

This is, of course, a legacy of one of the two hot wars in Cold War East Asia.
In both the Korean and Vietnam wars, a massively destructive and deadly civil
conflict was waged between a communist north and Western-aligned south.
Korean and Vietnamese identities are contingent on the different political and
economic development paths that followed those wars. A democratizing, glo-
balizing, and capitalist South Korea remained divided from the North, while
visions for unification are still hotly debated in domestic forums.[26] Vietnam
was unified under communist rule but remained largely isolated until it ex-
tricated itself from Cambodia and undertook reform (*Doi Moi*), opening to
international trade concurrent with domestic liberalization.[27]

Cold War divisions of nations throughout the Asian region weigh heav-
ily on national identity and offer several contrasts between South Korea and
Vietnam.[28] The United States was South Korea's Cold War ally but Vietnam's
Cold War enemy (and South Korean troops fought alongside their American

counterparts in the Vietnam War). While many Vietnamese feel pride in forcing out U.S. troops, some South Koreans feel shame in continuing to host
American bases. But the capitalist, U.S.-allied South Korea has proved much
more successful, economically and politically, since its civil war. Pride in
South Korea's rapid development has largely replaced a sense of victimization
at the hands of foreign powers, and the national shame associated with Korea's
inability to fully defend and unify itself. South Koreans are increasingly proud
of their global competitiveness, technological prowess, and popular culture
exports. The country's confidence grew alongside its regional role and identity.
Forging such a role and identity is a process that Vietnam has only recently
undertaken.[29] Its progress is noteworthy, especially since joining the ASEAN
in 1995 and the World Trade Organization (WTO) in 2007, engaging Vietnam
in a much wider range of international activity.[30]

South Korea and Vietnam offer two important examples of political reform under globalization.[31] Korea's incomplete unification versus Vietnam's
incomplete democratization and globalization have led to different types of
contestation in domestic politics.[32] National identity is largely shaped by history—especially by how history is taught, remembered, and used to articulate
goals for the future.[33] This is why incomplete reconciliation and the competing
"histories" involved are so important for national identity.

Such histories, in turn, inform debates on the requirements and benefits
of national membership. In both Vietnam and South Korea, native birth and
ethnic similarity admit one to the national community, which then demands
strong allegiance. Compared to other countries, national loyalties run strong
in both.[34] Depending on the wording of survey questions, Vietnamese score as
even more loyal to the nation-state than Koreans.[35] This is in part because most
Vietnamese see their state as coterminous with the nation, whereas many South
Koreans see the Republic of Korea (ROK) as an incomplete and imperfect representation of the Korean nation. What is more, Korean democratization en-
tailed formative and popular demonstrations in opposition to the state.[36] Issues
of reconciliation among subnational groups and debates over human rights
have been unpacked (and contested) in South Korea more than in Vietnam.[37]

In terms of the benefits of citizenship in the nation-state, modernization
in both South Korea and Vietnam has lifted millions out of poverty, freeing
people to debate the side effects of rapid growth, such as widening socioeconomic inequalities.[38] Disagreement over the entitlements of nationals—and
what counts as fair opportunity—is now central to debates on national identity. New communications technology only intensifies the fight as it clears the
way for voices from all parts of society—and from around the world—to be

heard. Since the Cold War, globalization has driven economic and political reforms in Asia.[39] Overseas Korean and Vietnamese communities (in the United
States in particular) are important bridges for exchange and commerce; within
Asia, meanwhile, significant flows of people are introducing transnational elements into national identity.[40]

Such globalization complicates what it means to be Korean or Vietnamese:
witness not only the budding multiculturalism in South Korea and efforts to
secure the rights of religious minorities in Vietnam, but also the rising expectations of both peoples to reap benefits they see other nationals enjoying.
With demographic and generational change in South Korea and Vietnam, citizens are contesting what their nation's distinctiveness should be under internationalization, and demanding their perceived share of social freedom and
economic prosperity.[41]

Building on this brief survey of the origins, contexts, and debates relevant
to national identity in South Korea and Vietnam, I proceed with a discussion
of how national identities in East Asia are changing relative to one another.
In the following section I consider South Korea–China, Vietnam-China, and
South Korea–Vietnam pairings of national identities, and ask which elements
of identity are shared or overlapping and which are in conflict.

Converging and Diverging Identities in East Asia

While South Korean and Vietnamese national identities are clearly multifaceted, it is possible to gauge if and how these identities are converging or
diverging with those of other nations by considering the aspects of identity
that are relevant or salient in bilateral relations.[42] In completing this exercise,
it is striking that both South Korea's and Vietnam's commonalities with China
appear to be in decline, while conflicting aspects of identity are in ascendance.
Conversely, shared aspects of identity between South Korea and Vietnam
demonstrate some increase, while conflicting aspects of identity appear to be
decreasing.

South Korea and China share Confucian influences, but these are not as
operative as before and are more often interpreted in different ways. South
Koreans tend to see China's neo-Confucianism of the 2000s as state sponsored
and politically instrumental. South Korea and China in many ways share faith
and pride in state-led economic growth,[43] but South Koreans are increasingly
uncomfortable with Chinese state capitalism and the market-distorting preferential treatment for Chinese state-owned enterprises (SOEs). Finally, anti-Jap-
anese sentiment is less prevalent in South Korea and China today, compared
to the height of the Yasukuni Shrine controversy in the mid-2000s.[44]

On the other side of the ledger, South Koreans increasingly object to the history and potential future of Sinocentrism in East Asia. There is consternation in Seoul over the extent to which China's economic weight will translate into political influence.[45] Meanwhile, Chinese handling of North Korean military provocations in 2010 and the death of Kim Jong-il in 2011 remind South Koreans of Beijing's role on the other side of the Korean War and Cold War, while shining a spotlight on North Korea's emphasis on stability over change, an issue central to South Korean national identity debates. Finally, China's domestic crackdowns after the Arab Spring, including forced repatriation of North Korean refugees, drew criticism in South Korea.

Longstanding similarities and contradictions between Vietnam and China make for a complicated relationship.[46] Traditional philosophies are no longer the glue they once were, nor is communist ideology. Chinese and Vietnamese party leadership have many points of comparison, as do their development strategies, but few Vietnamese would claim to follow a Chinese model.[47] Instead, conflicting identities are on the rise as Hanoi rejects a submissive relationship to Beijing. Also relevant is the "othering" of ethnic Chinese in Vietnam, and the intensification of territorial disputes and competing regional influence. Disagreement over Cambodia precipitated the 1979 war between Vietnam and China,[48] and the conflict still reverberates today, as Vietnamese grow anxious of China assuming the identity of regional hegemon. Vietnamese are very sensitive to incidents involving disputed islands with China and the Chinese harassment of Vietnamese boats in the South China Sea. Unprecedented anti-China protests in Vietnam in recent years also display the public's dissatisfaction with Chinese economic influence (e.g., extensive mining interests). These nationalist demonstrations show the Vietnamese government's willingness to allow such opinions to be voiced.

In contrast, there appears to be some convergence between South Korean and Vietnamese national identities. Both continue to share anti-colonial sentiments and pride in rebuilding their countries after civil war. Fears of class struggle and domestic disunity are on the rise in both countries. In terms of international orientation, South Korea and Vietnam are both developing middle-power identities in their interactions with global powers and East Asian regionalism. Meanwhile, what had been very different visions of economics tied to national identity (capitalism vs. communism) are less relevant to bilateral relations as Vietnam liberalizes and globalizes.[49] Cold War legacies are becoming less salient to Korea-Vietnam relations; so are differences over democracy and human rights, as Vietnam integrates with the community of nations from which it was estranged for decades after the Vietnam War.

TABLE 8.1

Bilateral comparison of national identity issues: South Korea, Vietnam, and China

	Shared aspects of identity	Conflicting aspects of identity
ROK-China	Confucianism and Buddhism ↓ State-led development model ↓ Anti-Japanese colonialism ↓	Sinocentric past/future of the region ↑ Memory of Korean War, Cold War alliances ↑ Vision of stability vs. change in North Korea ↑ Political freedom, human rights ↑
Vietnam-China	Confucianism and Buddhism ↓ Communist ideology ↓ One-party development model	Sinocentric past/future of the region ↑ Ethnic nationalism ↑ Territorial disputes, influence (e.g., Cambodia) ↑
ROK-Vietnam	Anti-colonialism; pro-independence Struggle to rebuild after civil war Middle power regionalism ↑ Fear of class struggle, disunity ↑	Different visions of economics, globalization ↓ Different sides of Cold War ↓ Political freedom, human rights ↓

Source: Author's compilation.

Note. The arrows indicate whether aspects of identity are increasingly or decreasingly shared or conflicting.

Finally, Vietnam and South Korea have not only experienced growing trade with China, but also have burgeoning economic relations with each other.[50] These involve larger flows of people and growing sympathies between the two countries. One example is the large number of Vietnamese brides in rural South Korea, whose experiences are often the subject of national media coverage and efforts to increase cultural understanding.[51]

The trajectories of these salient aspects of identity are summarized in table 8.1. In the next section I consider implications for East Asian geopolitics, viewing South Korea and Vietnam as middle powers between China and the United States.

Korea and Vietnam in the Context of U.S.-China Geopolitics

An undeniable trend in East Asian geopolitics is the phoenix-like rise of China, associated with Beijing's reforms beginning in the late 1970s and accelerating in the 2000s. South Koreans and Vietnamese appear uncomfortable with growing economic reliance on their larger neighbor and do not want to be pulled into a tighter orbit around China.[52] Policymakers in Seoul and Hanoi, concerned about the possibility of Beijing using economic leverage over national leaders and domestic groups, see relations with the United States as something of an insurance policy. For purposes of discussion, in this section I reduce the geopolitical situation at different periods in East Asia to a single-dimension analysis, wherein a middle-power's foreign policy moves along a spectrum between two great power poles.

During the Cold War, the two poles for Vietnam were the USSR and China, and for much of the Cold War, Hanoi moved closer to Moscow.[53] South Korea's security policy was almost entirely focused on North Korea, but the regional poles were the United States and Japan. While Seoul moved a bit closer to Tokyo due to Japan's economic predominance in Asia and episodic concerns about American military disengagement, Seoul still remained closer to Washington.

The poles for Vietnamese and Korean geopolitics changed in the immediate post–Cold War period with the disintegration of the USSR. For Vietnam, one pole consisted of the former Soviet Union states, and the other a grouping of the ASEAN countries and China, with Vietnam clearly moving closer to the latter. For Seoul the immediate post–Cold War spectrum had the United States and Japan at one end and China at the other. While Seoul remained closer to Washington and Tokyo in absolute terms, it moved relatively closer to Beijing.

The present situation is different from that during the Cold War and immediate post–Cold War period in two important ways. First, the poles for both Vietnam and South Korea are now the United States and China, meaning that the two countries are navigating the same geopolitical spectrum. Second, along this geopolitical spectrum, the positions of South Korea and Vietnam appear to be converging.

South Korea remains strategically closer to the United States in an alliance that leaders in both countries describe as "stronger than ever."[54] After having moved geopolitically closer to China post–Cold War, ROK-PRC military and diplomatic orientations remain far apart and are certainly not getting closer after recent North Korean provocations.[55] In contrast, U.S.-ROK military cooperation and diplomatic coordination have been high in the wake of the 2010 *Cheonan* and Yeonpyeong Island incidents.[56] However, domestic political debates inside South Korea demonstrate a strong reluctance to get "too close" to the United States at the expense of relations with South Korea's inescapable and giant neighbor.[57] Seoul thus may have found something of an uncomfortable equilibrium, well on the American side of the geopolitical spectrum, but looking to avoid tilting further in the direction of either Washington or Beijing.

Hanoi, too, is navigating between the U.S. and China poles. While geopolitically closer to Beijing than Washington, recent Vietnamese foreign policy—which involves more military exchanges and diplomatic coordination with the United States—suggests movement along the spectrum. Vietnam may be putting some space between its international position and that of China, making its position on the Sino-American geopolitical spectrum closer to that of South Korea.

Fully testing the hypothesis that the balance of shared and conflicting identities could explain this geopolitical movement is beyond the scope of this chapter (although important evidence is provided in other chapters in this volume). To make a causal argument, one would need to carefully process trace changing national self-conceptions and how these motivate government leaders' evolving positions on foreign policy. Meanwhile, geopolitics involves a more complicated geometry than a single spectrum with two poles (e.g., international institutions could reshape the playing field) and international strategies are hardly immune from domestic politics.[58]

Various other factors would need to be examined to rule out spurious correlations (such as changes in material power causing both changes in identity conflicts and geopolitical orientation). A more detailed study would likely find that the material power balance, cultural trends, and domestic political configurations all feed into the balance of shared/conflicting identities, which then might predict changes in geopolitical alignment. But then one would have to consider feedback (about changes in geopolitical alignment affecting identity, for example) and test competing explanations (such as the direct effects of material power balance on geopolitical alignment).

In the present hypothesis-generating exercise, I have shown the plausibility of a connection between identity and the positions of South Korea and Vietnam in the context of U.S.-China geopolitics. As shown in table 8.1, most aspects of national identity that South Korea and Vietnam share with China appear in decline, whereas conflicting identities are intensifying. This suggests that Seoul and Hanoi will increase their geopolitical distance from Beijing. In addition, the aspects of national identity shared between South Korea and Vietnam appear to be in ascendance, while conflicting aspects of identity between the two are receding. Changing identities thus appear to correctly predict geopolitical convergence between Seoul and Hanoi, which raises the question of what growing cooperation between these two pivotal middle powers might look like.

Conclusion: Middle Power Cooperation

It is easy to think of middle powers in Asia being "squeezed" between the United States and China, or between the forces of globalization and nationalism. However, far from being mere objects of Sino-American rivalry or functions of domestic political responses to globalization, South Koreans and

Vietnamese have great agency over the foreign policies of their nations. This is why it is important to better understand the trajectories of national identity debates inside such influential middle powers.

While those national identity debates appear to be creating some geopolitical distance between Seoul and Hanoi on the one hand and Beijing on the other, many South Korean and Vietnamese strategists recognize that hedging is not enough. The U.S. role in Asia remains strong but faces serious resource constraints. Washington will not always be willing to be played off of China. Seoul and Hanoi have to worry about both destabilizing Sino-American conflict as well as any great power cooperation that overlooks Korean and Vietnamese interests. It is likely that the leaders of both nations will look to improve or at least put a floor under relations with China without giving up too much in terms of national identity. From the perspective of this study, it will be particularly interesting to see if South Korean and Vietnamese identities build upon their modest convergence and whether this translates into deeper foreign policy coordination.

Numerous areas of potential South Korea–Vietnam cooperation exist. The two countries can take a more coordinated approach to multilateral dialogue with China via Track II dialogues, discussions with Washington over the so-called U.S. pivot to Asia, and, especially, the growing number of ROK-ASEAN meetings.[59] In addition to engaging Beijing on strengthening institutions for the rule of law and abiding by trade and investment agreements, coordination can also be increased on stable access to energy resources and shared responsibility for regional environmental standards. In the area of security, Seoul and Hanoi could jointly call for increased transparency of defense modernization, more detailed codes of conduct for safe and free navigation in the South China Sea, and stronger commitments to addressing territorial issues peacefully and in accordance with international norms.

Controversies over history and cultural stereotypes in East Asia may be somewhat assuaged by growing exchanges among students and scholars. More open and common markets can be expected to expand business links and public exposure to other countries' goods and cultures. National leaders and media, which largely shape the conversation about identity, may likewise promote understanding of regional neighbors. However, and perhaps even more likely, leaders and media may attempt to score points in domestic popularity by scapegoating regional rivals, with implications for the geopolitical positioning of middle powers.

In conclusion, two notes of caution are in order. One is that since identity is difficult to track accurately and reliably, scholars must be on guard against a normative bias in analysis. The importance of national identity should not be ignored just because it is difficult to measure; understanding identity calls for humility and closer investigation. A previous lack of understanding about national identities in the cases above helped precipitate and prolong the Korean and Vietnam wars. A second point of caution is that when the outcomes of interest involve geopolitics and international diplomacy, it is natural (and analytically efficient) to focus on elite perceptions. But as has been shown in careful historical analyses of postcolonial Vietnam and Korea, local circumstances and bottom-up forces can redirect history.[60] Further research is needed on how global norms and pressures are negotiated with the identities and preferences of local actors who are increasingly networked with social media technologies.[61]

The interests and policies of a new generation of leaders will be informed not only by material incentives and constraints, but also by national grievances and international reputational ambitions. It is thus essential to investigate how new leaders and their constituents understand history and look to reshape future national identities.[62] Middle-power identity and diplomacy are poised to be meaningful parts of that process for South Korea and Vietnam as both nations take on more significant roles in East Asia's international politics.

Notes

1 The author appreciates invaluable feedback provided by participants of the Shorenstein Asia-Pacific Research Center (APARC) Koret Conference held at Stanford in March 2012, and the excellent research assistance from In-young Park at Ewha University. A version of this paper appeared in *Pacific Focus* 27, no. 3 (December 2012): 421–42; reprinted here with permission.

2 There are at least three different approaches to defining a "middle power": a state (1) in between great and minor powers in terms of geographic size, population, gross domestic product (GDP), and military capabilities; (2) geographically situated between great powers, at an intersection of competing spheres of influence; and (3) that looks to be more influential than its material capabilities would allow by standing up to great powers using normative and institutional frameworks involving legitimacy and enforceable constraints. See David Capie and Paul Evans, *The Asia-Pacific Security Lexicon* (Singapore: Institute of Southeast Asian Studies, 2002), 161–64. On the growing interest in middle powers, see Cranford Pratt, ed., *Middle Power Internationalism* (Canada: McGill-Queen's University Press, 1990); Andrew Cooper, Richard Higgott, and Kim Nossal, *Relocating Middle Powers* (Canada: UBC Press, 1993); John Ravenhill, "Cycles of Middle Power Activism," *Australian Journal of International Affairs* 52, no. 3 (1998): 309–27; Denis Stairs, "Of Medium Powers and Middling Roles," in *Statecraft and Security: The Cold War and Beyond*, ed. Ken Booth (Cambridge, MA: Cambridge University Press, 1998); Eduard Jordaan, "The Concept of a Middle Power in International Relations: Distinguishing between Emerging and Traditional Middle Powers," *Politikon* 30, no. 2 (2003): 165–81; Mehmet Ozkan, "A New

Approach to Global Security: Pivotal Middle Powers and Global Politics," *Perceptions: Journal of International Affairs* 11, no. 1 (Spring 2006): 77–95.

3 The distinction between role identity and performance goes at least as far back as symbolic interaction theory in the 1960–70s. For details, see Peter J. Burke and Donald C. Reitzes, "The Link Between Identity and Role Performance," *Social Psychology Quarterly* 44, no. 2 (June 1981): 83–92; Kal Holsti, "National Role Conceptions in the Study of Foreign Policy," in *Role Theory and Foreign Policy Analysis,* ed. Stephen Walker (Durham: Duke University Press, 1987); Yaacov Vertzberger, *The World in Their Minds: Information Processing, Cognition, and Perception in Foreign Policy Decisionmaking* (Stanford, CA: Stanford University Press, 1990).

4 Joshua Spero, *Bridging the European Divide: Middle Power Politics* (Lanham, MD: Rowman & Littlefield, 2004); Nik Hynek and David Bosold, eds., *Canada's Foreign and Security Policy: Soft and Hard Strategies of a Middle Power* (Oxford: Oxford University Press, 2010); Richard Higgott and Andrew Cooper, "Middle Power Leadership and Coalition Building: Australia, the Cairns Group, and the Uruguay Round of Trade Negotiations," *International Organization* 44, no. 4 (1990): 589–632; Peter Vale, "South Africa: Understanding the Upstairs and the Downstairs," in *Niche Diplomacy: Middle Powers after the Cold War,* ed. Andrew Cooper (London: Macmillan, 1997).

5 To focus on South Korea and Vietnam, the present research deliberately puts aside questions of Seoul and Hanoi's relations with Pyongyang. Future studies could productively address how South Korea's identity politics in relation to North Korea, as well as Vietnam's historical relations with a fellow country in the Cold War communist bloc, figure into relations between Seoul and Hanoi.

6 In other words, the present research is a work of hypothesis generation that seeks to unpack elements of national identity and suggest how trajectories of identity perceptions among the policymaking elite in South Korea and Vietnam might affect the geopolitical orientation of these nation-states.

7 More authors are investigating the coalition-building role of middle-power states on functional issues. On the example of the Proliferation Security Initiative, see David A. Cooper, "Challenging Contemporary Notions of Middle Power Influence: Implications of the Proliferation Security Initiative for 'Middle Power Theory,'" *Foreign Policy Analysis* 7, no. 3 (July 2011): 317–36. On Seoul's role in regional security, see Woosang Kim, "Korea as a Middle Power in Northeast Asian Security," in *The United States and Northeast Asia: Debates, Issues, and New Order,* ed. G. John Ikenberry and Chung-in Moon (Lanham, MD: Rowman & Littlefield, 2008). On South Korea's role in global economic governance, see Andrew Cooper and Jongryn Mo, "Middle Power Leadership and the Evolution of the G20" (*Yonsei Hills Governance Center Working Paper* 11-02, Seoul, August 2011).

8 Analyses of the construction and evolution of national identity often differ in terms of which "significant other" is operative in a given case at a given time. The present analysis examines China (and to some extent the United States because of the geopolitical context) as a significant other for South Korea and Vietnam. Depending on the research question at hand, it might be appropriate to focus on different significant others. For example, to explain confidence-building problems for Northeast Asian security cooperation, it can be

useful to study how South Koreans differentiate their nation-state from North Korea or Japan as well as China. See Leif-Eric Easley, "Diverging Trajectories of Trust in Northeast Asia: South Korea's Security Relations with Japan and China," in *Asia at a Tipping Point: Korea, the Rise of China, and the Impact of Leadership Transitions,* ed. Gilbert Rozman (Washington, DC: Korea Economic Institute [KEI], 2012).

9 Gilbert Rozman, *Northeast Asia's Stunted Regionalism: Bilateral Distrust in the Shadow of Globalization* (New York: Cambridge University Press, 2004).

10 Gi-Wook Shin, *Ethnic Nationalism in Korea* (Stanford, CA: Stanford University Press, 2006).

11 For details of these historical processes during critical time periods during and since the Cold War, see chapter 7, by Brantly Womack, in this volume.

12 Shin, *Ethnic Nationalism.* This blurring of the "nation" and "state" concepts corresponds to a blurring of national and state identity, which aids government leaders and policymakers in the instrumental use of identity. The present research does not engage in epistemological or ontological debates concerning the nation and the state, but these are important questions in the political sociology literature, especially concerning transnational society. See William I. Robinson, "Beyond Nation-State Paradigms: Globalization, Sociology, and the Challenge of Transnational Studies," *Sociological Forum* 13, no. 4 (1998): 561–94.

13 U.S. Department of State, "Background Note: Vietnam," Bureau of East Asian and Pacific Affairs, U.S. Department of State, Washington, DC, January 2012.

14 Chee Kiong Tong, *Identity and Ethnic Relations in Southeast Asia: Racializing Chineseness* (Dordrecht: Springer, 2010).

15 Chaibong Hahm, "How the East was Won: Orientalism and the New Confucian Discourse in East Asia," *Development and Society* 29, no. 1 (June 2000): 97–109.

16 David C. Kang, *East Asia before the West: Five Centuries of Trade and Tribute* (New York: Columbia University Press, 2010).

17 Kyung Hwang, *A History of Korea* (New York: Palgrave Macmillan, 2010); Adrian Buzo, *The Making of Modern Korea (Asia's Transformations)* (London and New York: Routledge, 2008).

18 Michael J. Seth, *A Concise History of Korea: From the Neolithic Period through the Nineteenth Century* (Lanham, MD: Rowman & Littlefield, 2006), 224.

19 Hyung Il Pai and Timothy R. Tangherlini, eds., *Nationalism and the Construction of Korean Identity* (California: Institute of East Asian Studies, University of California, 1999).

20 John B. Duncan, *The Origins of the Chosôn Dynasty* (Seattle: University of Washington Press, 2000).

21 Donald E. Weatherbee, *International Relations in Southeast Asia: The Struggle for Autonomy* (Lanham, MD: Rowman & Littlefield, 2008), 44.

22 Samuel S. Kim, *The Two Koreas and the Great Powers* (Cambridge, MA: Cambridge University Press, 2006).

23 Gi-Wook Shin and Michael Robinson, *Colonial Modernity in Korea* (Cambridge, MA: Harvard University Asia Center, 2001); Mark Atwood Lawrence and Fredrik Logevall, eds., *The First Vietnam War: Colonial Conflict and Cold War Crisis* (Cambridge: Harvard University Press, 2007).

24 Carter Eckert, *Offspring of Empire: The Koch'ang Kims and the Colonial Origins of Korean Capitalism, 1876-1945* (Seattle: University of Washington Press, 1996); Bruce Cumings, "Japanese Colonialism in Korea: A Comparative Perspective" (Shorenstein APARC Working Paper, Stanford, CA, 1997), http://iis-db.stanford.edu/pubs/10061/Cumings.etc.pdf, 33–44.

25 Arthur J. Dommen, *The Indochinese Experience of the French and the Americans: Nationalism and Communism in Cambodia, Laos, and Vietnam* (Bloomington: Indiana University Press, 2002).

26 Key-young Son, *South Korean Engagement Policies and North Korea: Identities, Norms and the Sunshine Policy* (London and New York: Routledge, 2006).

27 Sujian Guo, *The Political Economy of Asian Transition from Communism* (Aldershot, UK: Ashgate, 2006).

28 Tsuyoshi Hasegawa, *The Cold War in East Asia, 1945–1991* (Stanford, CA: Stanford University Press, 2011); Michael Yahuda, *The International Politics of the Asia Pacific*, 3rd edition (London and New York: Routledge, 2011); Tuong Vu and Wasana Wongsurawat, eds., *Dynamics of the Cold War in Asia: Ideology, Identity, and Culture* (New York: Palgrave Macmillan, 2009); John Lewis Gaddis, *The Cold War: A New History* (New York: Penguin, 2006).

29 On Korea and Vietnam debating an Asian regional identity, see Gi-Wook Shin, "Asianism in Korea's Politics of Identity," *Inter-Asia Cultural Studies* 6, no. 4 (2005): 616–30; Nguyen Vu Tung, "Vietnam's Membership of ASEAN: A Constructivist Interpretation," *Contemporary Southeast Asia* 29, no. 3 (2007): 483–505.

30 On the regional concerns facing the ASEAN as an institution, see Donald K. Emmerson, ed., *Hard Choices: Security, Democracy and Regionalism in Southeast Asia* (Stanford, CA: Stanford University Press, 2008); Alice Ba, *(Re)Negotiating East and Southeast Asia: Region, Regionalism, and the Association of Southeast Asian Nations (ASEAN)* (Stanford, CA: Stanford University Press, 2009).

31 Kristina Jonsson and Catarina Kinnvall, eds., *Globalization and Democratization in Asia: The Construction of Identity* (London and New York: Routledge, 2002); Liang Fook Lye and Wilhelm Hofmeister, ed., *Political Parties, Party Systems and Democratization in East Asia* (Singapore: World Scientific, 2011).

32 See Alexander L. Vuving, chapter 4 in this volume.

33 Gi-Wook Shin, Soon-Won Park, and Daqing Yang, eds., *Rethinking Historical Injustice and Reconciliation in Northeast Asia: The Korean Experience* (London and New York: Routledge, 2006); Sheila Miyoshi Jager and Rana Mitter, eds., *Ruptured Histories: War, Memory, and the Post-Cold War in Asia* (Cambridge, MA: Harvard University Press, 2007).

34 See data on pride in national identification in the Asian Barometer surveys, http://www.asianbarometer.org.

35 Kazuya Yamamoto, "Vietnam from the Perspective of the Asia Barometer Survey: Identity, Image of Foreign Nations, and Global Concerns," *Memoirs of the Institute of Oriental Culture* 150 (March 2007): 326–12.

36 Namhee Lee, *The Making of Minjung: Democracy and the Politics of Representation in South Korea* (Ithaca: Cornell University Press, 2007).

37 A longer study might productively compare the status of national reconciliation in Korea and Vietnam and how these nations engage in the "Asian values" debate. On Asian

values, see Daniel A. Bell, *East Meets West: Human Rights and Democracy in East Asia* (Princeton, NJ: Princeton University Press, 2000); Ole Bruun and Michael Jacobsen, eds., *Human Rights and Asian Values: Contesting National Identities and Cultural Representations in Asia* (Richmond, Surrey: Curzon, 2000).

38 Duncan McCargo, ed., *Rethinking Vietnam* (London and New York: Routledge, 2004); Bill Hayton, *Vietnam: Rising Dragon* (New Haven, CT: Yale University Press, 2010); Ian Jeffries, *Contemporary Vietnam: A Guide to Economic and Political Developments* (London and New York: Routledge, 2011); Duck-Koo Chung and Barry J. Eichengreen, eds., *The Korean Economy Beyond the Crisis* (Cheltenham, UK: Edward Elgar, 2005); Jesook Song, ed., *New Millennium South Korea: Neoliberal Capitalism and Transnational Movements* (London and New York: Routledge, 2010).

39 Steven Levitsky and Lucan Way, *Competitive Authoritarianism: Hybrid Regimes after the Cold War* (Cambridge, MA: Cambridge University Press, 2010).

40 Rhacel Parrenas and Lok Siu, eds., *Asian Diasporas: New Formations, New Conceptions* (Stanford, CA: Stanford University Press, 2007).

41 On how the demands for national distinctiveness under globalization have encouraged cultural nationalism in Asia, see Hy V. Luong, "The Restructuring of Vietnamese Nationalism, 1954–2006," *Pacific Affairs* 80, no. 3 (Fall 2007): 439–53.

42 This section draws from the author's previous research on national identities in East Asia and conversations with Korean and Vietnamese policymakers and scholars from 2010 to 2012.

43 Eun Mee Kim, Big Business, *Strong State: Collusion and Conflict in South Korean Development, 1960–1990* (Albany: SUNY Press, 1997); David Hundt, *Korea's Developmental Alliance: State, Capital and the Politics of Rapid Development* (London and New York: Routledge, 2008).

44 Controversy continues to periodically spike in relations with Japan, however, over competing maritime claims, history textbooks, and adequate compensation and apology to wartime sex slaves euphemistically referred to as "comfort women."

45 Scott Snyder, *China's Rise and the Two Koreas: Politics, Economics, Security* (Boulder: Lynne Rienner, 2009).

46 Brantly Womack, *China and Vietnam: The Politics of Asymmetry* (Cambridge, MA: Cambridge University Press, 2006); Guo Ming, *Zhong-Yue Guanxi Xin Shiqi* [New era of China-Vietnam relations] (Beijing: Current Press, 2007); Priscilla Roberts, *Behind the Bamboo Curtain: China, Vietnam, and the World Beyond Asia* (Stanford, CA: Stanford University Press, 2006); Henry J. Kenny, *Shadow of the Dragon: Vietnam, China, and the Implications for U.S. Foreign Policy* (Washington, DC: Brassey's, 2002); Qiang Zhai, *China and the Vietnam Wars, 1950–1975* (Chapel Hill: University of North Carolina Press, 2000).

47 On comparison of the Chinese and Vietnamese reform models, see John Gillespie and Albert Chen, eds., *Legal Reforms in China and Vietnam: A Comparison of Asian Communist Regimes* (London and New York: Routledge, 2010).

48 It should be noted that while the 1979 war was seen in Hanoi and other capitals as a punitive policy by Beijing over Vietnamese involvement in Cambodia, the conflict had a different meaning for Chinese leaders who wanted to prevent Vietnamese hegemony over a greater Indochina that would threaten Chinese interests and self-image. See Xiaoming

Zhang, "China's 1979 War with Vietnam: A Reassessment," *China Quarterly* 184 (December 2005): 851–74.

49 Seoul and Vietnam recognize each other's strong, cohesive state structure focused on economic development. See Kyong Ju Kim, *The Development of Modern South Korea: State Formation, Capitalist Development and National Identity* (London and New York: Routledge, 2006); Tuong Vu, *Paths to Development in Asia: South Korea, Vietnam, China, and Indonesia* (Cambridge, MA: Cambridge University Press, 2010).

50 Ha Thi Hong Van, "Comparison of Vietnam and East Asia Countries (China, Korea, and Japan) Economic Relations," in *Japan and Korea with the Mekong River Basin Countries,* ed. Mitsuhiro Kagami (Bangkok: Bangkok Research Center, 2010).

51 Like other migration trends related to globalization and domestic demography, marriages between South Koreans and Vietnamese are not without problems. Vietnamese in Korea still face discrimination and challenges adjusting, and public opinion in Vietnam sometimes expresses resentment and damaged national pride over Koreans taking Vietnamese brides. On balance, however, the growing people-to-people connections appear to be increasing acceptance of a more multicultural society in Korea while increasing Vietnam's contact with and interest in Korea. See Choong Soon Kim, *Voices of Foreign Brides: The Roots and Development of Multiculturalism in Contemporary Korea* (Lanham, MD: Rowman & Littlefield, 2011); Eungi Kim, "Global Migration and South Korea: Foreign Workers, Foreign Brides and the Making of a Multicultural Society," *Ethnic and Racial Studies* 32, no. 1 (2009): 70–92.

52 See the Global Views Survey by the Chicago Council on Global Affairs, http://www.thechicagocouncil.org.

53 Nicholas Khoo, *Collateral Damage: Sino-Soviet Rivalry and the Termination of the Sino-Vietnamese Alliance* (New York: Columbia University Press, 2011).

54 Hyun-Mook Choi, "Obama: 'Korea is an Unprecedented Model of Development and Prosperity,'" *Chosun Ilbo,* August, 12, 2012, http://news.chosun.com/site/data/html_dir/2012/08/14/ 2012081400710.html.

55 Jung-Yeop Woo and Leif-Eric Easley, "Yellow Sea Turning Red: Darker Views of China among South Koreans," *Asian Issue Brief* no. 15, December 16, 2011, http://asaninst.org/upload_eng/board_files/file1_597.pdf.

56 In March 2010, 46 South Korean sailors were killed when North Korea allegedly sunk the ROK Navy ship *Cheonan.* In November 2010, North Korean forces fired artillery on South Korea's Yeonpyeong Island, killing two South Korean marines and two civilians, and injuring others. For details on the incidents and related developments, see the quarterly analysis of East Asian international relations provided by Pacific Forum's *Comparative Connections,* http://csis.org/program/comparative-connections.

57 This sentiment is a recurring theme in the author's conversations (2010–2012) with South Korean policymakers in both conservative and progressive camps.

58 On institutions, see T. J. Pempel, "Soft Balancing, Hedging, and Institutional Darwinism: The Economic-Security Nexus and East Asian Regionalism," *Journal of East Asian Studies* 10, no. 2 (May 2010): 209–38. On domestic politics, see Alexander Vuving, "Strategy and Evolution of Vietnam's China Policy: A Changing Mixture of Pathways," *Asian Survey* 46, no. 6 (November 2006): 805–24.

59 At the 13th ASEAN-ROK Summit in Hanoi on October 29, 2010, leaders agreed to elevate the ASEAN-ROK dialogue relations to a strategic partnership. On Track II dialogues, see the Council for Security Cooperation in the Asia Pacific, http://www.cscap.org; on the U.S. strategic "pivot" to Asia, see Hillary Clinton, "America's Pacific Century," *Foreign Policy*, November 2011; on ROK-ASEAN cooperation, see the Internet portal for official documents and exchanges by the South Korean Ministry of Foreign Affairs and Trade, http://www.mofat.go.kr/ENG/countries/regional/asean/overview.

60 David Elliott, *The Vietnamese War: Revolution and Social Change in the Mekong Delta, 1930–1975* (Armonk, NY: M. E. Sharpe, 2006); Susan Bayly, *Asian Voices in a Post-Colonial Age: Vietnam, India and Beyond* (Cambridge, MA: Cambridge University Press, 2007); Gi-Wook Shin, *Peasant Protest and Social Change in Colonial Korea* (Seattle: University of Washington Press, 1996).

61 Amitav Acharya, *Whose Ideas Matter?: Agency and Power in Asian Regionalism* (Ithaca, NY: Cornell University Press, 2009); Victoria Carty, *Wired and Mobilizing: Social Movements, New Technology, and Electoral Politics* (London and New York: Routledge, 2010).

62 The observed convergence of Korean-Vietnamese identities and geopolitical positioning in this study is necessarily tentative. The observed trend could be altered by the next Korean administration's efforts to improve relations with China, or by the next set of leaders in Beijing pursuing a more conciliatory policy toward Vietnam and Korea based on economic and cultural attraction, and reducing tensions between respective countries' fishermen and the nationalist media focused on territorial disputes.

9 Unhappy Nations: The Evolution of Modern Korea and Vietnam[1]

Tuong Vu

This chapter aims to identify and compare the major patterns of modern national and state evolution in Korea and Vietnam. Korea and Vietnam are located in the same geographical neighborhood. Both are (much) smaller neighbors of China and historically existed within the premodern Sinocentric cultural and political world. Premodern developments created an ethnically more homogeneous and politically more stable Korea than Vietnam. Their fates further diverged in the late nineteenth century, despite apparent similarities. Korea was colonized by a fellow Asian country (Japan) and Vietnam by a faraway Western one (France). Korea became a colony decades later than Vietnam, and was ruled under a unified administration. In contrast, Vietnam was broken up into three administrative zones under different laws. While both countries were divided during the Cold War into communist and anti-communist states, Vietnam was reunified under communist rule after a long and extremely violent war. The North Korean communist state also attempted to reunify the country by force, but failed after three years of savage fighting. South Korea eventually became a rich and democratic country in contrast to poor and authoritarian North Korea and Vietnam.

Interestingly, both Vietnam and South Korea have seen a strong resurgence of nationalism in the post–Cold War period.[2] It is understandable that a still-divided Korea frustrates many South Koreans, but why has a reunified Vietnam failed to satisfy Vietnamese patriots? The irony implied in the comparison between Vietnam and South Korea today brings to mind Leo Tolstoy's famous remark: "Happy families are all alike; every unhappy family is unhappy in its own way."[3]

Korea and Vietnam's tortuous path to modernity might well have something to do with their "middle-power" status.[4] Both countries are of medium size and situated between great powers. While Vietnam lies between India and China, Korea shares land or maritime borders with China, Russia, and Japan. Both Vietnam and Korea are across the Pacific Ocean from the United States. Their middle-power status makes them both geopolitically worthy for the great powers to fight over. At the same time, they themselves are big enough to dare to challenge the great powers, or—to use Donald Keyser's metaphor in the introductory chapter of this volume—to "punch well above their weights." Barely emerging from colonial rule, both Korea and Vietnam found themselves exactly where the Iron Curtain fell, which was not entirely a coincidence. U.S. military intervention in both countries was similarly not a coincidence. Both the Korean War (1950–53) and the Vietnam War (1965–73) were fought not only to contain the Soviet Bloc but also to protect the United States from facing communism on its borders. Lacking military capability but not ambitions, both North Korea and North Vietnam at that time chose to challenge the boundary imposed on them by the superpowers.[5] Their pride at being outposts of the socialist bloc and their bravado in standing up to the United States showed elements of middle-power behavior.

This chapter will be divided into three main parts. Following a brief discussion of premodern history, the first part concerns the development of modern national consciousness in Korea and Vietnam since the nineteenth century. In the second part I compare the process of modern state building in North Vietnam and South Korea. The literature on the political system of North Vietnam is scarce, and I will use primary data from an ongoing research project. In the conclusion, I discuss the lessons of Vietnamese reunification for South Korea. While Koreans in divided Korea may look to unified Vietnam with envy, they should be aware of the cost of Vietnamese-style reunification, which does not seem to have improved the lot of most Vietnamese.

Premodern Korea and Vietnam

Vietnamese and Korean relations to China in premodern times followed a similar course of initial subjugation and later independence. Today's Vietnam originated as a tribal society in the Red River Delta. This society fell under Chinese rule in 111 BCE and remained so until the tenth century.[6] During this period, significant Chinese migration and intermarriage took place. Chinese customs were absorbed, although the local culture retained certain distinguishable elements. After regaining political independence in 938 CE, Vietnamese kings maintained a tributary relationship with China. They successfully re-sisted several invasions from the north, such as the Mongolian invasions in the thirteenth century. For two decades, from 1400 to 1418, however, Vietnam fell under (Ming) Chinese direct rule, but regained independence afterward. While the nationalist scholarship makes much of Vietnam's "heroic resistance" against Chinese aggression, the premodern relationship between China and Vietnam was fundamentally peaceful, and periods of war were rare.[7]

Korea was also subject to direct Chinese rule from 108 BCE to the fourth century CE—only 400 years instead of 1,000 years as in Vietnam.[8] Following the collapse of Chinese rule was the Three Kingdoms period of 300 years, dur-ing which three centralized kingdoms—Koguryo, Paekche, and Silla—com-peted for domination of the peninsula. Silla first collaborated with China to defeat its "Korean" rivals, then later drove China out in 676. The subsequent tributary relationship between a unified Korea and China was marked by oc-casional conflicts, as between Vietnam and China. Korean rulers also resisted many Chinese invasions, but fell under Mongol rule in 1270–1356.

Vietnamese history after independence from China in the tenth century was marked by much greater disunity and political tumult than Korean his-tory. Korea was unified in the seventh century, never expanded its territory further, and underwent three dynasties before being annexed to Japan in 1910. In contrast, Vietnam's territory gradually expanded to the south from the Red River Delta, conquering the Hindu Champa Kingdom (today's cen-tral Vietnam) during the twelfth to the fifteenth centuries and the eastern part of the Hindu/Buddhist Khmer Empire (today's southern Vietnam) dur-ing the sixteenth to the eighteenth centuries. Most of the territory of today's Vietnam did not belong to it five centuries ago. During the sixteenth to the eighteenth centuries Vietnam witnessed two civil wars, first between the Mac and Le houses (1527–92), then between Northern Trinh, Southern Nguyen, and Tay Son lords (1627–1802). Together, the wars lasted 240 years—about the same length of time as the Three Kingdoms period in Korea a millen-nium ago. What Silla achieved territorially in 676, the Nguyen dynasty (the ninth or tenth dynasty after Vietnam's independence from China) achieved only in 1802.

Socially, an important difference between premodern Korea and Vietnam was the less hierarchical society of Vietnam. Vietnamese rulers were more suc-cessful than their Korean counterparts in eliminating the aristocracy, which they more or less accomplished by the fifteenth century. Nguyen's Vietnam appeared more centralized than Yi's Korea, where the *yangban* (aristocrats) formed a powerful group rival to kings.

Culturally, Vietnam, like Korea, was deeply influenced by Buddhism, Confucianism, and neo-Confucianism. As late as the nineteenth century, traditional Vietnamese elites still did not imagine or define their world in ethnic terms (that is, Vietnamese versus Chinese) but in cultural ones as "domains of manifest civility."[9] This world contained political boundaries but was united under a single cultural framework that centered on the "Northern Kingdom" (today's China) and to which "southerners" (today's Vietnamese) yearned to belong. As in Korea, borrowing Chinese political concepts and institutions helped Vietnamese rulers consolidate their rule, and they were proud of being part of the Sinocentric cultural universe.

Rise of the Modern Nation in Korea and Vietnam

Compared to Korea, Vietnam's geographic location exposed it to far more interaction with foreigners. Europeans were involved in Vietnam's civil wars from the sixteenth century. Facing Vietnam's rejection of its overtures for trade and missionary activities, France defeated Nguyen forces to occupy southern Vietnam in the 1860s. After a series of brief confrontations, the Nguyen king accepted French protectorates over the rest of the country in 1884. Until the end of the nineteenth century, Vietnamese mandarins who refused to accept defeat were busy organizing armed struggles to restore the monarchy. Modern national consciousness did not emerge until the 1900s, thanks mostly to intellectuals in exile in Japan and China (for example, Phan Boi Chau) whose work had only limited impact inside Vietnam.

In contrast, Korea was much more isolated when the imperialist age began in East Asia.[10] Like Vietnam, it resisted foreign pressure from the United States, France, and Japan to open up the country for trade. No foreign powers were particularly interested in colonizing Korea except Japan, who was not yet strong enough. In 1894 Japan defeated China and in 1905 it defeated Russia, both wars fought because of Korea. While Korea would eventually become a Japanese colony in 1910, the delay (compared to Vietnam) allowed Korean intellectuals to develop and spread a modern national consciousness while Korea was still independent. The most important work was done by the Independence Club during 1896–98. This club was organized by Philip Jaisonn (So Chae-p'il), a Protestant Korean intellectual who had obtained an American medical degree and U.S. citizenship before returning to Korea. The threat to Korea from Japan, a non-Western and anti-Christian power, made Protestantism appealing to Koreans.[11] In contrast, Christianity's presence in colonial Vietnam was mainly through the Catholic Church and was associated with the colonial power. Far from contributing to Vietnamese modern national consciousness, it frequently was a target of nationalist sentiment.[12] For this reason, the March 1, 1919, movement in Korea—in which the Protestant Church played an important role—would have been unthinkable in Vietnam.

In response to the March 1 movement, in which tens of thousands protested nationwide, Japan relaxed political control in Korea.[13] This policy (to be discontinued in 1931) resulted from the rise of democracy in Japan itself ("Taisho democracy") and from the aspirations of Japanese elites to emulate the West. From 1920 to 1925 Korea witnessed the birth of a vibrant movement for cultural reform.[14] A similar liberal policy was not implemented in Vietnam until 1936 (and lasted only until 1939), when the Popular Front came to power in France. Since a freer press and greater freedom of organization facilitated a stronger modern national consciousness, Korea was a decade or two ahead of Vietnam. An open organization like *Sin'ganhoe* (1927–31), which was tolerated by the Japanese colonial government and whose membership included both nationalists and communists, would have been possible in Vietnam only in the late 1930s, and then only in southern Vietnam (for reasons to be explained later).

During the colonial period, Koreans debated how to conceive of their nation using a wide range of approaches, including pan-Asianism, Darwinism, ethnic and civic nationalism,[15] and internationalism. (Gi-Wook Shin argues that Korean ethnic nationalism was a response to both colonialism and communism.) Similar debates were occurring among Vietnamese anticolonial activists at the same time, although less visibly, given the French colony's more restrictive political environment.[16] These debates tended to be confined to a small circle of activists whose views also shifted over time. Phan Boi Chau's writings, for example, combined pan-Asianism, Darwinism, and ethnic nationalism.[17]

Pan-Asianism lost its allure after Japan colluded with France to expel Vietnamese students sent there for study.[18] The anticolonial discourse eventually narrowed down to the rivalry between ethnic nationalism and internationalism. The narrative of ethnic nationalism drew from the Lac Long Quan-Au Co myth,[19] from claims of Vietnam's "4,000-year history of resistance to China," and from a fear of racial extinction derived from Darwinism. Internationalists were not a monolithic group. Like some communists in Korea at the time, many Vietnamese Stalinists believed in class struggle but saw ethnic nationalism as a powerful force useful for the fight against colonialism. They were able to briefly cooperate with the more radical Trotskyists.

The shift in Comintern policy in 1935 enabled collaboration between Stalinists and non-communist nationalists until 1948.[20] They founded the Viet Minh as a united front that used the language of ethnic nationalism to mobilize the masses.[21]

In Korea post-1945 politics created two opposing regimes in North and South Korea. In the North, Kim Il-sung set up a socialist state with the support of the Soviet Union and China. In the South, Rhee Syngman (a former member of the Independence Club) became president of an anti-communist republic. Both North and South Korea sought to use ethnic nationalism to consolidate their states and regimes.[22] Kim made it sound like his regime was pursuing not Stalinism but a unique socialism à la Korea. Rhee promoted the concept of "one people" to unite South Koreans against communism, which he once likened to a disease. In the early 1970s, following the Sino-Soviet conflict, Kim promoted the concept of *juche* ("one's own identity," often translated loosely as "political independence and self-reliance"; *chủ thể* in Vietnamese) as a guiding principle of the North Korean state, together with Marxist-Leninism. After seizing power in a 1961 coup, General Park Chung-hee of South Korea raised the slogan of "modernization of the fatherland" as the new doctrine of the state. This doctrine blended ethnic nationalism with anti-communism and developmentalism.

Similar manipulations took place in Vietnam during the Cold War. Ethnic nationalism helped Stalinists to seize power in late 1945 and to lead the independence struggle with the significant cooperation of many nationalist groups determined to resist French return. While working with certain nationalists, Stalinists executed or sent into exile anti-communist nationalists (the Dai Viet party), Trotskyist internationalists (for example, Ta Thu Thau), and advocates for civic nationalism (for example, Pham Quynh, labeled as a "collaborator").[23]

At the onset of the Cold War in Europe, Vietnamese Stalinists responded enthusiastically to a Soviet call for the communist camp to challenge imperialism.[24] They began to purge their government of non-communists and wholeheartedly embraced Maoism following the Chinese communist victory in 1949. A rural class struggle was launched in Vietnam during 1953–56 under Chinese supervision, and anti-Rightist and Great Leap Forward campaigns were similarly emulated (more briefly for the Leap). Nationalist struggles need not exclude class struggle; as General Secretary Truong Chinh of the Communist Party of Vietnam (CPV) said in an internal meeting in 1953, "Nationalist democratic revolutions are [essentially] peasant revolutions. Wars of national liberation are essentially peasant wars . . . Leading peasants to fight feudalism and imperialism is class struggle and nationalist struggle at the same time. It is class struggle within a nationalist struggle and under the appearance of a nationalist struggle."[25]

It took some time for the communist leaders to formulate a slogan to link ethnic nationalism to socialism. In the late 1950s, they came up with the formula "to be patriotic is to build socialism," making patriotism (a popular Vietnamese term for ethnic nationalism) serve socialism.[26] When they decided on launching the war for reunification, internal party documents viewed it in Marxist-Leninist-Maoist doctrinal terms as a revolution to overthrow a neocolonial regime to establish communism in the entire country.[27] In public, however, the war was framed as "the anti-American resistance to save the country."

North Vietnamese propaganda used both internationalism and nationalism, though emphasizing the first over the second, at least up to the mid-1960s. During 1955–59, for example, the four most published authors in North Vietnam were Lenin (40 titles), Stalin (29 titles), Mao (12 titles), and Ho Chi Minh (11 titles).[28] One out of every 100 copies of printed books was a work by Lenin.[29] A Communist Party document on the broadcasting system, issued in 1959, defined that the system's tasks were "to propagate and mobilize support for Party and state policies, to guide people in carrying out socialist revolution, to mobilize people in the whole country to struggle for reunification, to educate people about internationalism, to strengthen the international solidarity between our people and the socialist countries, and to strengthen the solidarity between our people and the other countries, especially those in Southeast Asia."[30]

An examination of the 1956 reading textbook for (typically six-year-old) first-grade students shows that 84 out of 328 lessons (25.6 percent) had political content.[31] Among those 84 lessons, 32 percent taught students about (dead) communist military heroes, 19 percent about "Uncle Ho," 10 percent about revolutionary and socialist life, and 7 percent each about the south, socialist brother-countries (one about young Lenin), and peasants' and workers' lives. Only two out of 328 lessons were focused on general patriotism and one on a historical hero (Tran Quoc Toan), compared to two lessons on land reform alone. The contents of this textbook suggest that Vietnamese students were taught less about patriotism linking to Vietnamese history than about socialism and its international connections. In general, the party wanted youths to have a strong belief in socialist values and a willingness to die for the socialist cause if told to do so by "Uncle Ho" and the party.

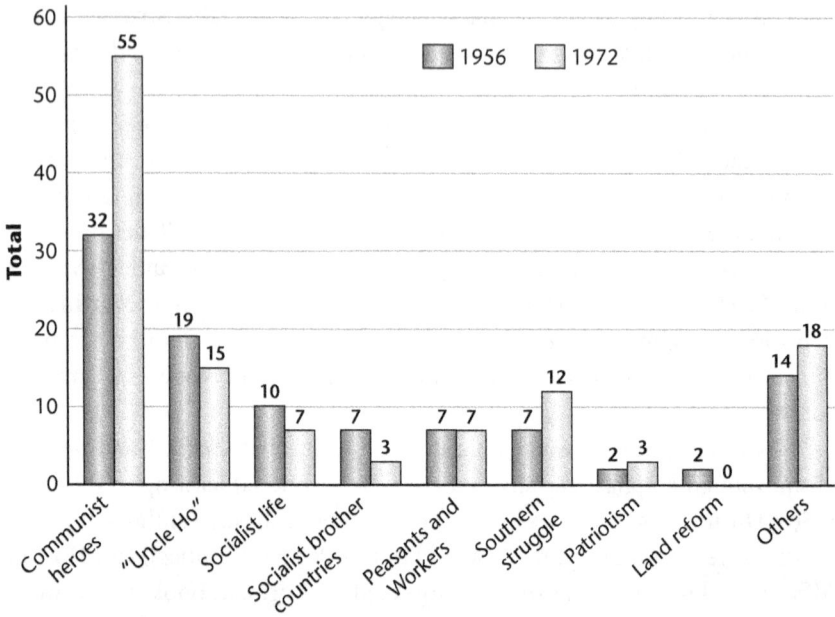

TABLE 9.1 Political content in *Reading Textbook for First-Grade Pupils*, 1956 vs. 1972
Source: Author.

Following the Sino-Soviet split, Vietnamese communists became less internationalist (but not to the extent of their North Korean comrades). They permitted a revival of the study of Vietnam's "feudal" past and came to reject Maoism as a threat to Vietnamese independence. They remained loyal to the global struggle against imperialism by rejecting Khrushchev's theory of coexistence as a sellout to the imperialist camp. This trend can be observed in the changes between the 1956 and 1972 editions of the same reading textbook mentioned above.[32] In the 1972 version published near the end of the civil war, 69 out of 236 lessons (29 percent) had political content. Fifty-five percent of those 69 lessons were about (mostly dead) communist military heroes, 14.5 percent about "Uncle Ho," 11.6 percent about unification or the south, 10 percent about revolutionary and socialist life, and 3 percent about "socialist brothers." The higher percentage of lessons with political content reflected a more politicized society due to the war. The higher number of lessons about communist heroes was also due to the war, which had produced many such heroes. "Uncle Ho" had died in 1969, and thus appeared less frequently in the 1972 edition. Significantly, the lessons about reunification were now three times more numerous than those about socialist brothers. At the same time, the numbers of lessons on general patriotism (two) and historical heroes (one) remained the same.

In South Vietnam, which was a separate country during 1955–75, President Ngo Dinh Diem declared colonialism, feudalism, and communism to be the three main enemies of the Vietnamese nation. He promoted "personalism" (*chủ nghĩa Nhân vị*), a theory developed by the lay Catholic French philosopher Emmanuel Mounier, as a third force between the two Cold War blocs' ideologies of liberalism and communism. Personalism aimed to protect and develop the dignity of the individual in contrast with liberalism (which offered false liberation) and with communism (which called for perpetual war).[33] By adopting an alternative to two Cold War ideologies, Ngo wanted to assert an independent national spirit despite his regime's dependence on the United States. However, cultural freedom in South Vietnam and the Ngo regime's lack of control over the educational system imposed severe limits on its attempts to manipulate nationalism. By the 1960s direct American intervention in the war led to a large anti-American movement in South Vietnamese cities.[34] This movement, which supported peace and reunification, was partly spontaneous and partly manipulated by North Vietnamese agents.

After reunification, the communist regime continued to mobilize ethnic nationalism in its war with China, which was portrayed as "chauvinist and hegemonistic." While the war with China was carried out in "the defense of the socialist fatherland," the invasion and occupation of Cambodia was for "the internationalist solidarity with the Kampuchea people."[35] Rather than stressing nationalism at the expense of communism as in the North Korean concept of *juche*, Vietnamese communists continued to make nationalism serve socialism, as evidenced in their identification of the national tasks as "construction of socialism and defense of the socialist fatherland." By the early 1990s, North Korea had dropped Marxism-Leninism from its constitution, making *juche*, and at times "Kim Il-sungism," the new doctrine. Parallel but more timid change occurred in Vietnam, where the thought of Ho Chi Minh was added to Marxism-Leninism as the ideology of the regime. Vietnam has thus far refused to drop Marxism-Leninism.

In South Korea anti-Americanism developed in the 1980s following the Kwangju massacre by the military dictatorship. A new ideology, *Minjung* (the oppressed masses; *dân chúng* in Vietnamese), which carried both Marxist and Christian connotations and conceptualized the masses as the core of the nation, guided the struggle for democratization until the late 1990s.[36] The *Minjung* movement supported reunification with North Korea while opposing military rule, anti-communism, and the South Korean alliance with the United States.[37] Led by a new generation of student activists, and thanks in part to the end of the Cold War, the movement achieved stunning success in forcing the generals to democratize.[38] The movement has since lost its steam, and left-of-center groups are now split between those fixated on reunification and North Korea, on the one hand, and those more focused on domestic issues such as labor rights, on the other.[39]

Interestingly, parallel changes in social consciousness are taking place in Vietnam today, two decades after those in South Korea. Spontaneous anti-China sentiment has surged recently; anti-China protests occurred in 2008 and 2011, despite being suppressed by the government. Protesters charge that the Vietnamese government is cozying up to China at the expense of Vietnam's national interest. While still fragile, their emerging movement has begun to link intellectuals to lower social strata, and domestic dissidents to anti-communist Vietnamese in exile. This movement suggests that ethnic nationalism is now struggling to escape the patronization of communists. In this struggle, it is aided by a rising demand for democracy among many groups in Vietnam. Vietnam today is not the South Korea of the 1980s, though, since Vietnamese democratic aspirations must confront a far more powerful and entrenched state—which is our focus in the next section.

Evolution of the Modern State

The evolution of the modern state in both Korea and Vietnam began under colonial rule, yet Japanese colonial rule in Korea was far more transformative than French rule over Vietnam. Japan removed the monarchy and created a unified administration and economy in Korea. In contrast, the French were ambiguous about the colonial project and slow in creating a modern, unified administration of Indochina.[40] In terms of the sheer number of residents and civil servants living in the colony and working for the colonial government, Japan maintained a presence in Korea ten times larger than France's in Indochina.[41] A smaller but significant contrast is found in the ratio of police relative to population: the Japanese police force employed one for every 400 Koreans, whereas the French had only one for every 850 natives in Indochina.

Southern Vietnam was granted the status of a full colony, where French staffed the administration and natives enjoyed many rights similar to French nationals. The Vietnamese monarch continued to maintain nominal rule over central Vietnam (Annam) and (through a viceroy) over northern Vietnam (Tonkin). In both Annam and Tonkin, a French *résident supérieur* oversaw the Vietnamese administration, although after the 1900s Tonkin was placed under the direct authority of Indochina's French governor-general. By separating southern Vietnam from the rest, colonial rule reversed the unification process begun under the Nguyen Dynasty between 1800 and 1860.

Both France and Japan built modern infrastructure in the colonies, but, again, Japan did much more. France built a trans-Indochinese rail network of 1,550 kilometers, or about half the length of the network built in Korea by 1945. The motor road network in Korea was also twice the length of that in Indochina. In addition, Japan promoted industrialization and urbanization, while France did not. Manufacturing (including mining and timber) accounted for 40 percent of Korea's total domestic product in the early 1940s, while the ratio for Indochina was about 20 percent in 1937.[42] More than 13 percent of the Korean population lived in cities (>20,000), with a working class numbering nearly 1.8 million, more than ten times the number in Indochina.[43] By 1937 there were 2,300 Korean-run factories, of which 160 employed more than 50 workers. Japanese policy thus created a new stratum of Korean entrepreneurs who would contribute to postwar industrialization in South Korea. In contrast, the most significant French contribution was not in industry but in agriculture. The French built 2,600 kilometers of canals, dug through marshes in Cochin China; these resulted in a quadrupling of the cultivated area for rice, a ten-time increase in rice output, and a five-time increase in rice exports during the period 1880–1937.[44] French policy created a sizeable landlord and middle class in Cochin China (many were ethnic Chinese), which contributed to the rapid development of commerce and capitalism in South Vietnam during the period 1954–75 (and today).

The politics of state formation from late 1945 up to the 1950s was more conducive to building a strong state in Korea than in Vietnam.[45] In particular, Korean elites were polarized into two groups led by extremists (Rhee Syngman and Kim Il-sung). The American occupation forces, in cooperation with Japanese-trained Korean police, carried out massive suppression of communists in South Korea and helped its government to consolidate early on. In contrast, Vietnamese elites cooperated with one another in late 1945 to create a nationalist movement for independence. This compromise resulted in a weak state with a divided leadership. However, with the launch of the class struggle in 1953 and establishment of a Stalinist-Maoist regime in North Vietnam after 1954, this country quickly overtook South Korea in the task of state building.

Elsewhere I have shown that President Rhee (1948–1960) built an effective anti-communist state through his Japanese trained police.[46] Prominent rivals such as Kim Ku and Yo Unhyong were reportedly assassinated by his agents. The National Security Law promulgated in 1948 (and still in force today) was designed to "prohibit all activities that aimed at subverting the state and denying private property" and "preventively detain" those deemed suspicious of "being dangerous and possessing unsound thoughts."[47] In 1949 alone, nearly 120,000 persons were arrested, and 123 social groups were dissolved from September to October.[48] Rhee implemented the *Podo Yonmaeng* program in 1948, which registered and monitored about 300,000 former communists and their families.[49] During the Korean War, the South Korean government imprisoned and executed tens of thousands of suspected or real communists, while Kim Il-sung forces did the same with anti-communists. The early and systematic suppression of communists helped consolidate the South Korean state. The killings of southerners and destruction of the south by northern forces generated intense anti-communist sentiment in South Korean society.

The military dictatorship under Park Chung-hee (1961–79) greatly expanded the political surveillance of the population through such measures as resident registration and residential associations.[50] Schools taught anti-communist thought in several courses. The populace was mobilized to participate in civil defense training in the 1970s. All young men were required to complete military service, which was a precondition for some kinds of employment. The regime maintained tight control over labor and labor organizations, especially during the Yushin period in the 1970s.[51] When necessary, the military relied on force to suppress protests, as in the Kwangju massacre in 1980.

Turning to Vietnam, there is no question that the force of nationalism, whether springing from the bottom up or mobilized from the top down, contributed to the success of the Vietnamese communists in building a strong state. Their leadership in the war for independence from France allowed Vietnamese communists to be strongly associated with the nation in the eyes of many Vietnamese. The U.S. bombing of North Vietnam and the presence of U.S. troops in South Vietnam convinced many Vietnamese that their nation was under foreign threat. This helped Vietnamese communists gain popularity and mobilize popular support for their policy. Yet I argue that an equally important but often neglected factor is the Vietnamese communists' use of overt violence, systematic coercion, and thorough indoctrination to generate compliance and loyalty to the state.

Capitalist South Korea was dictatorial and oppressive, but no match for communist Vietnam when it came to systematic violence, coercion, and control. To the Vietnamese communists armed with the class struggle theory, enemies were defined as entire social strata, not particular groups or individuals. As General Secretary Truong Chinh explained in 1948, enemies of the Vietnamese revolution included "counterrevolutionary feudal landlords and comprador bourgeoisie serving imperialism, and other traitors regardless of class backgrounds."[52] While peasants, urban petty bourgeoisie, intellectuals, "national bourgeoisie," and "progressive personalities and landlords" were considered allies of the revolution at the time, he forewarned that "when the revolution makes further progress, the ranks of our enemies and allies will change, and we will have to change those relationships." Truong Chinh's words were not mere talk. On the eve of the land rent reduction campaign in 1953, communist leaders issued a decree authorizing the execution of landlords in a ratio of one for every 1,000 people.[53] Not just political opponents but a percentage of the population as defined by the communist doctrine was marked in advance for extermination.

Systematic deployment of violence during the land reform of 1953–56 not only destroyed the social basis of potential opposition to the state, but also contributed specifically to state building. The first step was to launch a mass mobilization campaign to denounce and persecute the defined enemies. This step constituted several smaller tasks that involved the state bureaucracy throughout. One was to organize peasants' associations acting on behalf of the party to mobilize mass participation. A parallel task was to orchestrate the direct and enthusiastic participation or at least complicity of the masses in the violence. This was accomplished through intense propaganda work aimed at legitimizing mass violence against the enemies. Through teams of cadres assigned to live with poor peasants, and through the ubiquitous public speaker system and newspaper-reading teams, the "violent crimes" of the enemies were told and retold in graphic detail, desensitizing people and preparing them for the upcoming violence.

After people had been sufficiently aroused, the next step was to orchestrate public shows of terror during which denunciations and executions of targeted enemies were carried out, often by their very neighbors, relatives, and friends who had been coaxed or coerced into doing so. The third big step was to distribute rewards to supporters and construct new structures of power in the countryside. Zealous participants in the violence were rewarded with material goods such as land and positions in the new local bureaucracy, the military and security forces, and the local mass organizations. (Families of executed enemies, by contrast, were made subject to lifetime state monitoring through the personal dossier system.) This step was crucial to state building because it formalized the auxiliary mass organizations and added a permanent layer of state control over the local population.

Implicit coercion and surveillance were also far more comprehensive and systematic in communist Vietnam than in South Korea. Most important in urban areas were the neighborhood groups (*khu phố* or *tổ dân phố*), community police officers (*công an khu vực*) assigned to monitor a certain number of households, and the household registration system (*ho khau*). In the 1950s Vietnam created *ho khau,* modeled after the Chinese *hukou* and far more co-ercive than the Korean residential registration. Operated in combination with urban grain rationing and forced eviction from cities, *ho khau* maintained local police surveillance and controlled population movement between rural and urban areas and within urban areas. It bound people to their birthplaces, where the state could monitor them and their extended families. It served ef-fectively as a tool to reward loyal subjects (who could keep their urban reg-istration together with grain rations) and discipline disloyal ones (who were banished to the countryside forever).

The communist state not only maintained a political dictatorship but also attempted to turn most Vietnamese into state employees dependent on the state for jobs, food, and other necessities. Together with the nationalization of industry in 1958, North Vietnam launched the (forced) collectivization of ag-riculture and imposed a ban on private trade. Employment in the private sec-tor became scarce, and most individuals came to earn a living by working for some state units. To be sure, the black market on rice, ration coupons, scarce industrial materials, and so on, was vibrant and helped those not employed in the state sector to survive on the margins of society. On the whole, however, most individuals owed their livelihood to the state and had a strong incentive to be obedient.

While rural cooperatives in Vietnam were small and did not contribute at all to the Vietnamese economy, they appeared more important as a tool of surveillance and control.[54] In fact, they contributed decisively, if unexpect-edly, to North Vietnam's victory in the civil war. Working closely with local governments and army recruitment boards, cooperatives kept track of young men in each household and groomed them for as long as two years before they reached draft age.[55] Cooperatives made draft avoidance almost impos-sible for young rural men, but they could guarantee soldiers that their families would be taken care of if they served. A common slogan at the time suggested cooperatives' key political role: "Not a single kilogram of paddy short [of pro-curement quotas]; not a single soldier short [of recruitment quotas]" (*thóc không thiếu một cân; quân không thiếu một người*). While cooperatives failed in motivating peasants to work hard for socialism, they made sure that vil-lages surrendered to the communist state all able-bodied men needed for its war making (communist Vietnam lost about a million troops in the civil war between 1959 and 1975, out of a population of less than 20 million).

Communist Vietnam imposed strict control not only over politics and people's livelihood, but also in the cultural realm. In particular, the party required the complete submission of culture to politics and the promotion of values associated with the working classes. Early on the CPV implemented the Maoist method of *cheng feng* (or *zhengfeng*, literally "rectification," an approach involving forced self-criticism in a group setting) with great success.[56] State-controlled organizations were later formed to monitor and mobilize writers, artists, scholars, and other professionals. Writers whose works raised even vague doubts about socialist values or party policies would be swiftly and harshly punished. Public show trials in which dissidents were publicly scolded and shamed by their neighbors and colleagues were common (and are occasionally used today). Dissidents faced many other forms of punishment short of imprisonment, such as political and social ostracism, denial of food rations, a lifetime ban on publishing, harassment of family and friends, and banishment to the countryside.

By the mid-1950s, the government moved to nationalize private presses and media in North Vietnam (today Vietnam still allows no private newspapers and publishers). Media were organized as parts of the state bureaucracy and led by party organizations. Vietnamese were not just proscribed from reading unauthorized materials, but were forced to listen to what the state wanted them to hear. By 1957, 38 public address systems had been built to cover all towns and nearby rural areas. A CPV resolution issued by its Secretariat in 1959 ordered the extension of this system "further into the villages . . ., to produce small receivers that could tune into only our frequencies."[57] The public address system typically broadcast hourly and daily programs to every household within its range, whether people wanted to hear or not.

Education is ideally for enlightenment purposes, but in communist Vietnam (and, to a lesser extent, in anti-communist South Korea during its authoritarian period) it was primarily for indoctrination. Vietnamese schools became places to train future revolutionary heroes; "new socialist men and women" were nurtured from a very young age. The government not only banned private schools and textbooks, it also established Communist Party cells in each school—from elementary schools to colleges—to control faculty and students.

To sum up, in all areas, from politics to economy to culture, the North Vietnamese communist state ranked equal to North Korea, and far exceeded South Korea, in terms of its domination over society. After reunification, Vietnamese communist leaders sought to impose the entire Stalinist-Maoist socioeconomic system of North Vietnam upon the vanquished south despite the intense resistance of southerners. Not until the rise of Gorbachev and the subsequent collapse of the Soviet Bloc in the late 1980s did Hanoi abandon that system. As a result of market reforms over the past two decades, state domination over society has weakened greatly. However, the Vietnamese Leviathan today remains more powerful than its South Korean counterpart, even when compared to the latter's heyday of military authoritarianism. While extreme by standards of authoritarianism in the developing world, the South Korean leaders Rhee and Park were subject to regular elections (Park won elections twice by small margins). Alliance with the United States required accepting certain religious freedoms. The press remained largely privately owned and relatively free in the late 1950s and the first decade of the Park regime.[58] The state guided but did not control the economy, and rapid economic growth fostered the development of civil society. This is in contrast to the experiences of (North) Vietnam and North Korea, where the totalitarian mode of control stifled development in the long term, causing both countries to fail miserably. Yet state control in these two countries has survived numerous crises, while the South Korean state was forced to give up much control over society following democratization.

Conclusion: Lessons of Vietnam's Reunification for South Korea

Vietnam and Korea are in the same neighborhood and have traveled broadly similar paths from ancient history to the modern era: they asserted independence within the cultural-political world dominated by China, were victims of colonialism, and suffered national division. Yet a closer look reveals important divergences. The most glaring difference is that Vietnam emerged from the Cold War united but poor, while Korea remained divided but with one half rich and democratic. The recent surge of nationalism in Vietnam can potentially make this country more like South Korea if this movement can overcome the resistance of the Vietnamese state, which ironically is more like North Korea in its character.

Does Vietnam's reunification have lessons for South Korea?[59] The answer is yes—although most involve what *not* to do. Essentially, Korea should avoid repeating Vietnam's experience. The reunification of Vietnam was carried out by force and incurred staggering costs. Up to 3 million Vietnamese lives were lost on both sides. Economic and environmental costs, too, were enormous but have never been calculated. True, reunification brought a unified government, which is usually a benefit. In this case, however, reunification by force helped create a powerful and arrogant state that stifled society while pursuing a utopian vision that fostered national destitution and individual privations.

Meanwhile, Vietnam's reunification never ushered in the expected national unity. The Saigon regime may have been less popular than its Hanoi rival, but it was not without its loyal followers. Millions of southern civilians fled Vietnam after the communist victory and during the first decade after reunification, with thousands of "boatpeople" losing their lives on the trip. Having achieved reunification by force, Hanoi leaders brushed aside calls for national unity and sent hundreds of thousands of Saigon loyalists to hard labor camps. Many were released from prison only in the early 1990s, after the United States made it a condition for diplomatic normalization with Vietnam. Relations between the Vietnamese government and overseas Vietnamese communities remain tense despite individual efforts to reconcile on both sides. Former (communist) prime minister Vo Van Kiet, whose wife and two children perished during the war, recently admitted on the anniversary of reunification that while the day brought joy to millions of Vietnamese, it brought sorrow to millions of *other* Vietnamese.

In retrospect, perhaps the largest benefit that reunification brought Vietnam was peace. After three decades of turmoil, peace was truly welcome, even for the losing side. Yet peace turned out to be illusory: Vietnam was back to war—this time with Cambodia and China—in a mere four years. Though one can certainly blame Vietnam's neighbors for provoking it, Vietnam's tangled relationships with both nations cannot be separated from Hanoi's earlier manipulation of the Sino-Soviet rivalry and use of Cambodian territory for the Vietnamese revolution. Regardless of who is to be blamed, it is sadly ironic that a bloody war, waged in the name of reunification over two decades and costing 3 million casualties, bought only a short-lived peace. Why, it must be asked, should war have been waged in the first place?

The fate of Vietnam was shaped in part by the Korean War, not only because that war raised the stakes in Vietnam for the United States and deterred Stalin and Mao from supporting a similar war in Vietnam in the 1950s, but also because that war affected the calculations of North Vietnamese on how to conduct their own war for reunification. Rather than launching a frontal invasion across the demilitarized zone (DMZ) as North Korea did, North Vietnam chose to orchestrate a revolt in the south with the assistance of northern troops sent south by way of Laos and Cambodia. North Vietnam thus succeeded where North Korea failed. North Korea's failure allowed the survival and eventual economic success of South Korea. North Vietnam's military success led the country into a blind alley from which it has not yet fully emerged.

In short, the Vietnamese experience suggests that territorial and political reunification does not necessarily produce national unity. The goal of frustrated Korean patriots should be unity, not just reunification, however long it may take.

Notes

1 This chapter was written under the auspices of the Democracy and Development Program, Princeton Institute for International and Regional Studies, Princeton University. I am grateful to the program and to its directors, Atul Kohli and Deborah Yashar, for their support. I'm also indebted to helpful comments from Donald Emmerson, Donald W. Keyser, James Ockey, T. J. Pempel, Gi-Wook Shin, and David Straub on an earlier version.

2 For resurgence of nationalism in South Korea since the 1980s, see Sheila Miyoshi Jager, *The Politics of Identity: History, Nationalism, and the Prospect for Peace in Post-Cold War East Asia* (Carlisle, PA: US Strategic Studies Institute, 2007), http://www.strategicstudies institute.army.mil/pdffiles/PUB770.pdf. For a similar phenomenon in Vietnam recently, see Tuong Vu, "Southeast Asia's New Nationalism: Causes and Significance," *TRaNS: Transnational and Regional Studies of Southeast Asia* (forthcoming).

3 Leo Tolstoy, *Anna Karenina*, trans. Constance Garnett (New York: Barnes and Noble, Inc., 1997), 3.

4 See Donald W. Keyser's introductory chapter and also chapter 8 by Leif-Eric Easley for discussions of the concept of a middle power.

5 South Korean and South Vietnamese presidents Rhee Syngman and Ngo Dinh Diem also threatened to take their troops north to reunify their countries, but did not enact such aggressive policies as their northern rivals.

6 Keith Taylor, *The Birth of Vietnam* (Berkeley: University of California Press, 1983).

7 Keith Taylor, "The Vietnamese Civil War of 1955–1975 in Historical Perspective," in *Triumph Revisited: Historians Battle for the Vietnam War*, ed. Andrew Wiest and Michael Doidge (Hoboken, NY: Taylor and Francis, 2010), 17–28. For a critique of nationalist scholarship on Vietnam, see Tuong Vu, "Vietnamese Political Studies and Debates on Vietnamese Nationalism," *Journal of Vietnamese Studies* 2, no. 2 (Summer 2007): 175–230.

8 Michael Seth, *A History of Korea: From Antiquity to the Present* (Plymouth, UK: Rowman and Littlefield Publishers, Inc, 2011), chapters 1-2.

9 Liam C. Kelley, *Beyond the Bronze Pillars: Envoy Poetry and the Sino-Vietnamese Relationship* (Honolulu: Association for Asian Studies, 2005); Keith Pratt, "Politics and Culture within the Sinic Zone: Chinese Influences on Medieval Korea," *The Korea Journal* 20, no. 6 (June 1980): 15–29.

10 Seth, *A History of Korea*, chapter 9.

11 Kenneth M. Wells, *New God, New Nation: Protestants and Self-Reconstruction Nationalism in Korea, 1896–1937* (Honolulu: University of Hawaii Press, 1990), chapter 4.

12 Charles Keith, "Protestantism and the Politics of Religion in French Colonial Vietnam," *French Colonial History* 13 (2012): 141–74.

13 Seth, *A History of Korea*, 269–71.

14 Michael Robinson, *Cultural Nationalism in Colonial Korea, 1920–1925* (Seattle: University of Washington Press, 1988).

15 "Civic nationalism" is nationalism defined by common citizenship in a modern nation, as opposed to "ethnic nationalism," which is defined by shared ethnicity.

16 Gi-Wook Shin, *Ethnic Nationalism in Korea: Genealogy, Politics, and Legacy* (Stanford: Stanford University Press, 2006), 77.

17 David G. Marr, *Vietnamese Anticolonialism, 1885–1925* (Berkeley: University of California Press, 1971), chapters 5 and 6.

18 Ibid., 145.

19 This myth claimed that a dragon king and a fairy were the progenitors of the Vietnamese.

20 The Comintern reversed its earlier policy and ordered all communist parties in the colonies to form united fronts with nationalists in 1935.

21 Tuong Vu, *Paths to Development in Asia: South Korea, Vietnam, China, and Indonesia* (New York: Cambridge University Press, 2010), chapter 8.

22 Shin, *Ethnic Nationalism in Korea*; B. R. Myers, *The Cleanest Race: How North Koreans See Themselves and Why It Matters* (Brooklyn, NY: Melville House, 2010).

23 Francois Guillemot, "Autopsy of a Massacre: On the Political Purge in the Early Days of the Indochina War (Nam Bo 1947)," *European Journal of East Asian Studies* 9, no. 2 (2010): 229.

24 Tuong Vu, "From Cheering to Volunteering: Vietnamese Communists and the Arrival of the Cold War 1940–1951," in *Connecting Histories: The Cold War and Decolonization in Asia (1945–1962)*, ed. Christopher Goscha and Christian Ostermann (Stanford: Stanford University Press, 2009), 172–204.

25 "Bao cao cua Tong Bi Thu Truong Chinh" [Report by General Secretary Truong Chinh], in *Van Kien Dang Toan Tap 1953* [Complete collection of party documents] 14 (Hanoi: Chinh tri Quoc gia, 2000), 53–54.

26 Tuong Vu, "To Be Patriotic is to Build Socialism: Communist Ideology in Vietnam's Civil War," in *Dynamics of the Cold War in Asia: Ideology, Identity, and Culture*, ed. Tuong Vu and Wasana Wongsurawat (New York: Palgrave, 2009), 33–52.

27 Le Duan, "Duong loi cach mang mien Nam" [The revolutionary line in the South], August 1956, in *Van Kien Dang Toan Tap 1956* [Complete collection of party documents] 17 (Hanoi: Chinh tri Quoc gia, 2002), 783–825.

28 Alec Holcombe, "Stalin, the Moscow Show Trials, and Contesting Vietnamese Visions of Communism in the Late 1930s" (paper presented at the Workshop on Revolutions in Vietnam, University of California, Berkeley, November 11–12, 2011), 41.

29 Minh Tranh, "Nhung tac pham cua V. Lenin o nuoc ta" [V. Lenin's works (published) in our country], *Hoc Tap*, April 1960, 24–25.

30 "Nghi quyet cua Ban Bi Thu so 80-NQ/TW" [Secretariat resolution no 80-NQ/TW], July 14, 1959, in *Van Kien Dang Toan Tap 1959* [Complete collection of party documents] 20 (Hanoi: Chinh tri Quoc gia, 2000).

31 Bo Giao Duc [Ministry of Education], *Tap Doc Lop Mot* [First grade reading textbook] (Hanoi: Ministry of Education, 1956). Only one reading textbook was used in the whole country.

32 Bo Giao Duc [Ministry of Education], *Tap Doc Lop Mot* [First grade reading textbook] (Hanoi: Ministry of Education, 1972). No edition was published between 1956 and 1972.

33 Edward Miller, "Vision, Power and Agency: The Ascent of Ngô Đình Diệm, 1945–54," *Journal of Southeast Asian Studies* 35, no. 3 (2004): 448–50.

34 Ngo Dinh Diem resisted direct U.S. intervention, but by then he had been overthrown by his generals, with Central Intelligence Agency (CIA) support.

35 Truong Chinh, *Ve van de Kam-pu-chia* [On the Cambodian Issue] (Hanoi: Su That, 1979), 27, 33.

36 Kenneth M. Wells, *South Korea's Minjung Movement: The Culture and Politics of Dissidence* (Honolulu: University of Hawaii Press, 1995); Don Baker, "Christianity Koreanized," in *Nationalism and the Construction of Korean Identity*, ed. Hyung Il Pai and Timothy Tangherlini (Berkeley: Institute of East Asian Studies, University of California, Berkeley, 1998), 108–25.

37 Shin, *Ethnic Nationalism in Korea*, chapter 9.

38 Jager, "The Politics of Identity."

39 Gordon Flake, *The Rise, Fall, and Transformation of the "386": Generational Change in Korea* (Seattle: National Bureau of Asian Research, September 2008), 109.

40 Pierre Brocheux and Daniel Hémery, *Indochina: An Ambiguous Colonization, 1858–1954*, trans. Ly-Lan Dill-Klein with Eric Jennings, Nora Taylor, and Noémi Tousignant (Berkeley: University of California Press, 2009), chapter 1.

41 Vu, *Paths to Development in Asia*.

42 Carter J. Eckert and Ki-baek Yi, *Korea, Old and New: A History* (Seoul: Ilchokak, 1990), 210; Brocheux and Hémery, *Indochina*, 135.

43 Seth, *A History of Korea*, 285; Brocheux and Hémery, *Indochina*, 135.

44 Brocheux and Hémery, *Indochina*, 122.

45 Vu, *Paths to Development in Asia*.

46 Ibid., chapter 2.

47 Lim Chae-Hong, "The National Security Law and Anticommunist Ideology in Korean Society," *The Korea Journal* 46, no. 3 (Autumn 2006): 85–86.

48 Under the conservative government of Lee Myung-bak, this law was more aggressively enforced. In 2010, 151 people were interrogated on suspicion of violating the National Security Law, up from 39 in 2007. The number of people prosecuted for pro-North Korean online activities increased from 5 in 2008 to 82 in 2010. The number of domestic Web sites shut down for pro-North Korean content rose from 18 in 2009 to 178 in 2011 (compared to about 300 Web sites shut down by the Vietnamese police in 2009). Choe Sang-hun, "Sometimes It's a Crime to Praise Pyongyang," *New York Times*, January 5, 2012.

49 Seo Joong-Seok, "The Establishment of an Anti-Communist State Structure Following the Founding of the Korean Government," *The Korea Journal* 36, no. 1 (Spring 1996): 791–14.

50 Moon Seungsook, *Militarized Modernity and Gendered Citizenship in South Korea* (Durham, NC: Duke University Press, 2005), 30–43.

51 George E. Ogle, *South Korea: Dissent within the Economic Miracle* (London: Zed Books, 1990), 50–62.

52 Liberating Our People, Developing a People's Democracy, and Advancing to Socialism," in *Truong Chinh Tuyen Tap (1937–1954)* [Selected works by Truong Chinh] (Hanoi: Chinh tri Quoc gia, 2007), 725–26.

53 For an English translation of this decree, see *Journal of Vietnamese Studies* 5, no. 2 (Summer 2010). The actual number of executions is estimated to have been 15,000, or

approximately 1/1,000 of North Vietnam's population at the time. Vo Nhan Tri, *Vietnam's Economic Policy since 1975* (Singapore: ASEAN Economic Research Unit, Institute of Southeast Asian Studies 1990), 3.

54 Benedict J. Kerkvliet, *The Power of Everyday Politics: How Vietnamese Peasants Transformed National Policy* (Ithaca, NY: Cornell University Press, 2005). Cooperatives averaged about 60 households each in Vietnam in 1960 compared to about 5,000 households in China in 1958.

55 Kinh Lich, *Tuyen Quan Trong Lang Xa* [Military recruitment in villages] (Hanoi: Quan Doi Nhan Dan, 1972). "Grooming" means inviting them to events related to recruitment and other youth activities in support of the front, and talking to them and to their parents about government expectations for their enlistment.

56 Kim Ngoc Bao Ninh, *A World Transformed: The Politics of Culture in Revolutionary Vietnam, 1945–1965* (Ann Arbor: University of Michigan Press, 2002).

57 "Nghi quyet cua Ban Bi Thu so 80-NQ/TW."

58 Hong Yong-pyo, *State Security and Regime Security: President Syngman Rhee and the Insecurity Dilemma in South Korea, 1953–60* (New York: St. Martin's Press, 1999), 130; Ogle, *South Korea*, 32.

59 Reunification of Vietnam was carried out by force. The lessons from Vietnam are perhaps more useful for North Korea since it is far more prone to taking this violent course of action than South Korea.

Index

Next-11 (Bangladesh, Egypt, Philippines,
    Indonesia, Iran, South Korea, Mexico,
    Nigeria, Pakistan, Turkey, Vietnam),
    112n6
Nguyen dynasty (Vietnam), 155, 162
Nigeria, 112n6
Nixon, Richard, 40, 117
Nordpolitik (Northern policy; South
    Korea), 11, 17, 30, 41
North American Free Trade Agreement
    (NAFTA), 17
North Atlantic Treaty Organization
    (NATO), 4
North Korea (Democratic People's
    Republic of Korea; DPRK)
    and China-South Korea relations, 38,
        40–41, 44–46, 105, 140, 141
    economy of, 19, 20, 168, 169
    foreign aid to, 19, 33, 45
    founding of, 158
    ideology in, 18, 19, 20, 158, 161
    and Japan, 20, 110, 112n2
    military of, 19, 154
    and North Vietnam, 167, 168
    and nuclear weapons, 11, 15–18, 20, 33,
        99, 105, 108, 109, 110
    provocations by, 44, 45, 49, 51n14, 140,
        142
    refugees from, 34, 140
    and regional cooperation, 17, 18, 19–20
    and reunification, 19, 20, 33, 162, 173n59
    and UN, 19, 20, 38
    and U.S.-South Korea relations, 49
    and USSR, 19, 158
    and Vietnam, 18–20, 33, 67, 68n1, 160,
        167, 169
    and Vietnam-South Korea relations, 33
    and Vietnam vs. South Korea, 153
    See also China-North Korea relations;
        U.S.-North Korea relations
North Vietnam
    culture in, 166–67
    ideology in, 158–60, 165

and Korean War, 169
land reform in, 165
nationalism in, 158–59, 161
and North Korea, 18, 167, 168
and PRC, 66, 94n27, 158
state building in, 154
surveillance in, 165–66
See also Vietnam
Northeast Asia (NEA), 15, 18
new Cold War in, 16, 104, 105, 106
and South Korea, 6, 11, 14
and Vietnam, 7
and Vietnam-South Korea relations, 22, 34
Northeast Asia Cooperation Initiative
    (NEACI), 10, 15–17, 20, 99, 100, 102,
    103–11
    Presidential Committee on, 107
Northeast Asia Peace and Security
    Mechanism (NEAPSM), 16–17
Northeast Asia Project (dongbukgongjeong;
    PRC), 105
Northeast Asia Regional Forum, 18
Northeast Asia Security Dialogue
    (NEASED), 17, 101
Norway, 4
Nucelar Security Summit (2012), 2
nuclear energy, 17, 31
nuclear weapons
    and NEACI, 108
    and North Korea, 11, 15–18, 20, 33, 99,
        105, 108, 109, 110
    and PRC, 15, 53
    and Vietnam-South Korea relations, 33
    See also Six-Party Talks

Obama administration, 45, 126
Olympic Games (Seoul; 1988), 38
"On International Economic Integration"
    (Resolution No. 07-NQ/TW;
    Vietnam), 89
"On strategy for fatherland defense in the
    new context" (Resolution No. 8 of
    Central Committee; Vietnam), 90–91

RECENT PUBLICATIONS OF THE
WALTER H. SHORENSTEIN ASIA-PACIFIC RESEARCH CENTER

BOOKS (distributed by the Brookings Institution Press)

Sang-Hun Choe, Gi-Wook Shin, and David Straub, eds. *Troubled Transition: North Korea's Politics, Economy and External Relations.* 2013.

Kenji E. Kushida and Phillip Y. Lipscy, eds. *Japan under the DPJ: The Politics of Transition and Governance.* 2013.

Jang-Jip Choi. *Democracy after Democratization: the Korean Experience.* 2012.

Byung-Kook Kim, Eun Mee Kim, and Jean C. Oi, eds. *Adapt, Fragment, Transform: Corporate Restructuring and System Reform in South Korea.* 2012.

John Everard. *Only Beautiful, Please: A British Diplomat in North Korea.* 2012.

Dong-won Lim. *Peacemaker: Twenty Years of Inter-Korean Relations and the North Korean Nuclear Issue.* 2012.

Byung Kwan Kim, Gi-Wook Shin, and David Straub, eds. *Beyond North Korea: Future Challenges to South Korea's Security.* 2011.

Jean C. Oi, ed. *Going Private in China: The Politics of Corporate Restructuring and System Reform.* 2011.

Karen Eggleston and Shripad Tuljapurkar, eds. *Aging Asia: The Economic and Social Implications of Rapid Demographic Change in China, Japan and South Korea.* 2010.

Rafiq Dossani, Daniel C. Sneider, and Vikram Sood, eds. *Does South Asia Exist? Prospects for Regional Integration.* 2010.

Jean C. Oi, Scott Rozelle, and Xueguang Zhou. *Growing Pains: Tensions and Opportunity in China's Transition.* 2010.

Karen Eggleston, ed. *Prescribing Cultures and Pharmaceutical Policy in the Asia-Pacific.* 2009.

Donald A. L. Macintyre, Daniel C. Sneider, and Gi-Wook Shin, eds. *First Drafts of Korea: The U.S. Media and Perceptions of the Last Cold War Frontier.* 2009.

Steven Reed, Kenneth Mori McElwain, and Kay Shimizu, eds. *Political Change in Japan: Electoral Behavior, Party Realignment, and the Koizumi Reforms.* 2009.

Donald K. Emmerson. *Hard Choices: Security, Democracy, and Regionalism in Southeast Asia.* 2008.

Henry S. Rowen, Marguerite Gong Hancock, and William F. Miller, eds. *Greater China's Quest for Innovation*. 2008.

Gi-Wook Shin and Daniel C. Sneider, eds. *Cross Currents: Regionalism and Nationalism in Northeast Asia*. 2007.

Philip W. Yun and Gi-Wook Shin, eds. *North Korea: 2005 and Beyond*. 2006.

STUDIES OF THE WALTER H. SHORENSTEIN
ASIA-PACIFIC RESEARCH CENTER (published with Stanford University Press)
Gene Park. Spending Without Taxation: FILP and the Politics of Public Finance in Japan. Stanford, CA: Stanford University Press, 2011.

Erik Martinez Kuhonta. The Institutional Imperative: The Politics of Equitable Development in Southeast Asia. Stanford, CA: Stanford University Press, 2011.

Yongshun Cai. *Collective Resistance in China: Why Popular Protests Succeed or Fail*. Stanford, CA: Stanford University Press, 2010.

Gi-Wook Shin. *One Alliance, Two Lenses: U.S.-Korea Relations in a New Era*. Stanford, CA: Stanford University Press, 2010.

Jean Oi and Nara Dillon, eds. *At the Crossroads of Empires: Middlemen, Social Networks, and State-building in Republican Shanghai*. Stanford, CA: Stanford University Press, 2007.

Henry S. Rowen, Marguerite Gong Hancock, and William F. Miller, eds. *Making IT: The Rise of Asia in High Tech*. Stanford, CA: Stanford University Press, 2006.

Gi-Wook Shin. *Ethnic Nationalism in Korea: Genealogy, Politics, and Legacy*. Stanford, CA: Stanford University Press, 2006.

Andrew Walder, Joseph Esherick, and Paul Pickowicz, eds. *The Chinese Cultural Revolution as History*. Stanford, CA: Stanford University Press, 2006.

Rafiq Dossani and Henry S. Rowen, eds. *Prospects for Peace in South Asia*. Stanford, CA: Stanford University Press, 2005.

The authorized representative in the EU for product safety and compliance is:
Mare Nostrum Group
B.V Doelen 72
4831 GR Breda
The Netherlands